How to Lose Friends and Infuriate People

Jonar C. Nader is a digital-age philosopher and educator who has worked and consulted for some of the world's largest organisations, including Compaq and IBM. He was the co-founder of the Information Technology Society and the New Leaders Foundation. He is the author of *Prentice-Hall's Illustrated Dictionary of Computing*, and the technology writer for *Butterworth's Legal Dictionary* and the *Concise Legal Dictionary*.

Jonar is a highly sought-after lecturer and consultant in the areas of technology, leadership, management, thinking skills, teamwork, marketing, and politics. For more information about him, contact Jonar@Logictivity.com or visit www.Logictivity.com.

9/01 el.

HOW TO LOSE FRIENDS & INFURIATE PEOPLE

THE CONTROVERSIAL
bestselling book for thinkers

JONAR C. NADER

Penguin Books

Penguin Books Australia Ltd
487 Maroondah Highway, PO Box 257
Ringwood, Victoria 3134, Australia
Penguin Books Ltd
Harmondsworth, Middlesex, England
Penguin Putnam Inc.
375 Hudson Street, New York, New York 10014, USA
Penguin Books Canada Limited
10 Alcorn Avenue, Toronto, Ontario, Canada M4V 3B2
Penguin Books (N.Z.) Ltd
Cnr Rosedale and Airborne Roads, Albany, Auckland, New Zealand
Penguin Books (South Africa) (Pty) Ltd
5 Watkins Street, Denver Ext 4, 2094, South Africa
Penguin Books India (P) Ltd
11, Community Centre, Panchsheel Park, New Delhi 110 017, India

First published by Plutonium 1999

This edition published by Penguin Books Australia Ltd 2001

1 3 5 7 9 10 8 6 4 2

Revised cover concept by Cathy Larsen, Penguin Design Studio
Digital Imaging by Paul Fenton
Typeset in 10.35/15.74 pt Stempel Schneidler by Post Pre-press Group, Brisbane
Made and printed in Australia by Australian Print Group, Maryborough, Victoria

National Library of Australia
Cataloguing-in-Publication data:

Nader, Jonar C.
How to lose friends and infuriate people.

Includes index.
ISBN 0 14 100532 7.

1. Achievement motivation. 2. Leadership. 3. Psychology,
Industrial. 4. Interpersonal relations. I. Title.

158.1

www.penguin.com.au

HATS OFF TO THE HEROES

*A sign of intelligence to choose what you like
a sign of maturity to choose what is right,*

*A sign of character to voice what you like
a sign of integrity to voice what is right,*

*A sign of bravery to do what you like
a sign of heroism to do what is right.*

POEM WRITTEN BY THE AUTHOR AT AGE 16

THIS BOOK IS DEDICATED TO THE *heroes*
WHO KNOW THAT *nothing* IS EVER FINAL,
THAT POSSIBILITIES *are* ENDLESS,
THAT LIFE IS *never* SIMPLE,
THAT A ROLLING STONE *can* GATHER MOSS,
THAT A WATCHED KETTLE *does* BOIL,
AND THAT THOSE WHO CRY *last*,
CRY *the* MOST.

CONTENTS

part TWO
WORKING WITH OTHERS

part THREE
SURVIVING IN THE MODERN WORLD

FOREWORD

FOR MORE THAN FIFTEEN YEARS I have dedicated my life to learning more about leadership. In that time I have read hundreds of books, researched the topic passionately, and addressed thousands of people interested in how they can improve their life. Never have I come across a thinker like Jonar Nader whose work is challenging and revealing. He explodes certain long-standing theories in ways that will force you to take notice.

On the subject of leadership, Jonar delves into new insights about the function of leadership and its role in life, in business, and in society. He says that there is a big difference between being a "leader" and engaging in "leadership". He outlines the essential leadership skills that are required in the modern world, and he explores the functions of inspiration, motivation, and teamwork — saying that "teamwork" is useless until one constructs "teams that work".

Having worked with Jonar for many years, I know him to be true to his word. He tells it like it is and stands firm on his values and principles. As a result, I have watched him lose friends and infuriate people during our meetings. What is more important is that he produces extraordinary results.

No matter what the critics might think about this book, I can tell you what thousands of people have said about Jonar's inspiring lectures. Here are four of the hundreds of unsolicited comments sent to him via my office by those who attended his lectures:

> *You have no idea how*
> *you have changed my life.*
> *You will never know how powerful*
> *your presentation was for me.*
>
> •
>
> *Mind-expanding presentation.*
> *The lynch-pin that focused me on the possibilities.*
>
> •
>
> *That was the best presentation I have seen.*
> *You kept hitting me over the head — word after word.*
>
> •
>
> *That was fantastic. I could not believe that*
> *someone could open my eyes like you have.*

I have no doubt that the "establishment" will be outraged by this important piece of work. However, after the dust settles, it will be seen as an important contribution to the development of leadership skills for survival in these exciting and challenging times.

Take my word for it. Read it twice and read between the lines. This powerful book is packed with red-hot wisdom.

GORDON JACKSON
GENERAL MANAGER
J&J NEW LEADERS FOUNDATION

PREFACE TO NEW EDITION

THIS BOOK IS NOT ADVOCATING that people actually set out to *lose* friends, despite the title. *How to Lose Friends and Infuriate People* explains how to take control of life, success, and happiness. As a result, we might need to do things that sound like the opposite of how we were brought up to behave. All our lives we were taught to be patient, yet impatience is also a virtue in the networked world. We were encouraged to be tolerant, yet intolerance is a characteristic of successful people. We were told how important it is to win friends and avoid conflict, yet it is vital to learn how to lose those friends who sap our energy and stop us from achieving success and happiness.

INFURIATING MORE PEOPLE

It's now time to lose more friends and infuriate more people with this new edition. There are five new chapters based on what I believe to be important areas that successful people need to master if they are to maintain their lead. (The new chapters are marked in the Table of Contents with the symbol ➤.)

Chapter 8, "Another dirty word", investigates and revives the concept of ambition — whose popularity is declining because the politically correct among us would have us believe that *too much* ambition is a bad thing. In this chapter, I emphasise that if we don't know how to harness and use our ambition, we could miss out on the vital fuel that helps us get to where we want to go.

In Part Two, the idea for the chapter on hiring and firing came after observing organisations claim that "people are our greatest assets". What do they mean? After all, the whole purpose of hiring and firing is to focus on the bit that happens in the middle — working with talented people who can add value. Therefore, in the chapter called "Ready . . . aim . . . now what?", I investigate the important aspects of hiring, managing, and promoting people (and firing them, where necessary).

The three new chapters in Part Three address the following important questions pertaining to the networked world: 1) What will be the single most important asset?; 2) What future challenges will confront organisations?; 3) What will be more important than the bottom line?

HITTING THE STANDS

The first edition of this book took everyone by surprise. As a self-published author, I was amazed to find my book completely sold out within eight weeks. It hit several best-seller lists, including those of the *Business Review Weekly* and *Who Weekly*.

Within the first year I managed to find homes for over 70 000 copies worldwide. At the time of printing this second edition, the figure exceeded 100 000.

INFURIATING LAWYERS

Amidst the excitement of publishing the first edition, I had to battle costly legal issues with the owners of the book *How to Win Friends and Influence People* who strongly objected to the title. They said that my title was "unfair competition" and insisted that I withdraw all copies of my book from circulation.

I don't know why they thought that they could lay claim to the *opposite* of an idea. If an author writes a book called *How to Gain Weight and Keep It On*, what right would that author have to stop anyone else from writing a book called *How to Lose Weight and Keep It Off*?

WELCOME TO PENGUIN

I chose Penguin to publish this edition because the people there could see the big picture. They did not treat this book as a "product", but as an important contribution to life and society. With their publishing strength and support behind me, I am able to concentrate on writing more books.

Keep your eyes on my Web site for information about my future projects. As always, if you would like to share your observations, please write to me at Jonar@Logictivity.com or visit www.Logictivity.com. **Y**

JONAR C. NADER, 2001

PREFACE

THIS CONTROVERSIAL BOOK IS ABOUT personal achievement, management, and leadership in the new millennium. It is presented in three parts. The first part highlights some of the challenges facing people at home, at work, and in society. It covers important subjects that need to be understood by those who desire to fly higher — subjects that in themselves are taken for granted, but are often the root to many personal failures. They include motivation, inspiration, belief and conviction, self-control, brain power, creativity, and one's perception of the world.

Part Two delves into how people can work together, and how the leader can create synergy. This is important because we live in a world in which people must work better together, but unlike bees and ants we are not as well co-ordinated. We need to learn about human behaviour, how to interact, and how to work in teams. Chapters 9 to 15 explore the areas of leadership, teamwork, empowerment, and staff reward systems.

Part Three examines some of the pressing issues that organisations and individuals will face in the new millennium. Advice is given about what can be done to pre-empt (and succeed in) the new environment. Although each chapter in this book could be expanded to fill hundreds of pages, the pertinent points have been highlighted for you to explore. One might think that the modern world offers boundless opportunities. This is only true for those who can graduate from the old framework with flying colours. For example, those who do not understand the importance of customer service, and who do not currently deliver it superbly, will not be able to succeed in the modern world, regardless of how the Internet will change the face of service delivery. Incompetent organisations will not be able to survive, even with the help of the Internet. Instead, they will meet their fate much sooner than they had imagined.

EIGHT YEARS IN THE MAKING

There are far too many books that are nothing more than a compilation of articles and statistics from a myriad of journals and publications. They are interesting to read, but they do not cut to the heart of their respective subjects. Take a look at their bibliographies and you will see that all you are reading is a well-compiled list of other people's work, re-packaged in the form of a book.

How to Lose Friends and Infuriate People took eight years of solid work that involved investigation, testing, probing, study, and research. Although it is a definitive and prescriptive work that is easy to read, it looks neither like a report nor an essay. In some ways, readers who like copious footnotes and appendices might feel uncomfortable with its style. It is my view that books ought to provide well-considered advice from credible authors who offer their own opinion, not the opinion of others. Those who do nothing more than massage a collection of articles and anecdotes are better called writers, not authors.

THE NETWORKED WORLD

In *How to Lose Friends and Infuriate People,* references are made to the networked world. Networks have existed for thousands of years. We have had religious, royal, political, and social networks, as well as trade, criminal, and secret networks. We now also have powerful technological networks that have created new opportunities and unique challenges.

It is important to note that this book is not about technology. The use of the term "the networked world" refers to its broadest meaning — not only to its technological one. However, the new aspects of the networked world are highlighted in Chapters 20 to 24. These two chapters detail some of the specific issues that need to be understood if one is to survive in the *modern* networked world.

WHAT IS MEANT BY CEO?

Throughout the following chapters, I make reference to an organisation's chief executive officer (CEO). Naturally, different organisations use different titles. Therefore, the term is used generically to refer to the person who has the *power* and *control*. Depending on the situation and issue at hand, the term "CEO" could very well refer to any manager or project-owner who is ultimately responsible *and* who has the authority to act as required. In some instances, the term might refer to a government official, or the leader of a group.

A CONTROVERSIAL BOOK FOR THINKERS

The term "A controversial book for thinkers" was not placed on the front cover as a fancy catchphrase. It is placed there to warn you that this book *is* controversial, in the hope that you will be tolerant as you try to understand what is being expressed. I did not set out to write a controversial book. It just so happens that the information I need to share with you is often perceived to be taboo and/or risky or unconventional. You are encouraged to explore this book with an open mind, and to delve into each chapter in search of ideas.

The word "thinkers" is not used as a form of flattery. It highlights the fact that, although this book is easy to read, it requires careful consideration and contemplation. Almost every paragraph will challenge you to explore the subject in more detail. Rigorous mental activity is required, along with quiet reflection and meditation. When you can mentally zoom into each sentence and explore every word, you will begin to understand the concepts and ideas and recognise their profound meanings.

The combination of an open mind, reflective contemplation, and rigorous analysis will help you to make the most of this controversial book for thinkers.

WRITE TO ME

I have not written this book so that readers will say, "Oh yes, that's true", but so that they will say, "Wow, I had not thought of that before!"

What do *you* say? Write to me if you have had to lose friends and infuriate people. ◘

JONAR C. NADER, 1999

START HERE

SETTING *the* SCENE

IN A NUTSHELL,
WHAT THIS BOOK IS ALL ABOUT

L EADERSHIP, MANAGEMENT, AND self-development principles are taught at hundreds of colleges to thousands of students who read millions of books. Yet companies collapse, businesses blunder, and friendships fail, while individuals and organisations are enslaved to inefficiency, inaccuracy, and instability.

Why is it that so many popular techniques have a higher propensity to fail than to succeed? All this, despite the groundwork set by "gurus" who urged us to: go on a quest in search of excellence; win friends and influence people; engage in serious creativity; capture moments of truth; and develop the seven habits of highly effective people.

Beyond the hype, the real issues have been too controversial to communicate, too tough to tackle, and too risky to raise because:

1. *It is likely that motivated individuals willing to modify or change their habits would feel isolated and overwhelmed by the enormity of the tasks that lie ahead.*

2. *It is a tendency among colleagues and opponents to thwart anything that threatens the comfort of the status quo.*

3. *It is difficult to tackle well-entrenched and politically moulded standards of behaviour.*

4. *It is culturally accepted to follow the path of least resistance.*

5. *It is a mammoth task to single-handedly challenge the establishment.*

6. *It is a fact that social and cultural forces that accommodate mediocrity bond together to obstruct, frustrate, and dismantle any opponent through conflict or combat.*

Despite the efforts of commercialised gurus, it appears that individuals have not been properly guided in their pursuits. Misguided enthusiasts can be as menacing as non-believers. This results in a multitude of irritating graduates from "The Textbook School Of Bluffers".

STAND FIRM

The title, *How to Lose Friends and Infuriate People*, is about the fact that anyone who applies what is endorsed in this book is likely to do just that. It is envisaged that this book (and its supporters) will be ripped to shreds by supposed experts who among them think that they possess the collective wisdom of the universe.

Critics of this book will start to raise all manner of irrelevant and superfluous questions that will do nothing more than unequivocally prove the need for such a book. These critics are called *hindsight experts*. They are the kind of folk who would have naively: jailed Galileo for suggesting that the world was not flat; banned Pythagoras from enlisting mathematics enthusiasts into his club; ridiculed Alexander Graham Bell for his "contraption";

and told Henry Ford that his invention would never sell, except to "the rich and idle".

If you find truth in this book, do not let the critics intimidate you. Critics are those whose rich and condemning vocabulary largely consists of words like: never; impossible; not done; can't be achieved; unreasonable; unrealistic; will never happen. They have the audacity to place limits on the future. They encourage censorship and promote the "banning" of all sorts of things. They prize legislation and love thought-control, promoting themselves as mind-guards. Furthermore, they hide behind empty meaningless words which they do not understand — like morals, social standards, ethics, social behaviour, and political correctness. They have the gall to intimidate women, Jews, Christians, socialists, communists, capitalists, those of differing lifestyles, and those of atypical sexual desires.

Justice is an obscure word that has legitimacy to the one who applies it, and no useful function to the one to whom it is being applied

Righteousness. It is a timeless word that belongs to everyone. It is too bad it does not unite with "tolerance" and dance with "individuality" and blend with "acceptability" and stay away from "justice" — an obscure word that has legitimacy to the one who *applies* it, and no useful function to the one to whom it is *being* applied.

MAJORITY VERSUS MINORITY

The *majority-rule* society has produced nothing more than heartache and intolerance. Throughout the *majority-rule* period, members of the *minority* have made an impact. For better or for worse, it is the daring few who have shaped this so-called majority-rule society.

Inventors, pioneers, radicals, and visionaries have ventured from the lonely and costly camp of "minority" only to be obstructed by majority-rule concepts that tolerate inferiority, hinder progress, harbour injustice, and pose limits within the decaying status quo.

What is sad and insulting is that the majority basks in the benefits and riches that were originally afforded by individuals who sacrificed their sanity, their freedom, and their lives. When you start your journey of leadership in the modern world, you too might have to make some sacrifices.

IS THIS BOOK FOR YOU?

There are hundreds of books on offer, and collectively they explore every possible aspect of leadership, management, and self-development. Together they broach every conceivable topic, but they seem to lack one crucial ingredient — *truth*. Not that they endorse "untruth", but they fail to tackle the very roots of important issues about leadership, management, and self-development in the modern world.

How to Lose Friends and Infuriate People is for those who can, for example, study cosmology and then do three things *simultaneously*. First, marvel at the grandeur of the universe. Second, recognise the majesty of the infinitely small. And, third, doubt that we possess more than a nano-parcel of information about either subject.

This book is for those who are fed up with, and frustrated by, inefficiency, inaccuracy, inconsistency, and untruths. It is a tool for those who know that they have the potential to stretch the boundaries, have the creativity to break new ground, have the vision to shape new futures, have the determination to realise their dreams, and have the courage to break out of the social cast, even if it means that they'll have to bid farewell to friends and, along the way, infuriate the establishment.

If you acknowledge that nothing is ever final, that possibilities are endless, that life is never simple, that a rolling stone can gather moss, that a watched kettle does boil . . . this book is for you

If you acknowledge that nothing is ever final, that possibilities are endless, that life is never simple, that a rolling stone *can* gather moss, that a watched kettle *does* boil, and that those who cry last, cry the most, this book is for you.

I slam diplomacy as a waste of time. I blow the whistle on the corporate and political games. I discredit the rules that have done nothing more than nourish the lethargic, imprison new talent, and suppress freedom.

I expose protocol as a brick wall that protects the insecure and keeps at bay the bold. I call on those who *are* in a position of power to lift their game. I plead for action from those who have new ideas.

RUBBING SHOULDERS IN THE DARK

During the eight years of research, investigation, observation, and testing, not a single interviewee was aware of the making of this book. Not a single letter alluded to my authorship.

My research for this book has been authentic and comprehensive — encompassing a broad range of successful and unsuccessful artists, scientists, business managers, military leaders, political and government heads, ethical entrepreneurs, and shady ones, as well as students, the general public, and academics. Not one is named. The sound information gathered would not have been given if the subject being studied had known that the material or exchange was for a book.

Some books are written like a brochure and are full of praise for the author's clients or people whom the author would *like* as clients. This is a serious book, so unfortunately, there will be no profit from bulk sales to companies mentioned and praised here because *none* are mentioned or praised.

Authors of many popular books focus more on telling us *who* they know, than *what* they know. They want us to believe that they lead celebrity lifestyles, constantly bumping into the most successful people in the world. They expect us to believe that almost every aeroplane ticket that they have ever booked happened to seat them next to the founder of "Hero Corporation", and that the only blind person they have ever met went on to win a Nobel Prize.

Egotistical authors seem to bolster their own image. Their enthusiasm echoes a sense of ease rarely attained by struggling individuals.

Name-dropping and telling readers about dignitaries they met, what was said, and of the exalted circles they move in, dominate some books. (Just for the record, I have dined with the privileged and spent time with the outcast, poor, and addicted, including the homeless and the titled. Their spirits hover over each of the chapters in this book.)

. . . AND NOTHING BUT THE TRUTH

When I joined a large corporation as a manager of one of its divisions I read several books about the company. During my first week on the job I mentioned this to my manager who laughed and said, "Don't believe any of them." I was puzzled. Could it have been that my manager, a thirty-year veteran of the company, was embarrassed about what the books revealed? Well, despite the fact that some of the books were speaking about the company in disastrous terms, most were syco-phantic. I often wondered about his comment. Exactly two years, ten months, and fifteen days later the penny dropped. I realised what he meant, and why the contents of the books could not be believed. In due course I realised that *nothing* I read was true because the critical books could not be critical enough for fear of legal action while the sycophantic books were inaccurate because they were just sucking-up to the giant for reasons known only to each respective author.

How to Lose Friends and Infuriate People is not written so as to damage any company, nor to promote my friends, supporters, or worthy clients. It is written for readers who are committed to improving their situations and their environments.

SPEAKING OUT

As a long-time journalist, my first regular column was called "Controversials". Since then, most of the things I have said and done have been controversial. In the mid-1990s a respected publisher approached a small number of industry leaders for what were their predictions. I was chosen by the publisher to contribute my views which, needless to say, were controversial, so much so that when the publication was released, my then boss summoned me into his office and expressed his displeasure at my speaking out. He said, "Jonar, no matter what you think, you must not speak out." I asked him if he had agreed with what I had written. "Yes, you are right. I agree with you, but I would never tell anyone," he said. Well, so much for courage. He made me sign an official letter of reprimand. I now look upon that letter fondly and thank him for being one of the many people who drove me to speak out even louder.

Through the years my radio segments (although ethical and discreet) have had public relations departments scurrying with all sorts of unpleasant repercussions. They were tough days (as they still are), yet I have weathered the storms.

The big question will be how I am likely to be reprimanded for writing *this* book. I know that the more resistance I receive, the more that would prove that I have hit a nerve. Still, I will brace myself once more because I am not looking forward to the wrath of political, corporate, and academic establishments that might feel threatened by this book.

Although I could have included many more chapters in this book, the existing collection sets down a foundation. In due course, I will write more books about leadership, management, and personal achievement. I will also write about a wider range of subjects, so that more readers can lose more friends and infuriate more people. **U**

DEVELOPING *your* SKILLS

HAVE THE COURAGE TO LIVE AS IF *you* OWN YOUR LIFE

CHAPTER 1

WHAT CAN *you* SEE FROM THE BALCONY OF LIFE?

TIME IS RUNNING OUT

IMAGINE, WAY UP IN THE sky, a balcony that resembles a viewing platform where you and others stand looking down on Earth. You are but a spirit. From the balcony you can see the marvellous and wondrous things on Earth — spectacular surf, exotic fruit, delicious vegetables, tantalising ice-cream, mouth-watering pasta, remarkable flowers, awesome gardens, stunning animals, breathtaking mountains, splendid rivers, people in love, exquisite fashion, fast cars, exhilarating snow skiing, and romantic sunsets.

The one in charge, Spirit-Superior, approaches you with a clipboard in hand and says that the next tour to Earth is about to depart. The problem is, only 10 per cent of those on the balcony can be granted permission to go to Earth for a period not exceeding eighty years. Would you put your hand up? Would you ask to be considered?

Who is stealing your chance to walk barefoot in the sand?

Are you enthusiastic enough? Do you really want to wear a human body and experience the beauty of life on that planet below?

According to Spirit-Superior, all candidates promise to make the most of their time on Earth. They are eager to start their journey. They cannot wait to take their first swim, to enjoy a juicy orange, to bite into a scrumptious cake, to walk in the park, and to make love with a beautiful companion in symphony with the cool breeze. You push to the front of the queue and plead,

17

"Please pick *me*. I promise to make the most of life on Earth."

Well, here you are *on* Earth. Not long to go before you have to return to the balcony. Not long when you compare eighty-odd years to eternity. What are you doing about it? Did you bite into a delicious apple today? Did you take a swim? Did your heart skip a beat as the stars came out to bid the sunset a fond farewell? Or did you waste the day and insult Spirit-Superior by allowing anger, that elusive intangible, to take hold of your body and spoil your moment? You are not guaranteed the full eighty years. Only "now" is your guarantee. Tomorrow is not in the contract. You have no way of knowing when your tour will be terminated.

Every night, as you put your head to sleep, Spirit-Superior visits you and asks, "Would you like to go back from whence you came — back to the balcony of life where you will never again have the opportunity to come back to Earth? Or would you like one more day to give it another go?" What would you say? Most people say, "Oh please, give me one more day. Tomorrow I will live. Today I messed up, but tomorrow I will go to the beach and grab an ice-cream, and feed the birds, and make my friends laugh."

Doubtless, some do choose to terminate their stay. They cannot see what all the fuss is about. They want life no more. So, Spirit-Superior grants their wish and takes them back to the balcony. Tragically, others tamper with the process and take their own lives when they can no longer believe that tomorrow will bring relief. Some of my dear friends have decided to leave me behind by terminating their contracts.

Yesterday is gone, tomorrow is not yours, and today is already packed with drama

One young man of nineteen asked his mother for some money. As loving mothers do, she obliged and asked no questions. He bought a rifle, went back home, and did the deed. He used to love life, but a door shut in his face. He was convinced that the door would never re-open. Faced with that prospect, he bowed out.

Where are you at in life? Are you battling with time thieves? Are you being robbed of *your* moment? Who is stealing your chance to walk barefoot in the sand?

FLIGHT 101 NEVER RETURNS

In the airline business, everyone knows that once an aircraft departs, any empty seats on that flight cannot be filled again. The opportunity to recoup that lost fare has gone. This is why many airline companies overbook their flights. They do not mind inconveniencing their travellers, so long as they can be sure to pack the aircraft.

For undersubscribed flights, and since the advent of the networked world, airlines are trying to sell the last remaining seats via Internet auctions, hoping to fill every seat, even if at cost. It is better to cover costs than to fly with an empty seat, because empty seats cost money.

Your life can be likened to this challenge. Every day that you allow to slip through your hands is irretrievable. You cannot decide to return to yesterday or "turn back time" to mend the broken dreams. You cannot return to last Monday. So, yesterday is gone, tomorrow is not yours, and today is already packed with drama. Is this what you planned when you were standing on the balcony of life? If not, stand up and do something about it.

You know what needs to be done. You do not need "motivational" speakers to pep you up. This is *your* life.

Do you divide your day into work, rest, and play? Is work something you do out of obligation? Is rest something you do because you are exhausted? Is play something you do to forget about work? This is not a pleasant cycle.

No-one is authorised to upset you. This is *your* turn. No matter how generous you might be, you cannot pass it on to someone else. If you choose to skip a turn, you will not be doing anyone a favour. The one thing you will be doing is ringing the alarm bells in the control room, and Spirit-Superior will have to take a closer look at your files. (For more about motivation, see Chapter 3, "The secret destroyer".)

EVERY MINUTE OF EVERY DAY

Have you considered that the Olympic Games would not have progressed if it were not for technologists' ability to slice time into tiny bits we call a second, a tenth of a second, a hundredth of a second, and so on?

Electricity and the entire power grid, including street lighting and traffic controls, rely on disciplined and regimented pulses that must beat to time. The loss of one beat could stop a city. Traffic would grind to a halt, and the city could very well become grid-locked, meaning that no-one could move because no-one but pedestrians can move.

Computers operate to time. Not only for calendar and date-stamping purposes, but for internal microchip operation. One tiny beat out of rhythm and the computer fails.

Time, at its smallest, is precious. Even the big chunks we call day and night are great punctuation marks that herald a new week, a new month, a new season.

How well do we manage time? As a society, we manage it well. Things tend to work more often than not — despite that "year 2000 computer issue" that many will remember with fury and laughter as the "Y2Kaboom!"

How well do *you* manage time? Do you divide your day into work, rest, and play? Is *work* something you do out of obligation? Is rest something you do because you are exhausted? Is *play* something you do to forget about work? This is not a pleasant cycle.

Life is life. To allow manipulating hounds to steal your life at the office through bureaucratic and politically poisoned meetings is theft of the highest order. Life is now, not after work. Life is shopping, not when you get home. Life is every minute of every day. So, how well are you managing your life? How well are you managing your time?

Time management is not about a list of things in order of priority that must be completed by a deadline. (How apt that we call it a <u>dead</u>line.) Time management is about life management. The issue is not what you do, but where your soul is at.

Do you put your pleasures on hold when you clean the house? Do you accept misery and boredom as unavoidable traits of your work domain? Do you accept domestic unrest as your lot in life?

UPS AND DOWNS

Life management is not about a delirious state of affairs. You own your life, so only *you* can live your life. Take charge of it. This does not mean that you must seek to be happy at all times. This is impossible. Not because it is too difficult in this day and age, but because *happiness* can only mean something to you after you have experienced *sadness*. From a young age we are taught that if one achieves happiness, one has achieved something worthwhile. However, although sadness, pain, and sorrow are not mentioned, or undervalued, or avoided, they are *vital* for the attainment of more happiness.

Time represents seconds. The seconds measure the division between the sun and the moon and these, in turn, ultimately measure the distance between life and death.

After one of my presentations, a young man approached me to thank me. He had the brightest disposition. He told me that although his colleagues were looking to build their careers in medicine, business, and the like, he just wanted to be "happy", so it did not matter to him what profession he chose. He looked happy, but I knew that he did not know what he was saying. "How happy do you want to be?" I asked. "Very happy," he replied. We sat for a while as I explained to him that if he wished to attain ten lots of happiness, he would have to endure ten lots of sadness. He finally grasped the concept and became scared. He specifically does not want to be *unhappy*. So he froze. I felt sorry for him, but such is life. Eventually he began to understand and assured me that he would brace himself. He valued happiness because he had experienced much sadness. However, he was unaware that more happiness could only be appreciated in the wake of more sadness. Even then, the process is not automatic, and much building is required. The trick is to use the sadness to build for your-self tools that can help you to get back on your feet again. You need to be ready to attain additional wisdom, to build shields that protect you, to enhance your attitude to cope with the situation. This is important because sad-ness knocks you down, and it is much easier to stay down than to lift yourself against the inertia.

Life management is not about being happy through ignoring society, or shedding one's responsibilities, or resigning from corporate life to take up subsistence farm-ing, or filing for divorce. These things in themselves do not make you happy. They might be important steps that you choose to take, but on their own, they do not lead to happiness. Life management is about being *well adjusted*. This means taking the good and the bad, and being able to stand against the wind of disappointment. It is the realisation that solutions do not come from escaping. Running away from unhappiness does not build happiness. A well-adjusted person responds well to what life dishes out, and builds new shields. In responding well to what life dishes out to you, be sure to arrest those who steal time — the essence of life.

We are taught to be eternally tolerant, yet intolerance is just as important when you can use it to protect your life against time thieves

Time is not really the important element. It is what time represents that matters. Time represents seconds. The seconds measure the division between the sun and the moon and these, in turn, ultimately measure the distance between life and death.

LIVE BY HALVES

Although life is not so easy to measure, time *can* be measured. Assess your time and how you expend it. Do you really need to watch so much television? Is it important that you spend so many hours surfing the Internet? How about halving all of the things that do not add value to your life?

If you watch twenty hours of television per week, why not cut it back to ten? If the loss of your precious ring causes you to become angry for two days, try to get over it in one day. If the loss of your pet causes you to cry for six weeks, try to overcome your grief within three weeks.

By halving the things that you know are unproductive or soul-destroying, you are starting to manage your time. Continue to live by halves until you can take better control of the impact of your environment upon you. This does not mean that you ought not to spend your time any way you like. In fact, that is the point of the exercise. By ridding yourself of time-consuming life-wasters, you will have the time to do the things you really *want* to do, not the things that *force* themselves upon you, or command your attention without your permission, or that you do out of habit.

Some habits cannot be halved. They can only be amputated. The diseases of gambling, alcoholism, drug abuse, and the like, need to be obliterated without negotiation. Only the life-owner can choose to do that. If people's enjoyment of such things is greater than the value they place on their life, they are not ready to do anything about their addictions. In those cases, it is better that they do not try because the emotions and turmoil adversely affect the life of those around them as well.

In truth, time-wasters are life-wasters. Anyone who wastes your time is wasting your life. Do not stand for it. Typical time-wasters include: the way in which a meeting is managed; people's inability to stick to their word; not meeting deadlines; and being tolerant of people.

TOLERANCE VERSUS INTOLERANCE

If you consider tolerance a virtue beware you do not fall victim to virtues. Patience, tolerance, and empathy are all noble, important qualities in life. However, you need to learn how to set your boundaries. Supposing that you agree to meet a friend but that person does not turn up at the agreed time. How long are you prepared to wait? Ten minutes? One hour? Seven hours? Most people would not consider waiting seven hours. Well, why is ten minutes acceptable? Why not five? If you think that five minutes is a little harsh, then pray tell, would you leave at precisely ten minutes, or would you give your friend just a couple of minutes more?

The point to time management in such cases is to reduce the guesswork. You and your friend ought to have made an agreement that says if one of you is late by more than ten minutes the meeting will be cancelled. This has nothing to do with being nasty. It is all about setting expectations and understanding the boundaries.

Meetings at work should start on time. Do you start on time, or do you wait for the stragglers? I live a fair distance from the main city, so when people invite me to an early morning meeting in the city, I need to be up at 5:00 am to get ready and leave home before 6:00 am so that I can get there at 7:00 am. I need to do this even if the meeting is scheduled to start at 9:00 am because if I were to leave home at 8:00 am, I would not get through the unbearable traffic until 10:00 am. This is a tricky juggling act. So I arrive early, wait two hours until 9:00 am, and have to put up with life-wasters who say, "Oh, let's wait a few minutes for those who might be caught in traffic." Then they say, "Oh look, it's 9:30, why don't we have an early morning coffee break while we're waiting?" By 10:00 am, when the meeting starts, I would have been up for five hours!

At first, I give some people the benefit of the doubt, but I later become nonchalant, or do not arrive on time, or choose not to go. When will people learn that adults are just like children? If a child gets the chocolate after ranting and raving, that child is being conditioned. If chairpeople wait for late-comers, I would rather a few extra hours in bed, and they can wait for *me*.

Needless to say that most meetings are life-wasting rituals, devoid of content, lacking direction, and ultimately useless. The same is so for any meeting where the guest speaker reads a speech at me. If I have to get up early, iron my clothes, shave, shower, endure the heavy traffic, pay for petrol and parking, only to have some slow, uninteresting presenter read at me, I would prefer the speech be sent to me via fax or e-mail so that I can read it in the bath when I awake at a godly hour.

We are taught to be eternally tolerant, yet *intolerance* is just as important when you can use it to protect your life against time thieves.

WHEN TIME IS MONEY

Organisations measure the productivity of each employee. When they hire hundreds of people, they are effectively buying time. More people working on a project ought to result in greater output within the financial year. Productivity per head is one of the vital measures of success. If you are a chief executive officer (CEO), ask your financial analysts to estimate your corporation's profitability if your workforce were to double its output. What would become of your share price if you were twice as productive?

Sure, many organisations understand the need for more productivity. That is why they maintain the pressure and make everyone miserable at the same time while trying to improve productivity. Employees are having to work intolerable hours amid job insecurity and unfulfilling environments.

I long for the day when a senior manager congratulates the staff for a job well done without spoiling the whole ceremony with a plea for everyone to "work harder". And I cringe when I hear calls for employees to also "work smarter". How depressing. How ungrateful. Forget about working harder. Never mind about working smarter. If, as CEO, you want to improve productivity, start doing things by halves. Navigate your way through your spaghetti-like systems and policies and chop the time-wasters. Remove anything or anyone who steals time through bureaucracy, through stupidity, and through strangling red tape cast upon the masses by the almighty headquarters. Even if you cannot eliminate them, just halve them! What difference would that make? You do the numbers and work it out. If what you see does not make your blood boil, then you are sailing smoothly, and you have a well-adjusted organisation.

If you could double the productivity of your organisation, would such a project not be worthy of your attention? If so, get on with it. By the way, once you, as CEO, have removed the time-wasters, you need to search your soul and come clean with your conscience and check to see if you are the chief time-thief. Have you created an environment in which your actions create a domino effect?

It is laughable to see how many CEOs increase the revenue targets as a small buffer, so that their people strive harder for the bigger number, knowing that if they miss a little, the original target will be met, and the CEO will look like a hero in front of the board. I have seen numbers eventually doubled after they have gone through a buffering process from headquarters, to regional headquarters, to country, to division, to department, to individual. What a joke. At the end of the line the individual has to strive for a number that is twice as big as the original without the same level of growth in operating expense and headcount. This unrealistic target-setting is demoralising.

I have seen the aftermath of this wicked accounting process. The individual would have battled in spite of having unco-operative colleagues who are also stretched to unreasonable limits. The individual would have tried hard, increased the revenue by 70 per cent on the previous year's figure, but still be declared a failure because the ridiculous target was missed by a few dollars. How ungrateful the organisation is to make the employee work a miserable year with no time for life, no time for a decent lunch, and at the end of all that hard work, a slap in the face. Then, the chiefs of the land, who exceeded their revenue targets in real terms, end up scoring healthy bonuses. Every way you look at it, this is theft — and it starts at the top. Oh, the burdens at the top! **M**

CHAPTER 2

LIGHT AT THE *end* OF THE TUNNEL

INSPIRATION IS NOT KIND, BUT IT CAN BE GOOD

THERE WERE TWELVE PEOPLE AT a camp site. Independently and in their own pot, each was boiling an egg for breakfast. On close observation, one could see that each and every camper had sprinkled salt in the pot of water. Each had a very good reason for using salt. The young camper said that salt was used to flavour the eggs. Through osmosis, the salt would seep through the shell to provide for a delicious breakfast. Two of the campers used salt to make the water boil at a hotter temperature. While the first did this to save time by having the eggs boil faster, the second was more concerned with conserving what little gas remained in the gas bottle.

An older camper said that salt was used for the purpose of lining the shell of the egg to make it stronger, and therefore would make it less susceptible to cracking. The Mediterranean woman by the river used salt to increase the density of the water — enabling the egg to float a little more, thereby raising it from the strong flames which would have cooked the egg unevenly. Her husband insisted that he did this for a different reason. He was more concerned with increasing the density of the water in order for the egg to float so that it would not violently hit the base of his pot. Each of the remaining six campers had yet another reason for using salt.

SAME THING, DIFFERENT REASON

Isn't it amazing that so many people could do the same thing — each for a different reason? Each camper was expecting a different result while unaware of the other benefits that the same action brought.

This chapter defines the framework for inspiration. However, definition is a two-edged sword. On the one hand, definition allows us to capture the essence of the qualities that comprise a complex phenomenon (such as inspiration, leadership, hope, or love) while, on the other hand, it can imprison, stifle, and entrap both the spirit of the subject itself and the spirit of the one who is trying to play with it. At the risk of the latter, here are the secrets of inspiration.

The whole purpose of inspiration is to remind the heavy-at-heart that hope exists

Inspiration is like salt. To some, inspiration leads to *dedication*. To others, it could result in *determination, enthusiasm*, or *commitment*. To a large number of people, inspiration leads to *frustration* while others become *angry* in its presence. In truth, inspiration can yield each and every one of these outcomes. However, each individual might not be aware of the multifaceted nature of inspiration. At best, some can derive goodness from it, and at worst, others can become bitter as it stirs them to destruction.

What most people do not realise is that inspiration resembles a little cheeky girl, her hair in a ponytail. She lives in her own little world and is oblivious to her surroundings. When you least expect it, she pops her head around the corner, throws a sticky-date pudding in your face and giggles in her loud soprano, "You can't catch me."

INSPIRATION DOES NOT EXIST

Inspiration emerges to tempt the astute. It springs up in the face of the intelligent. However, it is the same intelligence that, most often, overcalculates the situation to the point of destruction. Inspiration is not kind. It is not fair. It is not helpful. It plays at one's conscience and torments the struggler. The whole purpose of inspiration is to remind the heavy-at-heart that hope exists.

Unlike a shooting star which is visible to all . . . inspiration is a one-on-one deal. If you miss it, you miss out.

It emerges and disappears like a mirage. It hovers long enough to remind the weary that there is light at the end of the tunnel. Its wide eyes stare threateningly lest one weaken and lose sight of the importance of the task at hand.

Many people go in search of inspiration, and this is a mistake. Inspiration cannot be found because it does not exist. Inspiration is a *carrier*. It is the medium through which we receive gifts. However, as salt is to campers, its gifts are singular, even though their application can vary depending on the state of the receiver.

When inspiration beckons, we may receive the spirit of dedication. This is the result of our basic values of loyalty. If at any point loyalty wanes, inspiration flashes its glimmers of hope, confirming our basic values.

When one least expects grace, one receives grace. When one least expects love, one is surprised by it.

If we are predominantly stubborn then, when inspiration knocks, we are overwhelmed with a sense of determination.

If faith is what drives an individual, then inspiration (should it visit unexpectedly) yields enthusiasm.

When inspiration persists with the mature, it manifests in a severe dose of commitment.

The haphazard are frustrated by random sparks of inspiration because it reminds them of what is possible if they were to exercise discipline.

To those for whom injustice exists, inspiration delivers anger.

IF YOU MISS IT, YOU MISS OUT

Inspiration is not contagious. It relies on your ability to see what no-one else can see. Each signal is coded for the receiver. Unlike a shooting star which is visible to all who look, inspiration is a one-on-one deal. If you miss it, you miss out. Catch it, and it will do to you what you *expect* it to. The more you expect of it, the more you will receive.

Best of all, if you know how to catch inspiration, you will be able to use it to recharge your soul. It can be your silent partner, and your source of energy. Unfortunately, no-one will ever see what you see. No-one will ever appreciate what life means to you. Inspiration cannot be shared. It cannot be recycled. What it does to you will be instant. No second chance. With this in mind, you must be at the ready; but herein lies the dilemma. Like love, inspiration will not go near the expectant.

When we least expect grace, we receive grace. When we least expect love, we are surprised by it. Similarly, when we least desire a whip up the backside, we are blessed with another glimpse of the red rag that fires the spirit with inspiration.

Inspiration is not kind, but it can be good. **U**

CHAPTER 3

THE *secret* DESTROYER

WHAT'S YOUR POISON?

N O-ONE CAN MOTIVATE YOU. You cannot even motivate yourself — even though you have a *motive* for everything you choose (or choose not) to do, say, or feel.

What *motivates* an alcoholic to become an alcoholic? Nothing. No alcoholic sets out to become addicted — just like no-one sets out to catch cancer. The question is, what motivates a person to drink to such a degree that alcoholism eventually takes hold? Very often the answer has to do with one of two things — *hope* or *escape*. In some situations, fear acts as the third element.

Finding an escape can be a good thing. Unfortunately, it is when an escape becomes your master that you realise there is no escape thereafter.

Hope is the thing that vanishes moments before people commit suicide. Such people are unable to see what lies ahead, other than what is at hand. If what is at hand (the here and now) is displeasing or agonising, they choose to bow out because they do not like (or cannot cope with) the status quo. Alternatively, if they *do* happen to have a vision for what lies ahead, they are frightened or disgusted by it.

Many of us enter periods when the status quo is not to our liking, but the thing that keeps us going is either the belief that the chosen path will lead to a better life, or the hope that a new path will emerge in due course.

Some people take drugs in the hope that they will be accepted by their peers, or in the hope that they can relax or change their behaviour with a view to attracting a new friend.

The other motivator is "escape". It is something that we do for release, whether we are trying to release pressure or anxiety, or trying to suspend the status quo by entering a cocooned environment, even if for a brief moment. To some degree, life-threatening sports offer people an entry into another environment by *forcing* them to escape from the status quo. Sky-diving and the like offer a rush for several reasons, including the immediate and urgent shift in focus to the risk at hand.

Very often the thought of the task ahead is more exhausting than the task at hand. This situation is temporarily suspended when we engage in an activity that focuses the mind sharply on one thing. Some people can do this through meditation, social outings, gardening, or reading. Others try alcohol and drugs in search of an escape.

Finding an escape can be a good thing. Unfortunately, it is when an escape becomes your master that you realise there is no escape thereafter. For example, once alcoholism grips, it will never let go until you find a motive to beat it.

The motivation to kick a habit, or to write a book, or to take up painting, or to file for divorce, needs to come from within you. It cannot be given to you by another person. The best that others can do is offer an incentive, or bribe you, or intimidate you, or threaten you with something you fear or hold dear. These things are not motivation — they offer a "reason" for action. Note also that there is a difference between "motivation" and an "incentive". The former must come from within while the latter comes from external elements.

Watching hair grow is tedious, and it would be unlikely that one could notice the microscopic growth. Similarly, the path to destruction is often as subtle.

If people say, "We would like to lose weight but we need more motivation," they are not serious. The only thing that will motivate them to lose weight is the promise of an attractive environment which they cannot enter until they lose weight. Sometimes the promise comes through fear — such as the fear of death, with the promise of extended life if they lose excess fat.

TO FEAR OR NOT TO FEAR

Fear plays a major role in life. It is unfortunate that people are easily motivated by it. Fear is a feeling that most societies consciously promote and develop in their members. Although fear is a good trigger that cautions us to examine our judgement before taking action, it needs to be balanced with courage. Sadly, courage is not something that society encourages.

When one quickly understands the taste of fear while

unable to taste the glories of courage, the stronger force (in this case fear) will dominate. If the converse were true we would lean towards courageous decisions.

The healthy state is a *balanced* state wherein we work neither out of fear nor out of courage, but out of *conviction*. When a balanced person understands the consequences and still takes a course of action, that person is said to be acting with *confidence*. Confidence is fuelled by *faith*, and faith is fuelled by *belief*. Belief comes from *knowledge*, and knowledge comes not from logical calculations, but from *emotional* certainty. Emotional certainty comes from an *unshakeable existence* — where mind, body, and soul are fuelled by the spirit.

It can be argued that belief does not always come from knowledge. There might be times when belief seems to come irrationally and illogically. This is owing to the forces of a different kind of logic — such as the logic of love, or the logic of hate, or the logic of fear. However, such belief cannot fuel faith because it is not really "belief". Belief must come from knowledge, therefore anything else that resembles belief might turn out to be an opinion, a desire, a suspicion, an idea, an expectation, or an assumption.

Most addicts acknowledge that their path will lead to destruction. Despite that knowledge, they lack the *urgency* to act because they do not see the damage taking place. For example, watching hair grow is tedious, and we would be unlikely to notice the microscopic growth. Similarly, the path to destruction is often as subtle. Because there is no evidence to show, it makes it impossible to reason with an addict. Furthermore, as one's senses and health begin to deteriorate, even the willing can no longer wrestle with addiction. (It would be a different matter if every time addicts had ciga-rettes, they felt unbearable pain, akin to someone bashing their thumb with a hammer. The immediate consequence would discourage the act of smoking because the resulting pain would be immediate and unbearable.)

Motivation is not a force or power, but an impetus. Those who delude themselves and seek it as a source of strength never find it because it does not exist for that purpose.

Amid subtle consequences, deteriorated physical and emotional faculties, and a lack of urgency, the motivation for overcoming an addiction or affliction needs to be stronger than all of these forces. Herein lies the dilemma. If motivation needs to come from within, how can we obtain strength from a state of weakness? It is doubtful that this would be possible except for balanced individuals who possess extraordinary physical and emotional strength. Therefore, the solution is *not* to seek motivation to rescue you from the grip of addiction or to project you towards your desired outcome. Seeking motivation at this stage is far too late in the process. *The secret to motivation is not in searching for it, nor in acquiring it, but in examining it when it initially comes your way.*

This little secret has puzzled as many people as it has destroyed. Motivation is not something that you ought to seek *after* you realise that it is needed. Rather, it is something that you ought to examine before everything that you choose (or choose not) to do, say, or feel. Note that motivation is something that would have come and gone by the time you realise that you need to examine it.

A STITCH IN TIME

You need to examine the motives behind your decisions, actions, and reactions *before* they happen — not seek to find a reason to reverse them *after* you have made your move.

Whether it is something you are about to do (or not do) in hope, or in fear, or as an escape, you need to understand the motive behind your action. Once you are cognisant of what is motivating you, it is vital that you pre-empt the consequences. If you understand the potential consequences and still have the desire to proceed, knowing that the path is not an ideal one, you will need to examine what it is that is driving you toward the decision. If it is hope for a better future, or fear of the current state of affairs, or an escape for temporary pleasure, you will need to examine the root cause. What is causing you to have hope or fear?

If you can identify the root cause, you will realise that motivation has done its job. It emerged, did its deed, and the rest is up to you.

Motivation is not a force or power, but an impetus. Those who delude themselves and seek it as a source of strength never find it because it does not exist for that purpose.

Once you understand the function of motivation, you will realise that it is not there to boost or assist you, but to challenge you to arrive at the root cause — the real reason behind anything you do, say, or feel.

If you can reach a balanced state of *unshakeable existence* — where your mind, body, and soul are fuelled by the spirit, you will have arrived at wisdom. Nothing can withstand the forces of wisdom. Therefore, once motivation meets wisdom, the correct decision will emerge naturally and peacefully, with spontaneity. ▪

CHAPTER 4

BELIEVE IT *or* NOT

ARE YOU READY
TO SACRIFICE YOUR LIFE?

S O MANY SUPPOSED GURUS SPEAK about "belief" as if it is a choice. They say things like, "You must start to believe in yourself." This is incorrect, impossible, and damaging because it confuses a lot of people and misleads them into thinking that "belief" is something they can choose to have.

You cannot choose to believe something that you do not believe. It is that simple. No matter how much of a "positive thinker" you might be, optimism has nothing to do with belief.

Therefore, if people speak about the need to believe, and they are sincere in their communication, they are speaking about a matter of fact. They are saying that if you do not believe, you will be unable to progress. They are not asking you to believe because that is impossible. You cannot choose to start believing, any more than you can choose to feel satisfied when you are famished. You cannot believe that you are not thirsty when you are. In the same way, you cannot choose to believe in something that you do not really believe in.

Belief is not blind. It is not hope. It is unequivocal, unshakeable knowledge.

Belief manifests itself to you through supreme knowledge and faith. Belief is not blind. It is not hope. It is unequivocal, unshakeable knowledge that what you hold to be true is true — or what you seek will be found.

Here is an analogy. Supposing someone walks up to you and insists that you are carrying ten dollars in your pocket when you know that you are not. Notwithstanding trickery, you know the truth. This means that you *believe* that you do not have the money. Do you hang on to your belief in the hope that the more you believe it the more likely it is that you will be right? Of course not. It is pointless to even engage in such brain activity because you know the facts. You are steadfast in your belief. That firmness gives you conviction which, in turn, is powerful. That is what is meant by the "power of belief".

THE POWER OF BELIEF

Many people can only believe when they know something to be true through evidence (either past or present). When something has not yet happened, people find it difficult to believe. They might have doubts because they reason that no-one can be sure of the future. Well, anyone who thinks that about any issue is entitled to do so, and that simply means that they do not believe it, no matter how much they would desire it to happen. Still, if you believe, such doubt would never enter your mind because you would have as much conviction as knowing that you are now alive.

Conviction alone does not help you because it is merely there as a question for you to answer. It is part of the checklist that helps you to determine the truth. Ask yourself if you believe in your project, or in your art, or in your idea. If your answer is uncertain, the answer is "no". And you cannot do anything about it. However, the truth will set you free, and you will know in your heart the secret of your conviction or lack thereof. If your answer is an unequivocal "yes", that too is your secret. The state of "believing" is for your knowledge, not for others to understand.

To believe is to give all you have. When you have given your all and seem to have nothing else, you are left with one thing — your life.

Having determined where you stand, you can make decisions that will help you to progress. If you choose to sit back and not do what you ought to do, nothing will happen. Believing in something that requires intervention from you will not progress without your input. Therefore, your desire to see it happen rests with your decision to take the necessary action.

If you encounter failure, it is up to you to rectify the issue. Failure cannot be called "failure" if it is in something you believe. It is merely an obstacle or a delay. It is up to you to observe, learn, and try again. Your setback will not shake your belief.

YOU'LL KNOW WHEN IT HAPPENS

No-one can tell you what belief means until you experience it. When you believe in something, you will know it, and you will know what I mean. Until then, have hope in the power of belief, and stand at the ready.

To believe is to give all you have. When you have given your all and seem to have nothing else, you are left with one thing — your life. If you believe in something, and go after it with *passion*, you will give your life also. Passion is like rocket fuel. You will not know what hit you — nor would it matter. ◼

CHAPTER 5

IF *you* DON'T CONTROL YOURSELF, SOMEONE ELSE WILL

THE PLIGHT OF THE CANDLE IN THE WIND

IMAGINE BEING IN A HOT-AIR balloon, moving briskly through the sky in very strong winds amid a beautiful sunset. You look down and see your friend waving to you from the rooftop of a tall lighthouse on the beachhead.

You prepare to engage in an experiment you have planned that involves you and your friend each lighting a candle to determine how far you can travel in your balloon and still be able to *see* each other's flame.

You can go with the flow without losing sight of your goals, without compromising your position, and without changing your values

Your friend on the rooftop of the lighthouse strikes a match, but the wind is far too strong, so the moment that the flame appears it is blown out by the wind. Your friend tries several times to no avail.

What chance do *you* have of lighting the match in the balloon when the wind is even *stronger* at your altitude? You give it a go and strike the match anyway. To your surprise, you can light the match with ease, and your candle is lit effortlessly.

How can a tiny flame survive in such strong winds? The answer lies in its *environment*. The balloon moves gracefully *with* the wind and *becomes* part of it. The flame is at ease because it is *protected* from the wind *by* the wind.

Is the flame in control of the wind, or vice versa? Neither, because within the right environment, some things can co-exist in harmony, even if those things would normally clash with each other under different circumstances. Within the right environments, incompatible tangibles (such as the tiny flame and the strong wind) neither support nor obstruct each other. In this context, one might begin to understand the benefits of "going with the flow".

Deciding to go with the flow of life ought *not* to mean that you have given up the fight, nor given in to the stronger force. You can go with the flow without losing sight of your goals, without compromising your position, and without changing your values. Going with the flow does not mean *avoiding* opposition and distraction, but *co-existing* with them. This state of affairs is called "peace". The law of peace governs the co-existence of elements. Peace is an intangible state that reflects one's *life* in relation to one's *environment*.

PEACE BE WITH YOU

To be at peace neither guarantees happiness nor removes difficulties. To be peaceful removes neither conflict nor trials and tribulations. These things are part of life, and can be good for you. They are only bad when they spin you out of control.

One can still be in control in the face of difficulty and unhappiness. Trials and tribulations can also be addressed without losing control. To lose control is to lose peace. To have control is to be at peace.

Although you cannot control *when* difficulties arise, you ought to control when you allow things to *affect* you. Timing becomes an important factor in controlling your peace. Timing does not refer to "time" itself, but to *when* and *where* you decide to react to a situation.

This chapter deals with the issue of timing, so that you can control your life and how you live it.

WHERE DO YOU LIVE?

When you live, where do you live? This is not a question of geography but of "state" — meaning where does life take place for you, and in which state of affairs do you live?

Where do you hurt when you lose your loved one, suffer embarrassment, or feel unloved? Can you put your finger on it and say, "my pain comes from this part of my anatomy"? No, you cannot. Hurt is intangible. It exists nowhere on your body — yet it consumes it. Emotions live neither *on* you nor *in* you, but *with* you.

Given that life is mostly . . . about intangible things, does it not make sense to learn to control them — things such as thoughts, desires, anger, curiosity, love, hurt, and sorrow?

Many people who study tangibles (things you *can* see and touch) and intangibles (things you *cannot* see and touch) believe that tangible things are easier to control. This is generally true. Notwithstanding unfortunate accidents or natural disasters, we tend to control the tangible world around us. However, given that life is mostly about *intangible* things, does it not make sense to learn to control them — things such as thoughts, desires, anger, curiosity, love, ambition, motivation, sadness, hurt, and sorrow?

Although we live in a tangible world, life itself occurs within our mind, spirit, and soul. If life and most of its issues are intangible, we could live a better life by controlling these intangibles — *what* we feel, *when* we feel, and *how* we feel.

CONTROLLING YOUR NET

Long before the term "net" became synonymous with the Internet, I was using it to refer to our "shield". We all have a shield, yet some of us use it effectively while others do not use it at all. Learning to control your net (shield) enables you to control the intangibles of life.

First, it is important to become *aware* of your net — what it is and what it does; how strong it is; where it is weak; how big it is; how flexible and elastic it is; and what size the holes are. Some nets (like tennis nets) have big holes that allow big things to pass through. Some nets (like hairnets) have smaller holes that catch most things that come by. Some nets (like mosquito nets) have even smaller holes, and allow very little to penetrate unnoticed.

Second, it is important to learn how to *change* the size of your net's holes. You need the ability to make the holes a different size to suit different issues or environments. If your net is tightly woven your life is likely to become cluttered and tense because you end up catching everything that comes your way. You become superbly observant and overly sensitive to what is going on around you. This can be an asset, but it can also be a burden, especially if most of the things you catch are neither important nor relevant to you, or untimely in your life.

There are many things in life that stare you in the face, but you allow them to pass through your net unnoticed

Third, it is important to learn *when* to change the size of the holes. This gives you greater control of what you let into your life.

Fourth, it is important to note that your net is not only used to control what you let *into* your life, but what you allow *out* as well. The size of the holes used for incoming signals might need to *differ* from the holes used for outgoing signals.

Therefore, becoming *aware* of your net, and learning how to *change* the sizes of its holes, and *varying* those for incoming and outgoing signals, and taking control of *when* you change them, are the four vital starting points to controlling your life. For information on "observation skills", see Chapter 7, "Can you speak another colour?"

AWARENESS

The next important aspect is "awareness" because your net will only catch things of which you are *aware*. For example, when you buy a new car you become acutely aware of other cars on the road that are the same model. Those cars were there before, but you had not noticed them because your net let them pass through. Once you become aware of that model, your net traps it — until you lose interest.

There are times when your observation acts like a snare — catching things that are relevant to you, but not to those around you. For example, although a word, phrase, or gesture might pass through everyone else's net, you catch it because it means a lot to you. It could be something that disturbs you, while others look on, unable to understand why such a little thing means so much to you. "Why are you over-reacting?" they'll ask. To them, the incident passed right through their net and they do not even recall what it was. "What brought this on?" they'll demand to know.

Notice that when you learn a new word, you tend to hear it that night on the news. When a friend of yours mentions a new song or the name of a band, you are amazed when you read about it that evening. Had your friend not mentioned the band, or had you not become aware of that new word, your net would not have caught that word of which you are now aware.

There are many things in life that stare you in the face,

but you allow them to pass through your net unnoticed because you are unaware of them. Another example of this happens at the cinema. Almost everyone has seen a film on the big screen. However, how many have noticed the scene-change signal that flashes during the film? I often ask my students: "How many of you can tell me, while watching a film, when a scene is about to change?" Many put their hand up. Some say that the music tends to give it away. Others say that it is often obvious because of the predictability of the plot. "No," I emphasise, "these things might work, but I am talking about really *knowing* when a scene is about to change." No-one can say. All the hands go down. "How can this be?" I challenge them. "The signal for a scene change is right there in front of you. Have you never seen it? It is a real signal that everyone can see!"

I proceed to tell them about the circular flash that occurs at the top right-hand corner of the screen three seconds before a major scene change. The flashes occur several times during the film to warn projectionists (using manual systems) to prepare the second projector. "How many of you recall seeing that circle?" I ask. Very rarely does anyone remember seeing it. The signal, right there in front of their eyes, slips through their net every time. They cannot remember ever seeing it.

"Oh, well," I say, "next time you go to see a film, take a good look at that top right-hand corner of the screen and you will notice it."

Within a matter of weeks I receive many calls and e-mails from students who are amazed at that flashing circle. "I started to laugh when I noticed it," said one young lady, "because I realised that I must have seen twenty movies this year, but never noticed it. The funny thing is now I am *unable* to ignore it." This kind of response is typical.

A TIME TO LAUGH, A TIME TO CRY

Why should others have the right to penetrate your emotions when *they* feel like it and disturb you when *they* decide to do so? It is *your* life, so you ought to have the right to decide *when* someone can upset you, if at all.

If someone wants to start an argument, it ought to be your choice whether you allow their strategy to work on you. Being able to control what enters or escapes your net gives you control of timing. With better timing, you are able to choose the right environment in which your issue can be addressed. Selecting the right environment can enable you to deal with a difficult issue in a way that gives you greater control — just like having the ability to light the match at a high altitude while in the balloon.

I am not suggesting that you do not become angry about situations that anger you. I am saying that through net-control you will be able to choose *when* you become angry. Learning to control your net will enable you to decide *when* and *what* you catch with it. You will also be able to control what goes out — *what* you say, *when* you react, and *how* you feel.

Comedians understand the dynamics of timing. Often an audience will surrender itself to the comedian and allow the jokes to be processed immediately. Those in the audience who are troubled or distracted might not find much to laugh about because they do not give the joke any priority. The joke might slip through the net unnoticed.

There is a fine line between declaring someone to be calm and accusing them of being insensitive

Those who have control of their net can hear a joke (or receive input) and hold on to it until they are ready to process it at a time that suits them. After years of practice I am now able, quite naturally, to process inputs when *I* am ready to do so. For example, it is common for me to be sitting in a public place (like an airport lounge or an aeroplane) and burst into laughter. It so happens that I might have been ready to process a joke told to me several days earlier. If it is funny, I sit there laughing to myself. Onlookers might wonder about my sanity. While my colleagues might have found the joke funny at the time it was told, I could have been *focusing* on something else at the time, even though I was *aware* of the joke being told. The capacity to be *focused* while *aware* is an important skill to practise. (For more on focus and awareness, see Chapter 16, "Management styles are out of fashion".)

Consider the situation experienced by Tom, a young chap who cares deeply about his dog. Tom waves goodbye to his dog and leaves for work at 8:00 am. He enjoys his day, goes out to lunch, has lots of fun with his colleagues, and later goes out to a birthday dinner. All along, Tom is happy until he arrives home to discover that his dog has died. At that point, Tom becomes distraught.

What connection does the dog's death have with Tom's life? None! There is no connection between the two because, if there were, Tom could not have had such an enjoyable day while his dog was lying lifeless at home since 10:00 that morning.

Tom becomes sad about the loss of his dog the *instant* he becomes aware of its death, not before. There is nothing wrong

You can be angry without showing signs of anger, and appear to be furious when you are very calm. This is self-control at its most supreme.

about feeling sad, and nothing unusual or unhealthy about grieving. The question is one of timing. It is obvious that Tom was able to enjoy his day even while the dog was dead. So it proves that Tom's life is independent of the dog's life.

If Tom were able to control his net, he would have grieved when *he* deemed it to be the right time, not the moment that he found the dog on the kitchen floor. (Unless that was the right time for him.) The time to cry, or to feel sad, or to grieve ought to be controlled by Tom, not by the incident.

There is a fine line between declaring someone to be *calm* and accusing them of being *insensitive*. Not becoming hysterical when a major incident occurs might be seen by some as insensitivity and a lack of caring. Tom would not be accused of insensitivity if he applied his self-control to save victims of a horrific car accident. The ideal situation is to be at peace — meaning to co-exist with the situation and decide to react to it when *you* feel that the timing and environment are right for you.

Even after you manage to control the environment for, and the timing of, your reaction, it is important for you to reflect later on how long you grieved. Whether it is the death of your dog, or the theft of your car, or the breaking of an expensive vase, you need to be aware of the *length* of time it will take you to overcome the sadness or concern. Being aware of the length of time, and then being able to control it, is an important part of gaining control over your life. (See the section about how to "live by halves" in Chapter 1, "What can you see from the balcony of life?")

When you can start to control your reaction to what comes *in* and what goes *out* of your life, and the timing and environment in which things take place, you will have started to take control of your life. You can then go one step further and start to control the length of time that an issue occupies your life.

To advance even further would be to put into practice the ability to remove feelings from reactions and reactions from feelings. This means that you can be angry without showing signs of anger, and appear to be furious when you are very calm. This is self-control at its most supreme.

Learning to take control of your net takes as much energy and effort as it would take to learn how to become brilliant at tennis or mathematics. It requires dedicated training. However, beware the dangers of control. Self-awareness ought to precede self-control. The converse could lead to self-destruction. ◭

Beware the dangers of control. Self-awareness ought to precede self-control. The converse could lead to self-destruction.

CHAPTER 6

ACHIEVING *intellectual* SIMPATICO

USING LOGIC AND CREATIVITY TO REACH LOGICTIVITY

THE LOGIC OF CREATIVITY AND the creativity of logic is a study I call "logictivity". It is a term I've coined to describe a very complex discipline that requires a book all its own. However, in Chapter 9, "Leadership", I mention that the single most important factor in leadership is creativity. Although this is true, it is important to touch on *logictivity* because those who wish to develop their leadership skills need to develop both their logic *and* their creativity — in equal doses and to equal proportions. Although both are powerful on their own, a lot of synergy can be created when both logic and creativity are used simultaneously. Synergy is the creation of a new substance. When logictivity is in play, it is altogether a different substance to its component parts.

A person who is 100 per cent creative is only operating at a capacity of 50 per cent. A person who is 100 per cent logical is only half as effective as is otherwise possible. A person who boasts to be one and *not* the other does not realise the synergy that both can bring. It is like having a television without a signal, or signals without a television. Claiming to be supremely creative may seem to be a colourful way to describe oneself, but it admits to a supreme ignorance of logic. And vice versa. To one who knows better, such a display of ignorance is greeted with as much contempt as the notion that reading is superior to writing, as if it were true that reading and writing can be mutually exclusive!

Logic says, "I'll believe it *after* I see it." Creativity says, "I'll believe it *then* I'll see it."

Logic asks, "What if?" Creativity asks, "Wouldn't it be great if?"

Logic keeps your life on track, while creativity fuels it.

The creative proposition, "I can talk to you from anywhere in the world", is acceptable because our logic is aware of how the telephone can make this proposition possible.

The creative proposition, "I can speak to millions of people at the same time" is also acceptable to our logic because of our understanding of how television can be used.

What would happen to these creative propositions if our logic did not know about the telephone and the television? If we were untrained thinkers, we would come to a

Once you have developed both your logic and creativity, you can engage in logictivity — the ability to use both skills simultaneously (and at lightning speed) without having to be conscious of the rapid swing from one to the other.

standstill — as many people do when confronted with such seemingly impossible propositions.

LOGICTIVITY CAN BE LEARNT

Logic and creativity are systems of learning. They are as important as learning to speak, or learning to walk. Some people possess very little creative or logical energy. Others tend to lean to one side or the other, while many boast to be one and *not* the other.

The important thing to realise about logic and creativity is that both skills can be acquired. This argument is about as true as the one that says that anyone can learn to ride a bicycle. The person who cannot yet ride a bicycle will not find it easy to learn, and might fall off several times during training. In the same way, a person learning the skills of logic and creativity might find it difficult at first, or might make mistakes that bruise emotionally, intellectually, or even physically.

Those who possess an over-abundance of creativity will find it just as difficult to learn about the structure of logic because people are not born "logical" or "illogical", nor are they born to be "creative" or "uncreative".

You will never learn to ride a bicycle until you first have the *desire* to do so. A *decision* to take action must then be made. Third, the *determination* to ride is necessary to see you through. These three attributes alone are insufficient to give you the skills to ride a bicycle. However, they will prepare you for your *development*. Cycling requires special muscles, special co-ordination, hours of training and practice, balance, an understanding of the road rules, and a place to ride from and to.

Learning to be logical or creative also requires the *desire, decision, determination,* and *development*. In the same

We tend to go in search of that which confirms our own position. We rarely volunteer to go in search of that which might expose us to ideas that go against our own beliefs.

73

way that a skill is never complete or whole, being logical or creative is a never-ending development. It is exciting that the more creative you become, the more you enjoy being creative; and the more logical you become, the more you enjoy being logical. But such enjoyment cannot reach a sustained level until the energy of both logic and creativity *balance*. That balance is what I call "logictivity".

Be warned that once you practise the processes of thinking "logictively" you will be unable to return to the old method of thinking.

Remember that logic and creativity are extremes. The mind swings between them. On the one side, logic acts as the science of reasoning, processing everything in binary — meaning that something is either true or false, up or down, possible or impossible. Computers are powerful logic machines because they work using binary systems. Logic is our understanding of what is possible and what is impossible. It relies on previous knowledge (hindsight). Logic starts to work against creativity when we introduce fear, confusion, and irrationality.

On the other side, creativity is about creating, making, inventing, crystallising, and going beyond the status quo; it brings into being that which was not there. This applies to our thoughts, ideas, actions, behaviours, attitudes, and imagination. The limits to creativity are lack of vision, lack of foresight, lack of understanding (or an imperfect understanding), and lack of knowledge (or an imperfect knowledge). In addition, logic itself can be a barrier to creativity, just as creativity can be a barrier to logic!

Once you have developed both your logic and creativity, you can engage in logictivity — the ability to use both skills simultaneously (and at lightning speed) without having to be conscious of the rapid swing from one to the other. In fact, once you practise logictivity, you no longer need to swing from one to the other. A trapeze artist fights against gravity by swaying left and right. Eventually, a balance is found. Balance is calm, it does not fight against other forces. It is a new force. When you find the balance of logictivity, you also find a whole new thinking process.

At first, logictivity requires a conscious effort. This is like asking you to tap your head with your left hand while rubbing your stomach with your right hand. Many people find this difficult at first. If they are able to control this motion, they can eventually do it without any conscious effort. The same applies to people learning to play the piano. At first, they find it a challenge to use both hands simultaneously to play a different set of notes. After much practice, the desired dexterity is achieved.

A NEW DIMENSION TO BRAIN POWER

Logictivity is definitely a complex (and worthwhile) skill to have. It adds a new dimension to your processing skills. It also makes you realise that those who are preoccupied with left-brain/right-brain development have far to go.

Logictivity requires an open mind. An open mind hints at the possibility of changing one's mind about certain issues.

Changing one's mind is the hardest thing to do in life. By listening with an open mind, we stand to learn something contrary to our long-held notions.

Changing one's mind is the hardest thing to do in life. By listening with an open mind, we stand to learn something contrary to our long-held notions (assumptions). In general terms, we tend to go in search of what confirms our own position. We rarely volunteer to go in search of what might expose us to ideas that go against our own beliefs. Those who love tennis do not go in search of reasoning that opposes tennis. Instead, they seek new ways to attain new pleasures from tennis.

Intellectual simpatico goes beyond "left brain and right brain" to recognise and use the brain as a *whole* — not as an instrument comprising two halves.

The agonising and liberating aspect to `logictivity is that it seeks neither to support nor oppose your existing assumptions. It does raise new thoughts and ideas that might go against your existing assumptions. It is this dilemma that you must be ready to accept if you wish to engage in logictivity. However, be warned that once you practise the processes of thinking "logictively" you will be unable to return to the old method of thinking. ▣

CHAPTER 7

CAN *you* SPEAK ANOTHER COLOUR?

USE MONO-THOUGHT TO SHARPEN YOUR BRAIN-SPEAK

THIS CHAPTER WILL INTRODUCE YOU to three powerful tools that relate to the development of leadership skills. These are "mono-thought", "brain-speak", and "colourful thinking". These are terms I have coined in order to describe these complex, yet essential, leadership skills.

During party conversations that centre on dreams, someone eventually asks if you dream in black and white, or in colour. This offers a good opportunity to engage in an experiment. Try to keep the conversation alive by asking if they can dream in hologram or only in red.

Try to stretch the boundaries and ask if they can dream in mirror image. I have not been able to take it beyond this point. However, if ever I find a group of people with a higher tolerance for my experiments, I would like to ask if they can dream in fast-forward. Then, for some self-inflicted torture, I would be curious to see their reaction when I ask if they can dream in reverse (as if rewinding a film).

The more you know, the more likely it is that others will irritate you

At a social gathering, there seems to be a sense of urgency to respond immediately to all questions. Awkward humour and witticism might emerge. Before you know it, the group will start to poke fun at the questions and, in no time, a new subject will command their attention.

The purpose of this social experiment has *nothing* to do with dreams. It is designed to observe the thinking process that someone gives to new ideas and strange questions. Above all, notice that there seems to be a sense of obligation to respond instantly to these interesting questions. Rarely would someone produce a note-pad to write down the question with a view to thinking about it and responding to it at a later stage.

At the other extreme are moments when friends and colleagues go through excruciating processes to arrive at a conclusion. They might be afflicted with hesitation or guilt thereby finding it difficult to take a stand. There are those who jump to conclusions without affording the subject sufficient analysis. The saddest of all are those who can no longer hold their *own* thought. They find it sinful to stand firm on a decision, except for socially approved norms.

Society enjoys social norms. As a result, those who gravitate towards the comfort zone are likely to sink into socially acceptable thinking processes. For example, at school I was conditioned to write essays that were devoid of my opinion — only authorities on the subject could be quoted or referred to. At work, I was encouraged to canvass several options and show flexibility in my views. The former says that one's opinion is not important while the latter says that a lack of flexibility-in-thought amounts to unwelcome stubbornness.

THINKING IS SUCH A PAIN

It is true that the more you know, the more you realise how much you do not know. Similarly, the more you know, the more likely it is that others will irritate you.

The more you think, the more you realise that there is very little competition in this sphere. The painful aspect comes when certain truths become known to the thinker while these revelations remain undiscovered for those who do not engage in rugged thinking. This results in a sense of loneliness for the thinker.

There are thousands of shades of grey, and unless one knows which shade is being referred to, one is merely saying that life is complex and far too difficult to cope with

Despite the revered qualities of intelligence, thinking is generally not understood, and is therefore not encouraged. Taking one's time to think might be seen as not knowing the answer. Stopping at work to stare out the window to think might label you as a daydreamer. Those who slow down to think about a solution might be called procrastinators. Sadly, those who require periods of inactivity are generally seen as lazy or unproductive.

Mind you, there are those who are so slow in their deliberation that they infuriate others by staring or appearing so vague that they make others uncomfortable. Slow thinkers ought not to discard social graces. They still need to be able to multi-task whereby they acknowledge the presence of others around them, and communicate the fact that they will need time to think through the implications. Simply not responding can be rude, if not off-putting.

IN WHICH COLOUR DO YOU THINK?

Regardless of what others do, this chapter is about you and your thinking processes. What do *you* do? What thinking processes do you engage in to arrive at your conclusions? Are you uncomfortable with holding on to a thought for fear of things changing around you, necessitating a change of mind? *Is your "thought" the derivative of "thinking" or do you hold thoughts that may have been born through someone else's brainwaves?*

Has anyone accused you of being simplistic when you have reduced complex thoughts into clear solutions? Have others tried to make you feel inadequate and accused you of being "black and white" when you have cut through complicated situations? Have you been told that you must deal with life's "shades of grey"? Have you been reminded about "the facts of life" when you have tried to synthesise issues? Have your colleagues told you to "get real"? Do your actions still cause people to plead with you to "be realistic"? Or, have you been accused of being: a dreamer; idealistic; futuristic; or too courageous in your thinking?

If you have suffered these hurdles, chances are that you are a thinker (or a real loony who has not come to grips with the facts of life). If you are a thinker, and are brave enough to venture to the next lonely level, come on a journey as we explore the *infuriating* and *liberating* concept of mono-thought — a process of thinking that boils everything down to one element. If it were possible to observe thinking under a microscope, mono-thought would be equivalent to observing complex compounds at their atomic level.

Mono-thought goes beyond the "black and white" and ventures through every shade of grey to colourful thinking, enabling you to arrive at the single thought or single word that best describes the answer. Mono-thought is a mental discipline that analyses an issue, concept, object, or thought, so that one arrives at the *single most important element*.

I became interested in this subject when, as a youngster, I had to battle with those around me who accused me of being "black and white". I had not heard this term before, so I was not sure what they meant. Later in life I was told that the world has many shades of grey, as if to suggest that there are many solutions to a problem. To me, I was neither being "black and white" nor was I ignoring the many shades of grey. In fact, I got to the point where I knew exactly which shade of grey I was referring to (meaning that I knew precisely what the issue was).

There is nothing wrong with being a private individual. However, the person you can least afford to lie to is yourself.

There is no point in knowing that the world contains shades of grey if you do not know which shade you are thinking of. There are thousands of shades of grey, and unless you know which shade is being referred to, you are merely saying that life is complex and far too difficult to cope with.

Through the years I was not only able to pinpoint the exact shade of grey, I was able to see the different colours as well. When I began to see the world in colour, my ability to inadvertently infuriate people, and they me, became heightened.

THINKING IN COLOUR

The best way for me to explain what it means to be able to "think in colour" is to refer to music or mathematics. If you are trained in music, you can quickly look at a score and hear the music in your mind. Notes may appear as black symbols on paper, but their meaning to those who can read music is brought alive in their mind. Those who are advanced at mathematics can calculate numbers in ways that make others marvel at their dexterity.

Similarly, words also mean more to the reader than just the characters of the alphabet. To those who can read English, the word DANGER means so much more than a string of letters. *Words bring thoughts to life*. The more words we have in our vocabulary, the better we can articulate meanings and nuances. However, an advanced command of the language through an increased vocabulary does not guarantee one the ability to communicate any better. In fact, it might retard the communication process if the recipient of the message is not so advanced.

So it is with mono-thought and the ability to think in colour — you will be able to see thoughts, ideas, and truths manifest out of thin air, just like 2+2 conjures up the number 4 whether you like it or not.

WHAT LANGUAGE DO YOU SPEAK?

Those who speak several languages are invariably asked about their "thinking language". If you can speak Italian, French, and English, others wonder which of these three is dominant. When you think and speak to yourself, which of the three languages do you engage in? What language do you dream in? Doubtless, for most bilingual and multilingual people, a dominant language emerges — just as it is that most people are either right-handed or left-handed, and rarely ambidextrous.

Beware the misconception that the more you know, the more you are revered or respected. In fact, the converse is true.

Mono-thought is about "brain-speak" — the natural language of the brain. Not English, nor Japanese, nor French, but "Brain". It is a language of the brain that is neither constrained nor restricted by human-made language. Brain-speak is an activity of the brain that manifests into thoughts that describe for us how we relate to our existence, reality, or environment.

Brain-speak is fast, it is accurate, it is vivid, and sometimes scary because it opens up a part of our world that is difficult, if not impossible, to explain in words. English, and the like, are artificial codes. These are nothing more than utterances born of the manipulation of vocal chords. Despite the wonders of oration and literature, the richness of the brain cannot be expressed adequately through vocal means.

Brain-speak is not related to intuition. Intuition is about input emanating from *external* signals and involves guesswork, heuristics (rules of thumb), analysis, and assumption — but not suspicion, or ESP (extra-sensory perception), or telepathy. Intuition leads to conclusions, meaning that after all the inputs have been processed, intuition arrives at an end-thought (that might lead to an action). You cannot engage in intuition without arriving at a conclusion. Intuitive processes can take place in split seconds. One of the experiments I use to demonstrate this requires members of the audience to place their fingers inside a door jamb, near the hinges. If the door were to close, their fingers would be crushed. I ask them to stand still and then I start to slam the door shut very quickly. Within a split second, everyone pulls their hand away, in fear of a painful encounter. The process they went through to arrive at the decision to remove their finger from the door jamb is an example of intuition. No-one could be certain of what I was about to do. No-one knew if I would intentionally hurt them. They calculated that their fingers were placed in a dangerous position, and that my motions seemed to point to a painful outcome. They observed, they processed, they made some assumptions, and then made a decision — all within a split second.

Unlike intuition, brain-speak is not about a conclusion. It is about input emanating from *internal* signals. Its purpose is to communicate with oneself — not necessarily to arrive at conclusions.

Those who argue that their words adequately describe their thoughts might be ignorant of brain-speak — and ignorance is bliss. For example, not knowing how to speak Greek is fine for millions of people. However, imagine how much richer their vocabulary and thought process might be if they could use that language. It is this kind of logic that best describes the beauty and wonder of brain-speak. Imagine how much richer one's *creativity* and *logic* could be if one were able to speak Brain!

If you are still unsure about what brain-speak means, first consider the nature of feelings. Imagine seeing an attractive person for the first time. You look at that person and within a short period of time you say to yourself, "I like that person!" The thought had never existed in your mind before because you had never seen that person before. When you decided that you liked that person, you expressed that thought to yourself in English. However, where did that thought come from? Before being able to form the words in English, you had that thought. It emanated from your feelings. Many people understand what feelings are, and they can agree that feelings have a language of their own.

The process of constructing music is an example of how the brain can function without the aid of the English language. Like brain-speak, music has a language of its own. Those who understand music, and are able to construct a tune or a symphony in their head, are not using the English language to do so. If you can appreciate that the brain does many things without the aid of the social language, you will start to accept the possibility that brain-speak exists. Like music, brain-speak happens in the privacy of your mind.

BRAIN-SPEAK IS NOT UNIVERSAL

Brain-speak is the most useful, unconstrained, and liberating form of thinking. However, it is not universal, it cannot be exchanged, and it is different for each person — meaning that it is a private affair that cannot be exchanged with others. This limitation is upon us until we discover a breakthrough that will free us from the shackles of the tongue. If, one day, we are able to communicate with each other through electronic brainwaves (e-brain, as it might become known) we would be able to know what each person is thinking. Imagine what a new world that would be.

E-brain would impact society a million times more than all the inventions and discoveries since the beginning of time. Imagine the power of truth. No longer would we need to search awkwardly for the right words. No-one would need to hide personal feelings and thoughts because it would become impossible to disguise them through the tricky veil of words. What would become of court cases? Of saying (or not having to say) "I love you"? Of affection and fondness becoming known? How would you feel if your disdain and dislike for others became evident in their presence? No more diplomacy, no more lies, no more hypocrisy, no more assumptions, no more speculation. Can the world survive in its current form? Definitely not! E-brain would do to social structures what a million exploding nuclear bombs would do to physical structures — obliterate them.

Imagine how much richer one's creativity and logic could be if one were able to speak Brain!

Alas, e-brain is not yet with us. However, *brain-speak* is here. But brain-speak is an individual process that must still battle with the bottle-neck of social language — if its revelations and outcomes are to be expressed to another person. One way to communicate brain-speak to another person is through *mono-thought*. Brain-speak is the most complex of thinking processes, hence it requires the simplest of decoders. Mono-thought is encouraged because it is the simplest way to net complex thoughts down to one single element.

SHARPEN YOUR BRAIN-SPEAK

Just as it is possible to learn how to add numbers very quickly, and it is possible to learn how to read music, it is possible to hone one's skills to engage in colourful thinking through brain-speak. This does take practice and years of hard work. In this short chapter I am unable to teach you how to *stop* thinking in your language and to *start* thinking in your own brain language. However, I can give you some clues to explore. For a start, you must work on some of the prerequisite subjects. The three primary areas that must first be sharpened are observation, memory, and analysis. These could take years to improve. The process cannot be a casual one. As with music, it could take ten years just to realise that you are ready to "play with" music, not just "play" music.

Furthermore, the development of your observation, memory, and analytical skills requires sustained practice to the point where they are exercised subconsciously. This means that your ability to think in these three ways would resemble your ability to see 4 every time you see 2+2.

Having become accomplished in these three primary skills you will possess the mental agility to forgo your dominant social language. Once you have let go of your social language (such as English) you will have a void. However, the brain is too clever to allow a void to exist. It will spring into action with its own unconstrained brain language that I call "brain-speak". (By the way, there is something I call "spirit-speak", but that is a subject for one of my future books.)

As you begin to use brain-speak to *think* in colour, you will have an urge to *speak* in colour, and unless you are communicating with someone who is at your level, you will infuriate people, and they in turn will irritate you. To minimise this confrontation, you need to understand mono-thought.

WHAT IS MONO-THOUGHT?

As previously explained, mono-thought is a mental process that analyses an issue, concept, object, or thought, so that one arrives at the *single most important element*. It is used to examine an issue and net it down to one element through one word or one phrase so that it eliminates as much doubt as possible. Mono-thought tries to take away ambiguity. Its simplicity is designed to remove misunderstanding and misconception. Mono-thought exposes an issue, so that its intent becomes clear and unequivocal.

Mono-thought demands and forces the communicator to make tough choices. This can be likened to the question, "Who would you prefer was killed, your mother or your father?" Supposing that you love them both equally, you might be tempted to plead with the killer to choose neither. You might even offer your own life as a sacrifice. However, mono-thought is stubborn. It demands an answer, not an alternative. In this scenario, you would be obliged, and forced, to make a choice between one parent or the other. Imagine the difficulty of having to choose which of your loved children would have to suffer brutal torture and death. Although this is an unpleasant analogy, it best describes the single-minded and focused decision process that you will be forced to make when you engage in mono-thought. This decision-tree approach to decision-making cuts through the nonsense. Your thoughts will have to stand naked and away from the clutter.

If used properly, mono-thought offers rich rewards. Like any profound revelation, its manifestation cannot be ignored. For example, you cannot choose to forget your name. You cannot decide to disbelieve in the existence of motor vehicles. Once you become aware of the power of mono-thought, you cannot decide to ignore it. You cannot even decide to disengage from it.

The practical application of mono-thought helps you to get to the bottom of things. You will be able to prioritise your tasks in ways you had not imagined possible. You will be able to arrive at conclusions at a speed similar to the way you arrive at 4 every time you see 2+2.

Mono-thought demands the answer to complex questions. Why are you choosing to do this or that? What is the real reason that you want to get married, or buy that car, or take a holiday? You must be honest with yourself. Even though people know the truth behind their motives, they rarely admit the situation to themselves, let alone to their friends or colleagues. There is nothing wrong with being a private individual. However, the person you can least afford to lie to is yourself. You need to use mono-thought to really interrogate why you are making a decision. Why do you really want to get married? Is it love, or money, or sex, or security, or do you fancy the idea of moving out of home and leaving your demanding parents? Is it something society expects of you, or are you trying to hide your homosexuality by being seen to wed someone of the opposite sex? Any answer that is right for you is acceptable. The point of this chapter is not to ask you to *change* your life or your choices. It simply challenges you to *confront* your real motives so that you know what you are doing, and *why* you are doing it. You need not confide in anyone, nor divulge your thoughts. (For more on motivation, see Chapter 3, "The secret destroyer".)

E-brain would do to social structures what a million exploding nuclear bombs would do to physical structures — obliterate them

In work-related environments, mono-thought does become uncomfortable because, although it does not demand that others divulge their thinking process, it does demand that they make a choice. Why must we advertise this product? Is it to increase awareness, or to increase sales? You cannot say both. If it is to increase sales, by how much do you expect sales to be increased? At which point would you cancel the campaign? All the answers must be explicit, single-minded, and direct. No slippery or wishy-washy responses can be tolerated.

THE BLACK-AND-WHITE DAYS

Those who engage in mono-thought will eventually be accused of being "black and white", despite the fact that mono-thought was born of brain-speak. It is the product of thinking in full colour. Those whom you infuriate might even curse you for being bloody-minded. Part of the infuriation might come from misunderstandings. It could spring from frustration when you expose the truth and possibly stifle someone's hidden motives. It could also emerge from impatience when others realise that they will have to re-work their proposals.

EXAMPLES OF MONO-THOUGHT

Many times I have heard lecturers preface a series of questions with the comforting remark that "there are no right or wrong answers". In mono-thought, there *are* right and wrong answers. When situations arise that depend on personal issues, the answers will still demand truth, but that truth would be known only to you. For such personal issues, or for issues that relate to your unique environment, your mono-thought will be right for you if you so *believe, understand,* and *accept*. These three stages are vital in your comprehension. You need to *believe* that what you are saying is true for you. You need to *understand* that what you are saying is true for you. You need to *accept* that what you are saying is true for you. When you have tested your environment, and processed your situation via another round of observation, memory, and analysis, you will arrive at *knowledge*. You will then reach the supreme level of mono-thought — where you will *know* that what you are saying is true.

By all means, mono-thought is difficult. For example, try to determine the single most important organ in the human body. Think about it or discuss it with friends, but do arrive at a conclusion that you believe, understand, and accept; and one that points unequivocally to a single organ. If you are not medically versed to make such a decision, try to determine what, for each of the following, is the single most important element: 1) formula-one motor racing; 2) political elections; 3) business; 4) disease management; 5) religion; 6) the Opposition; and 7) customer service.

Ask motor-racing experts and they will tell you that, all things considered, it is excellence in braking that determines the winner. Most political elections are won and lost as a result of how well one sells to the marginals. The single most important element to a successful business is execution. Prevention is the key to disease management, and faith is the lynchpin for religion. Your opinion may differ. For example, if fear is what you attribute to religion, that is correct if you so believe, understand, and accept. An Opposition party's single most important mission is to tear the Government down so that it can get into power. It is not there to help make the country a better place. The single most important element in customer service is speed.

When we talk of leadership, creativity is the most

important element. As for technology, the most important element is application, meaning how one applies the technology to solve a problem or to create an opportunity.

If mono-thought is applied to everyday questions, you will see how controversial it becomes. For example, in an organisation, what is the *function* of staff? To me, staff members are there to execute management's plans. From "execute" we arrive at the word "executive". Staff members are the executives.

What is the function of capital? To generate wealth. The function of industrial labour is to generate capital. Of course, many would argue with these conclusions. However, ask them to arrive at their own mono-thought. See how they cope with having to net the question down to one single thought — not for academic reasons, but for truth. Why do they do what *they* do?

For me, the single most important function of management is to "pre-empt". As for sales, the single most important function is to "sell". This comes as a surprise to many sales folk who had hoped it was something more elaborate than this.

The function of marketing is not "to market". There is no such thing. Those who speak of the four-Ps are showing their ignorance and their rigid textbook thinking. There is no such verb as "to market" despite messy thinkers who say things like "we must market this product to children". There are many functions to marketing, as with everything in life, but the single most important function of marketing is to "engineer the future".

The function of technology is to "create an advantage", meaning that if you are using technology, and you are not doing so for the purpose of creating an advantage, you are either a victim of the "law of saturation" or you are an ignorant sucker.

UP AND OUT

The more knowledge you have, the further out you will be. Beware the misconception that the more you know, the more you are revered or respected. In fact, the converse is true.

There is an old Chinese story that speaks of a young man who lives in a village with his family. They enjoy a simple life, and they know nothing of how other villagers live. They are content. One day the young man ventures to another mountain in the distance. There, he is exposed to bigger, better, brighter things. Better food, cleaner water, happier people, fresh air, and a greater sense of joy.

Some time later, the young man returns to his family whom he loves. He pleads with them to join him in the new-found land. They do not listen. They are content, and do not wish to venture further. He is now caught between his current state of affairs, and knowing that the other mountain could offer him a better life.

Despite his immense love for his family, he decides to leave them. He knows that he could not live with himself if he does not go to the mountain and enjoy all that it offers. His mind has now expanded, and it is impossible for him to ignore what he now knows to be true.

Brain-speak, colourful think- ing, and mono-thought are all elements offered by the other mountain, awaiting the adventur- ous. If you leave your current comfort zone in search of these, you will be forced to bid farewell to your dear friends whom you will be forced to love from a *distance* because they might choose to ignore your invitation to join you.

If you are using technology, and you are not doing so for the purpose of creating an advantage . . . you are an ignorant sucker

The more you know, the more likely it is that others will irritate you, and the more likely it is that you will infuriate the establishment. Sadly, you will also, inadvertently, be considered an outsider who "does not understand" when, in fact, it is you who can see what others do not see.

Mono-thought, brain-speak, and colourful thinking are liberating, but liberation is cruel to the status quo. Choose carefully because your subsequent choice might be forced upon you. **K**

CHAPTER 8

ANOTHER *dirty* WORD

AMBITION — POWER WITHOUT MERCY

I ONCE HEARD A CEO of a large organisation criticise military establishments for their obvious reverence for visible ranking. This sparked my curiosity about the benefits of displaying one's rank through pips and stripes. What does such categorisation do? Is it there to inflate one's ego, or to communicate the reporting structure? Is it a way to seek respect and discipline? Does it keep subordinates eager? Or is it so steeped in history and tradition that it has lost its meaning?

The CEO presented a cogent argument about "respect for all", not just for the chosen few. He advocated equality, and criticised the ways in which military personnel flaunted their rank.

The slight ring of truth in his argument dissipated when I started to realise the hypocrisy of his statements. Upon close examination, it was clear that he flaunted his position in more ways than his accused. His business card advertised his impressive title; his name was followed by a series of letters signifying his academic qualifications and industry associations; his supposed equality afforded him a much-desired parking space for his chauffeur-driven car; his spacious office was adorned with certificates and photographs; support staff catered to his whims; and he enjoyed a myriad of corporate accessories and fringe benefits that other comrades lusted for, including exclusive memberships, first-class travel, and his own washroom!

The authority he wielded attracted sycophants desperate for his approval. His influence and lifestyle had a glossy exterior that many found attractive and desirable.

His executives seemed keen to acquire the trappings of the ivory tower. They focused more on climbing the corporate ladder than on engaging in an exciting industry — all the while aware that their skills and intellect (or lack thereof) had very little to do with their prospects for promotion.

This does seem to be a harsh way to describe his managers. One would think that among them were a few keen, enthusiastic professionals. Yes, there were but, typically, such individuals did not last long. Their refusal to "play the game" landed them in hot water.

This destructive game lured executives with the promise of a possible stint on the throne, although anyone who threatened the incumbent received the fatal sting. He expected his followers to be ambitious — but not *too* ambitious.

The pecking order was re-set every time the boss went away on business. A much-awaited memo would give all the right signals to those who knew how to read the cryptic clues. It would decree who was to "fill in" for the boss. Interestingly, complete power was never vested in just one person. A typical memo would read, "Jane has my *functional* authority, while Bob has my *financial* authority . . ."

In my developing years I had the misfortune of working with just such a person of discriminating power. I was too young to know better at the time; however, I became puzzled when, one day, the operations manager came into my office and moved the large pot plant to the outside of the glass wall. "What are you doing that for?" I asked.

"Sorry, Jonar. Your level does not allow you to have a plant in your office."

That must have been a tribal hint to which I was completely oblivious. Whatever I did to trigger that pettiness was still threatening the boss, because a few weeks later the telephone that I had inherited was replaced. I was not permitted to use it because it contained a calculator, which in those days was a serious executive perk reserved for the privileged few. I recall seeing it thrown into a box full of junk in the storeroom. It was better for it to sit there and collect dust than to have a lesser ranked employee use it. To top it off, I had to buy a calculator at my expense because when I requisitioned one from the company, I was told that my choice was limited — managers at my level were not permitted to order calculators that contained more than twenty-one buttons. A few months later, the round table in my office was replaced with one that was slightly smaller in diameter.

Although we executives did not wear our rank on our sleeves, there was no doubt about our pecking order.

CLIMBING THE LADDER

In order to understand how *ambition* interconnects with *rank*, I undertook part of my research at a military airforce base where I met sergeants and officers, including pilots and the Air Commodore.

One of my visits was especially memorable. An officer and I were lured onto the tarmac by the roar of the F111s.

Within seconds two airmen ran towards us shouting. They did not dare touch us because they did not know who we were. So they stopped, saluted, as befitted their rank, and asked us to move back. I did not pay attention because my eyes were fixed on a jet that was making its final approach to land. A third airman arrived. Realising that he was the more senior officer, he told us to "get the hell out of there" in crude and no uncertain terms.

By this time, the F-111 had just landed on my right. The officer grabbed our arms and abruptly dragged us away. I felt a rush of adrenalin. What was all the panic about? As the jet taxied past us and made a sharp right turn, we hit the ground. Just over our heads the scorching after-burner put everything into perspective. I felt the heat-wave from those merciless flames and realised that we could have been burnt to a cinder.

Strangely enough, despite the intensity of that near-death experience, and the many fascinating conversations I had with all sorts of military personnel during my research, the one event that made the biggest impression on me was a conversation I had with a sergeant. I asked him about his career and what he was doing to elevate his status. To my dismay, he said that he had no desire to become an officer. I could not understand his response. "Why are you serving in the air force if you do not want to be promoted?" I asked. I could not understand why he was so uninterested in furthering his career. Was he unhappy? Did he lack ambition? Was he complacent?

I must admit that my esteem for him plummeted. For years I remained disappointed by his response. I was under the impression that the whole purpose of working within such an environment was to seek promotion and climb the ladder.

In years to come, I began to learn that ambition is not about wanting a bigger title or a higher rank. The sergeant was content with his work. He loved what he did. He was not wasting his days trying to escape his job. I remember him saying, "I like the action at my level. I don't want to be an officer because I will lose touch with the men and might end up a pen-pusher."

TOO MUCH OF A GOOD THING CAN'T BE BAD

There is a disease in life called "too much". Often we hear of someone drinking too much, spending too much, or thinking too much. Some of us are said to be too clever for our own good. Alas, some of us even *love* too much. Those who fall from a great height are sometimes branded as too ambitious — which makes one wonder just how much is too much?

Is ambition something that needs to be moderated? Why is it a dirty word when it is essential for success? If ambition is so important, why is too much ambition a bad thing?

Evidently, ambition is fraught with danger. It is one of those personal ingredients that often lead to theft, dishonesty, selfishness, and short-sightedness.

WHAT IS AMBITION?

Ambition is nothing more than fuel that we can use to help us get to where we want to go. It drives us to improve the tangible things in life, such as where we live, what we drive, and the work we do. We can use it to enact change that is material. It helps us to take practical action to learn and develop. As with many fuels, it needs to be mixed with other oils. The two oils that mix well with ambition are *perseverance* and *greed*.

Ambition mixed with perseverance leads to devotion. Ambition mixed with greed leads to insatiability.

Ambition mixed with perseverance leads to *devotion*. Ambition mixed with greed leads to *insatiability*.

Used properly, ambition can help people to reach their target so long as they know when to switch the engines off. If they do not slow down at the right time (usually well before they reach their destination), they are likely to overshoot the mark. Some people do not recognise their target as they approach it because it looks different upon closer inspection. Others bypass it when a more alluring jewel distracts them. Consequently, their target is always distant because it is like a horizon at sea — ever present yet far away.

The desire to climb higher and travel further can become so distracting, that one becomes enamoured by the lure of the distant dream, thereby losing sight of the surrounding riches. As a result, people will lack contentment and peace; they will never feel a sense of belonging. Whatever their situation, they are dissatisfied with it. Their material wealth never seems to be enough. They do not value their self-worth. If you do not understand your self-worth, it is like having a box full of trinkets — you throw out all the diamonds in search of a penny.

At this point, ambition is used to fuel an insatiable appetite. Those within the grip of insatiability seldom correct their ways until they hit a brick wall — physically or emotionally. They can't stop until something stops them. That sudden shock will either destroy them, or help them to reset their values and become enthusiastic for life.

However, life is not a balance between "realities and dreams", but between "addiction and grace". Paradoxes such as these keep us alert to the meaning of life.

Addiction to bigger and better ideals generates hope, which in turn provides purpose. Addiction becomes destructive when it no longer seeks "bigger and better" but hunts for "more, more often".

Grace fosters satisfaction and brings charm to modesty. It dignifies the status quo and greets each waking moment as one would greet a dear friend. Its only shortcoming is its propensity to be complacent.

SO WHAT'S WRONG WITH TOO MUCH AMBITION?

While ambition can take us to new and unfamiliar territories, *too much* ambition can take us to places that are
beyond our capabilities. The reason that we do not
acknowledge the latter is that we tend to harbour two
diseases — *pride* and *denial*.

The main function of pride is to convince us that we
possess certain things that in fact we do not. The main
function of denial is to convince us that we do not possess
certain things that in fact we do.

At the crossroads of life we have to greet "addiction
and grace" and "pride and denial". The complexity of this
balancing act will determine how and when we use our
fuel to reach our desired destination. Perfect balance is
best reached after we learn about these necessary (but
potentially lethal) paradoxes. We can only master them
after making mistakes and refining our judgement. In the
same way that it is impossible to teach children how to
ride a bicycle merely by describing the process, it is impossible to teach people how to balance these paradoxes until
they each experience the process for themselves.

When addiction and grace fuse, we arrive at *gratitude*.
When pride and denial fuse, we arrive at *consciousness*. If
we are mature, we will be able to fuse the blessings of
gratitude and consciousness to enjoy a *zestful life*.

When we understand the function of ambition, we
can see that there is no shame in being ambitious for a
zestful life.

WHAT IS THE MEANING OF SUCCESS?

Those who use ambition to help them climb the ladder of success will never be satisfied because the ladder is a magical one that has no end point.

Those who believe that success is measured by "rank" will never feel successful because they will always aspire to a higher rank.

Although people truly desire success, they cannot reach it until they understand its characteristics and laws.

Are you successful? If you answer yes, then the next question is are you working towards *more* success? If so, what does that mean? How will you measure your success?

First, success has nothing to do with material wealth, position, or status. If you are desperately trying to seek profits, you will not reach your goal anywhere near as quickly and as joyfully until you can engross yourself in your craft, and love your environment and the people with whom you interact. When you do what you do well, with wholesome intention and superb attention, then success comes your way. Success comes to you, you don't go to it.

When you do what you do well, with wholesome intention and superb attention, then success comes your way. Success comes to you, you don't go to it.

Also be aware that success is not concerned with what you *amass*, but with what you *discard*. There are several levels of success. The primary level is to discard the things that detract from a zestful life. The secondary level of success develops the mind and expands the soul in search of that which is bigger, better, and purer.

Without an understanding of the meaning of success, people tend to use ambition (the fuel) to amass trophies in the form of material wealth and rank. Unfortunately, what they do not realise is that while they are growing their assets, they are also growing their burdens. Such people bemoan the fact that they are busier than ever, under more pressure, and have more weight on their shoulders. If growing one's asset portfolio results in growing the pain, then this is the epitome of futility.

WHAT DIRTY WORD?

In summary, let me reiterate that the primary level of success is reached when we can use ambition to help us to alter material conditions so as to strive for a zestful life by reducing the things we dislike, and increasing the things we enjoy. Mind you, what we enjoy is not necessarily good, and what we dislike is not necessarily bad. The ability to ascertain the difference is called perceptivity. The ability to resist the temptations is called wisdom.

The secondary level of success is associated with increasing our capacity to absorb more of the beauties of life. This enables us to share generously, travel steadfastly, laugh louder, love more deeply, and rest more nourishingly.

At any point in time, you have a limited quantity of energy. You can expend it in search of rank and status, or use it wisely to subdivide your life into manageable portions. When selecting your desired portions, seek what your heart desires, not what your ego demands. Satisfying your heart is fulfilling. Kowtowing to your ego is depleting.

Seek what your heart desires, not what your ego demands

When you look at the potential of how ambition can be used, you might agree with me that ambition is not a dirty word. Furthermore, too much ambition can only assist us to live an enchanted life. ∎

PART TWO

WORKING *with* OTHERS

CONTROL IS A
WONDERFUL THING.
BUT YOU *don't*
HAVE CONTROL
WHEN YOU
HAVE A COMMITTEE.

CHAPTER 9

LEADERSHIP

THE WRONG QUESTION
WILL LEAD TO
THE WRONG ANSWER

FOR SOME REASON, "LEADERSHIP" HAS been well-branded. As a single word, it commands great respect. Remarkably, most people would be happy to be dubbed a leader, despite the popular notion that some leaders are good and just as many are evil. The term is used respectfully in business, sport, government, and in battle.

In the presence of too many would-be leaders, and to stand out from the crowd, some disown the ambiguous title and bestow upon themselves something humbler, like "servant-leaders" who prefer to engage in "stewardship".

Not every giver is generous. Not every fighter is a warrior. Similarly, not all leaders appreciate the values of leadership.

When the tribe follows and copies, things must change once more. To stand apart, the proud invent another branch of leadership such as: *effective* leadership; *breakthrough* leadership; *strategic* leadership; or *situational* leadership. There are those too who bow out gracefully, leave it all behind, and refer to themselves as "mentors".

As it is with marketing, management, and politics, there are many who claim to be experts on leadership — making it difficult for the keen student to find a source of knowledge. Uncertain of a direction, seekers entrust their hearts to gurus who promise to enlighten the faithful with pearls of wisdom.

For such an old subject, it seems strange that so many

new books proliferate annually while seminars run unabated. What is it that makes the subject of leadership so fascinating? Why is it that whenever the subject is discussed, the word "management" needs to be defended and put into its own box. Why does this subject always result in the question about leaders being *made* or *born*?

The fascination with the subject of leadership is multi-pronged. There are those who *know* that they are leaders and go in search of new ideas, so that they can fuel their dreams; those who *think* that they are leaders and go in search of buzz-words, so that they can fool some of the people some of the time; those who would *like* to be leaders, so they study as much as they can to grow and to enter the ranks in due course. There are also the humble few who are curious about leadership and seek to understand it, so that they can become better followers.

By and large, this book is of no use to those who delude themselves. The humble could benefit from an understanding of their environment, so that they do not infuriate their leaders (and others) with ignorance. However, this book is most valuable to those who engage in leadership and are challenged by the modern world, looking for clues about how to navigate its terrain. As for those who would *like* to be leaders, they can use this book to learn more about what they aspire to be. It is possible that they, too, might be deluding themselves if they go in search of something about which they know little. The danger is that they might harbour delusions about the environment in which leaders must survive. Some assume that there is glamour associated with being a leader. Alas, the moment you become a leader, you will be hit with the "law of paradoxicality", feeling rich and poor, liberated and opposed, free and restrained, proud and humble, popular and lonely — simultaneously.

WHAT IS A LEADER?

Here it is important to introduce a new thought by stating that the word "leader" and its function is different to the word "leadership" and its function. This means that a *leader* is not necessarily one who *engages in leadership*. Therefore, please take note of the ways in which these two words are used throughout this book. There are major differences. In fact, there are no similarities. This is explained below.

> *We are what we think, we think what we know, and we know what we can articulate*

Leaders are pathmakers — those who *cut a new path,* with or without the help of others; for their own sake or for the sake of others; for monetary gain or otherwise; for adventure or duty; in misery or delirium.

When a *leader* cuts new paths, most often the outcome is *tangible*. On the other hand, *leadership* defines the *framework* (the condition under which paths are carved); and most often this is *intangible*. The principles of the tangible and intangible worlds are explored throughout this book.

If *leaders* are pathmakers, what is *leadership?* This is a difficult question. The difficulties do not lie in the answer, but rather in the question. To ask "what is leadership?" poses all sorts of hurdles because it is the *wrong* question to be asking. The wrong question will lead to the wrong answer. After reading this book, I expect that you will realise that the question ought to be "*why* leadership?"

WHY LEADERSHIP?

There is a major difference between "what" and "why". Hundreds of books have dealt with *what* leadership is. Obviously very few authors agree, otherwise so many publications would not have eventuated. In life, to find the right answer, one must ask the right question. If it were merely a question of "what" then anyone who fulfils the criteria, or those seven habits, could claim to be engaging in leadership. If it were possible to agree on the definition of *what* leadership is, and let's say that it is doing X, Y, and Z, then anyone who does these things could be said, erroneously, to be engaging in leadership. Surely leadership is not as superficial as fulfilling a list of criteria.

Leadership is not *what* is done, but *why* it is done. The "why" penetrates to the truth behind an action. The act of giving can be unwholesome in the light of why it is done. It is in itself open to judgement until its roots are exposed, because the reasons behind an action far out-weigh the worth of the action itself. It is the truth behind the action that makes it wholesome or unwholesome. Leadership cannot exist in the presence of the unwhole-some, just as integrity cannot exist in the presence of corruption or deceit.

In presenting this concept through the years, it prompts people to ask for an explanation about how we can account for brutal dictators whose actions are considered to be unwholesome. Please note that such people were *leaders*, but they did not engage in *leadership* because leadership cannot exist in the presence of the unwholesome.

Not every giver is generous. Not every fighter is a warrior. Not all players are champions. Similarly, not all leaders appreciate the values of leadership.

Furthermore, leadership is not a layer. It is not a cloak. One cannot put it on and take it off when convenient. Leadership is either *present* or it is not. Like many of the intangible human qualities, it exists on its own terms or not at all. It is a quality that permeates one's every waking moment. Its existence is constant and unshakeable. Also note that the concept of "situational leadership" is a mis-nomer. Yes, it is possible to have a situational *leader*, but it is impossible to engage in situational *leadership*. Leadership is not alternating. It is rock-solid.

A *leader* might choose to behave or react in certain ways, depending on the situation. However, one who engages in *leadership* never deviates from the *values* of leadership.

Leadership is *not* about "doing". One can engage in leadership while idle. Leadership is not about activity and action. Although the essence of leadership often results in action (whether it be by oneself, or with others, or through others), action is merely the *result* of leadership, not the *mark* of leadership.

As for the question of *good* leadership versus *bad* leadership, it must shatter many myths to declare that there is no such thing as good or bad leadership — nor anything called *real* leadership. I am appalled at the misinformation that is propagated about this. It sickens me to hear lecturers ask students to name some leaders, in the hope that Adolf Hitler's name is mentioned. From this, the lecturer points out that Hitler's leadership was bad. That is hogwash. Hitler might have been a *leader,* but he did not engage in *leadership*. Remember that there is a huge difference between being a leader and engaging in leadership.

Innovation comes not from conformity. Genius is harnessed not from mediocrity.

A *leader* can brave new paths, and these can lead to good or evil. The leader can be: a happy builder or a miserable destroyer; shrewd or foolish; temporary or permanent; recalcitrant or respectful; revered or feared; hated or loved; acclaimed or despised. A leader can be self-appointed, anointed by others, or one who earned the position through rank.

Leadership is something altogether different. There is no such thing as *good* leadership or *bad* leadership.

Leadership is a word that resembles "leader" but has no association with its diversity. Leadership, as a personal characteristic, stands on its own. It is not always correct to say that a *leader* is one who engages in *leadership*.

It is possible for a leader to be devoid of leadership qualities and values. Such nuances make all the differences in the world. Minute detail can sink ships. A comma and a full stop look similar, but their function is different. You would agree that the joy of seeing a million dollars written on your bank statement hinges on the tiny plus sign (+). If it were governed by the similar minus sign (–), its value would be different.

Leadership is not something that can be *bad*. It cannot even be *good*. It just *is*. It is pure and neutral. It does not seek to build nor to destroy.

Leadership defines the framework and the condition of an intangible human characteristic whose values are immovable, whose quality is consistent, whose charter is unwavering, and whose presence is constant.

One must realise that leadership is not about *leading*, it is about *creating* — another nuance that makes all the difference!

THE VISIONARY, THE DREAMER, THE REVOLUTIONARY, AND THE LEADER

Words have fascinated me since childhood. I have come to the realisation that our words are our definition. They determine our thoughts. We are what we think, we think what we know, and we know what we can articulate. We must not treat words with contempt, nor unnecessarily colour our language flamboyantly.

People are sometimes described as visionaries, dreamers, revolutionaries, and leaders, or a combination of these — although rarely with any justification. It is important to understand these words and how they are associated with leadership.

Visionaries are those who can see a distant paradigm that is *different* to the one they currently embrace. Leadership can enable visionaries to see a *better* paradigm.

Dreamers have the capability to design *new* frameworks. Leadership can enable the dreamer to design *better* frameworks.

Revolutionaries dislike the *current* path and seek to destroy it. Leadership can help revolutionaries to discern which path is the better one to destroy.

Leaders are those who know how to construct *new* paths. Leadership can enlighten leaders to construct *better* paths.

THE MOST IMPORTANT QUESTION IS THE THIRD

In the modern world, the margin for error has been narrowed while the time frame for evolution has been compressed. To operate within the framework of leadership, the most important question that one must answer is "why?" However, it is the *third* "why" that gets one nearer to the root and closer to the truth.

When someone in your organisation proposes a course of action, ask them *why* they are making that suggestion.

Leadership is not about <u>what</u> is done, but <u>why</u> something is done

After they give you the top-level response, ask them *why* that is so. After that has been explained, ask them *why* for the third time. For example, someone might say, "Let's paint this office and make it look better." *Why?* "So that we can impress the client." *Why?* "So that we can give them the impression that we are a successful and credible operation." *Why?*

It is this third question that will open the way for a more detailed and frank discussion about the root of the matter. Does the client currently have the impression that you are *not* a credible operation? If so, would painting the office suffice? Are you competing against a polished competitor whose plush offices reflect success? If that is the case, can you compete on image or should you find a more convincing angle? Furthermore, if it is *credibility* you must project, perhaps your representative's mode of dress and professional conduct ought to be reviewed, not the condition of the walls. Another example will illustrate this. If your friend suggests that she would like to study science at a distant university, you would ask *"why?"* She might say that she enjoys science. But *why* not study science at the local university? She might respond, "Because I really want to get out of this district." *Why?*

"Because I want to leave home." The picture is starting to change. At first it was for the love of science, and now it emerges that it has something to do with an unhappy environment at home.

Be careful not to interrogate people. You must handle this line of questioning delicately, compassionately, sensitively, and discreetly. Do not bombard people with a series of questions that is likely to make them feel under attack. It is important to really understand what is happening around you. Very often, by the third "why", things begin to look different.

Finding the root at an early stage saves a lot of agony and heartache down the track. This discipline is something you must be able to apply to yourself first. *Why* do you feel the way that you do? *Why* are you choosing this course of action?

It takes perceptive people to be honest with themselves, and courageous ones to be honest with friends, family, and colleagues. A lot of courage would be required to overcome the sometimes bombastic and foul elements that charge ahead without reasonable analysis or with hidden unwholesome intentions. This is why it is so much easier to go with the flow. However, innovation comes not from conformity. Genius is harnessed not from mediocrity.

DEFINITIONS

Let us now summarise what the words "leader" and "leadership" mean, and define what is meant by "management".

First, a leader is a pathmaker — one who carves a new path, finds or designs new ways, and moves in a new direction. A leader is one who invents a new solution to an old problem, or invents a new solution to a *new* problem. A leader might even invent a new problem, with or without a new solution to match. The leader can be anybody who chooses to lead. However, when you lead, you are exercising your right to accept or demand the authority needed to act. A leader cannot lead without first having or taking the authority.

Remember that leaders might lead others, or might just lead themselves. Leaders who work through others are not necessarily always said to be *leading* others. Those people whom the leader works with to accomplish a mission are not necessarily *followers*. They might just be workers, contractors, or consultants who might not understand the bigger picture. They might be working for a salary, a fee, or voluntarily.

The leader could very well be the mail clerk who decides to change the whole mail distribution system. That mail clerk could become a leader by marshalling support to form a new union to fight for workers' rights.

Anyone who leads does so for the duration of the project. This might be ten days, or ten years. However, it is during the act of leading that one is deemed to be a leader. In other words, a leader is only a leader when *leading* — when carving a new path. The moment that a new path has been carved and the leader completes the task, that person is no longer a leader (until the next project). This is why people cannot be grouped into leaders and followers, or leaders and non-leaders. Meaning that the roles, functions, and responsibilities of a leader expire the moment that the mission has been accomplished, or when one has a change of heart or when one dies. It is for these reasons that it seems trite to categorise or to flatter people with the title of "leader". They cannot be leaders unless they are carving new paths. The fact that someone was a leader, or had successfully carved a new path, does not make that person a leader forever. No matter what people did in the past, they cannot be called leaders today unless they are in fact leading today.

This explains the reasons behind once-great leaders who move from victory to failure. Their failure puzzles others who cannot understand how it was possible that the person who accomplished great things in the past is now unable to repeat that performance. You might have heard about prominent leaders who were great when in battle, but less effective in times of peace. The staggering thing is that people are still trying to fathom this phenomenon. A leader in war ceases to be a leader when the war is over. If that person tries to carve a new path once more, success is not guaranteed.

One is not a leader first, and a carver second. Instead, one is a carver and, as a result of this, one is called the leader. This means that the title of leader is not something that can be bestowed or given, or claimed, without the act of carving new paths.

This is the major difference between a manager and a leader. The manager is one who is appointed. A manager can hold on to the authority of the office for a set duration, or until that title is withdrawn. A manager is a professional, meaning someone whose job it is to undertake certain tasks agreed by the boss who appointed the manager.

It takes perceptive people to be honest with themselves, and courageous ones to be honest with friends, family, and colleagues

It is possible for a manager to be a leader within the scope of management, or to be a leader externally, meaning that a sales manager of one organisation can be a community leader who carves a new path to freedom and equality. An office worker could be the leader who makes major reforms that lead to new laws enacted in parliament.

A manager cannot be called a leader simply because that manager has fifty staff. Having people reporting to the manager does not make that manager the leader of the group. The group might not have a leader. On the other hand, the group might have one or more leaders who lead within the scope of their job, or who lead externally.

Having defined what it means to be a leader and what it means to be a manager, it is now important to define leadership. It was outlined earlier in this chapter that it would be incorrect to ask, "what is leadership?" Leadership is not about what is done, but why something is done.

Leadership is a quality similar in nature to integrity. Leadership is inextricably linked to values.

In summary, leadership is about operating to a set of rock-solid wholesome values, all the time, every time. There are different levels of leadership and we begin to learn more about leadership with maturity, experience, and blessings. However, there is only one kind and one style of leadership. The person who is blessed with leadership might operate in life as a manager or as a leader. That person might choose to operate within certain styles, but you cannot deviate from leadership and still be within the framework of leadership. Those who deviate from honesty are no longer honest. Those who deviate from honour are no longer honourable. Leadership, like honesty and honour, is not a layer. It is not alternating. Deviation spells destruction.

There exists a famous notion that "to lead, one must follow". This is fallacious. To lead, one must follow one's spirit faithfully, not other people.

Finally, leadership is about *creating* something that was not there before. Within the framework described above, people engage in leadership when they create. Most often, these creations are intangible.

The other major difficulty in defining leadership is that it is ultimately an intangible itself that cannot be described to those who cannot see it. And people cannot see it until they have it. Like wisdom, or love, or honour, words alone cannot describe it sufficiently, no matter how eloquent the description. Imagine how difficult it would be to describe a colour to someone who has never seen that colour before. Or imagine trying to invent a new colour that you have never seen before. Try it, and you will realise how difficult, if not impossible, this is.

Ultimately, leadership can only be recognised when it knocks on your door. When the spirit of leadership knocks on your door, the best that you can do is be at the ready to identify it. If you let it in, you will be blessed by it. If you reject it, that is your choice. However, cursed is the one who turns it away without knowing what is being turned away!

WHAT IS THE MOST IMPORTANT FUNCTION OF LEADERSHIP?

Getting to the bottom of things is a skill that not many have. It requires practice to be able to sift through the layers of defence and ambiguity to arrive at the root. (For more about getting to the root, see Chapter 7, "Can you speak another colour?")

It is important to understand, believe, and accept that the *most* important function of leadership (at its supreme level) is to *break barriers*. This goes against the grain of many admirable Chinese philosophies. However, remember that some of the respected Chinese philosophies raise the question about the supreme *leader*, not about supreme *leadership*.

The supreme *leader* is one who overcomes difficulties via the path of least resistance. Being able to achieve one's goal without conflict is better than engaging in conflict. Conserving energy is paramount. That is a correct course of action for leaders. However, as far as *leadership* is concerned, the most important level, one that might take years to attain, is the one that *obliterates* the barriers.

After stumbling over a rock, it would be wise to inform those behind you, so that they do not stumble. But this only warns those immediately behind you and leaves the way open for others to trip at a later stage, long after you have left the path. You would do better to place a sign to inform future travellers, and this might offer a longer-lasting warning to the unsuspecting. The noblest and ultimate action would be to *remove* the stone, so that the possibility of stumbling over it no longer exists. This is the supreme level of leadership.

The barrier might be a physical one or a social disorder. It might be temptation or aggressive opposition. Removing the stone might necessitate a battle. Supreme leadership must do what is necessary to remove these barriers for the benefit of those who are unable to fend for themselves, or who are weaker and less confident to traverse the area.

WHAT IS THE MOST IMPORTANT FACTOR OF LEADERSHIP?

What is it that supreme leadership hinges on? Distilling this question, I arrive at *creativity*. This does not refer to

colour and right-brain theories. Creativity in this context refers to the creation of opportunities, systems,
procedures, shields, desires, as well as tolerance, acceptance, understanding, and awareness.

Creativity in leadership is about *crea-*
tion. The single most important
factor of leadership is to *create* — to
bring into being that which was not
there before.

It is very difficult to bring into
being something that was not there.
Therefore, it would follow to ask the
next question: "What is the most
important factor of *creativity*?"

When you drill down to the roots

It takes a
brave person
to do something
different,
and an
audacious one
to do something
differently

of creativity, you will see that its most important factor
is *courage*. This, in turn, demands *audacity* — involving
boldness and daring. Audacity is a marvellous elixir. It has
the power to shatter barriers. However, most gentlefolk
become awkward at the thought of audacity because it
requires them to say and do things that they would otherwise never contemplate. To be audacious might require
them to push their way into places where they are not
invited, or to express a thought that they would otherwise have been too polite to express. Audacity requires a
break with tradition and a deviation from one's normal
decorum.

If leadership is about creativity, and creativity brings
into being that which did not exist before, it stands to

reason that change must follow. Change means doing something *different* or doing something *differently*. It takes a brave person to do something different, and an audacious one to do something differently. (For more on logic and creativity, see Chapter 6, "Achieving intellectual simpatico".)

WHAT IS THE BEST KIND OF LEADERSHIP?

There can be as many *kinds* of leaders as there are leaders. Each leader operates within a personal framework; leaders each adopt a different set of behaviours, depending upon their own ethics, principles, and values. The word "kind" refers to a class, type, sort, or variety. There can be many kinds of leaders (such as autocratic or democratic) who use different *styles* (such as compassionate or ruthless), depending on their personalities and dispositions. However, there is only one kind of *leadership*, just as there is only one kind of honesty and one kind of integrity. For this reason the question of the "best kind of leadership" is phrased incorrectly. Better put, the question ought to be: "What is the best *level* of leadership?" (Naturally, the best level is always the highest. However, it is important to understand what that level is.)

It stands to reason that personal qualities (such as maturity and wisdom) begin as seeds. As each seed grows (if it grows), it develops step by step, stage by stage, until it reaches various levels. The level that one reaches determines how and what decisions are made.

So, although there is only one *kind* of leadership, there are several *levels* of leadership. The ultimate level is to have leadership that is *unattributable*. Indeed, Chinese philosophies speak of the best leader as one who is invisible. However, there is a difference between invisibility and unattributability. The former denotes the existence of a leader who is not visible or not known, but who, upon closer scrutiny, can be found. The latter refers to an inability to attribute or credit an action or a creation to any individual. By the way, there exists a famous notion that "to lead, one must follow". This is fallacious. To lead, one must follow one's spirit faithfully, not other people.

Leaders attract *followers*. Leadership attracts *travellers*. A follower is one who consciously chooses a path that is important to the destination. A traveller is one who is unaware of the path, and not overly concerned with the destination, but enjoys the fruits of the journey.

Although followers are attracted to leaders, travellers are oblivious to the leadership that created their environment. This does not constitute ignorance on the part of the traveller, but supremacy on the part of leadership. ◨

CHAPTER 10

forget ABOUT TEAMWORK

GIVE ME TEAMS THAT WORK

SOME MANAGERS SEEM TO THINK that one way to survive the corporate world is to keep one's head down. They figure that they can do this by ensuring that all of their direct reports (and those within their matrix management structure) work well together to avoid complaints and arguments. To such managers, it is important to suppress problems and to keep all conflicts out of public view. I once attended a meeting where one such manager called all his senior managers to a three-day off-site conference for the purpose of setting the ground rules about how he wanted to operate as the new group manager.

The meeting opened with the group manager's announcement that he wanted all his managers to work together as a "highly effective self-led team". He thought that this would make us feel important. He supposed that we would feel happy about directing our own destiny. In his own awkward way, he was silently pleading with us to get along famously and co-operate so that we did not make a fuss that might embarrass him with headquarters.

Never mind "teamwork". This is not possible in modern organisational terms. What one ought to strive for is a "team that works".

The group manager announced his desire to build us into a highly effective self-led team and proceeded to quiz us about what this might mean. Holding a workbook in hand, and following one of the exercises step-by-step, he asked us to outline what we thought were the essential qualities of a self-led team. No-one was brave enough to break the ice, so I put my hand up as a gesture of co-operation to get the ball rolling and to save him from panic. "What do you think, Jonar?" he asked. "Fun," I said. With that, he felt relieved and happily approached the white-board to scribe this three-letter word.

Now that the ice was broken, others needed to make their mark. One chap shouted, "Integrity", another "Co-operation". As if a dictionary had been opened, one by one words were bandied about while the scribe filled the white-board with fancy expressions. Soon the list began to look impossible. How could any team possess so many noble qualities? The list included honesty, trust, support, honour, vision, com-promise, patience, and others I did not understand. After ten minutes of furious co-operation, the word-count began to slow down. At that point, I raised my hand for the second time. Now I was ready for my real contri-bution. "Jonar, what do you think?" said the scribe. "A strong leader!"

Any group that does not have complete authority to make its own decisions cannot be called a team

I exclaimed. The group manager quickly realised that this would bring the whole edifice tumbling down. He stopped writing and shouted, "No! A self-led team does *not* need a leader. It relies on teamwork."

Those who were looking forward to this new era of freedom nodded and agreed with him. They were intimidating in their rejection. "A strong leader defeats the whole exercise", said one manager. "If we work well together, we do not need a leader", shouted another.

My goodness, what a nerve that hit. The most striking thing about this exercise was the fact that by 4:00 pm on the third day, the group had not agreed on a single initiative. They had spent three days chatting and arguing about the split of budgets, who ought to have sign-off authority for the different countries' budgets, and who ought to be the sacrificial lamb and agree to a higher target to appease head-quarters' demands that we increase our revenue.

I looked at my watch and realised that we had one hour to wrap this up. In defiance, in disgust, and in amazement, I put my hand up, waited for everyone to cease the chatter, and said in a zombie monotone voice, "I think we need a strong leader."

Teamwork is useless

Teamwork does not work in organisations that set targets for individuals or divisions. It is useless to expect teamwork to work when individual goals are vital for individual survival.

Furthermore, teamwork is useless in organisations that depend on rank because rank brings with it some privileges. Why should anyone work to assist another when the rewards and privileges will not be shared equally?

I am not advocating the abolition of rank. Rank is vital. Nor am I suggesting that teamwork is not powerful.

I am saying do not expect teamwork to work in the context of an organisation that sets individual targets and individual rewards. (See Chapter 14, "Fluid shares".)

Do not confuse workers by setting strange goals. If they are given a job to do, they focus on that job, especially if their salary depends on certain targets being met. This means that they have no incentive to co-operate within a team environment.

Many chief executive officers (CEOs) realise that teamwork does not work when there is a choice — meaning that workers will choose to focus on the things that matter most to them — their salary, their rank, or their hidden agenda. As a result, CEOs look to ways of *forcing* individuals and divisions to work together. They make them *interdependent,* forcing them to co-operate. This is a perverse way of trying to engender teamwork.

YOU DON'T NEED TEAMWORK — YOU NEED TEAMS THAT WORK

The stupidest element of teamwork is the way in which it is espoused amid contradiction and hypocrisy. For a start, sporting analogies must not be used to express organisational desires. There is a great difference between a sporting and governmental or commercial organisation. Also, the structure of a sporting team is vastly different from the structure of a division.

Even in the sporting arena there are crazy behaviours that make a mockery of the principles of teamwork — such as the variance in salaries, and the special recognition given to the "player of the match". How can such recognition be reconciled with the theory of teamwork? A sports group comprises skilled individuals who combine their talent and energy to strive for a common goal. Yet, the rewards are not shared equally.

In the computer industry, it has been said that if cars had developed at the same pace as computers, today a Ferrari would cost $5.50, drive five million kilometres on one litre of petrol, and park comfortably on the head of a pin. In organisational terms, sporting analogies are farcical because if they are to mean anything on the corporate or organisational front, sport would have had to endure the same changes and challenges that a typical business has had to cope with. This would translate into a typical baseball team having to function without a coach, halve the number of players, play twice as many games per season, with each game lasting double the original duration. Many more meetings would be required mid-game, as well as the introduction of robots or some mechanisation to replace players.

How would a baseball or soccer team cope with industrial action mid-game, or with having to answer e-mails at half time, or breaking the team into smaller divisions from which they would have to negotiate services?

Do not pin your hopes on teamwork. People are not interested in teamwork when it is forced upon them. No-one wants to be bothered with other people's projects.

The work environment is full of contradictions. On the one hand, teamwork is espoused yet, on the other hand, groups are formed for the purpose of focusing on specific products or projects. The very act of forming a division says "focus". Yet each division is asked to work with another, thereby spelling "distraction".

Never mind teamwork. It is not possible in modern organisational terms. What we ought to strive for is a team that works.

A ROSE BY ANY OTHER NAME

A rose by any other name would smell as sweet, but a team that does not have the authority to act independently ceases to be a team. Any combination of bodies does not form a team. Any structure or group dynamic cannot be called a team.

A team must have access to vital elements within its domain. Does your marketing department have complete authority for its advertising budget? Or has some bright vice-president decided to create a separate group to handle advertising? And what about public relations? Is this headed by a different manager? Are there now three separate groups that must work together to jockey or beg one another for attention, resources, and permission?

There is no way that a group can be called a team until it has all the autonomy, authority, and capability to operate independently, swiftly, and to its own tune, without any interference or obstruction by another group. One team must not be dependent upon another. Therefore, if your organisation has interdependent divisions then no-one belongs to a team, and no team exists.

Any sign of manipulation needs to be confronted with all the opposition you can muster

If the marketing, advertising, and public relations divisions can each operate independently, three teams do exist. However, their ability to serve the organisation successfully would be questionable because the profession of marketing requires that advertising and public relations be integrated within the objectives set by the marketing division. The team's success now hinges on the dynamics of the organisation and, more so, on the dynamics of the competitive landscape.

Chief executive officers delude themselves with terms like cross-functional teams. There is no such thing. Any group that does not have complete authority to make its own decisions cannot be called a team. Therefore, cross-functional teams cannot be interdependent. If they are, they are merely cross-functional groups that together might comprise one large team (if one leader exists).

Note also that interdependence here refers to the inability to make an independent decision. Obviously no group can exist without another, meaning that an organisation cannot exist without the services of the electricity utility, or without a telephone service. Marketing cannot function without the help of manufacturing. However, one cannot have a marketing team if that team is dependent upon manufacturing. A marketing team can only exist if it can make all the decisions, after receiving all the input. It might mean that the marketing manager might choose to contract the manufacturing process to an external organisation if the internal manufacturing facility cannot meet the current requirement. If that level of authority does not exist at the hands of the marketing manager, that manager does not have a marketing team. Rather, only a group of professionals exists, and they work with the group from manufacturing. Together they might make a team if one leader exists. Individually, they are only groups.

Teamwork is about synergy. It often deals with intangibles that can bring a team to victory or to its knees. The outcome rests with the leader.

CONSTRUCTING TEAMS THAT WORK

On several occasions I have been contacted by executive search firms who have tried to offer me a job of some kind. Eventually, I lose interest when I find out that, during their hunt for a managing director or group leader, they are in the process of hiring other senior staff who would ultimately report to the role in question (the one that they wanted me to accept).

How can this be? How is it that the corporation has the gall to hire the sales director, the finance director, and the marketing director before they have hired the managing director? These appointments ought to be the responsibility of the new managing director who would need to hire direct reports of choice.

Often the search firms are responsible because they are eager to complete as many placements as possible before the new head arrives. The new managing director might prefer to use other search firms, or might delay the hiring process. However, the board of directors is ultimately to blame for being so naive and manipulative. The board might feel that it can count on greater loyalty from the direct reports — just in case the new managing director does not work out. The board is particularly keen on making its own choice of finance director, so that it can have an insider working for it should the managing director not play the game by its rules. This style of operation is doomed to fail, and deserves to fail. Placing a managing director amid manipulative frameworks of doubt explains a lot about organisational mistrust.

CEOs delude themselves with terms like cross-functional teams. There is no such thing. Any group that does not have complete authority to make its own decisions cannot be called a team.

If you want teams to work, you need to realise that a group can only be a team if it has all the authority and resources it needs to perform its tasks. Do not bother with a matrix structure. (See Chapter 13, "Cut across the dotted line".) A team must be able to perform its function completely and make its own decisions within the boundaries, ethics, and scope of its charter. Note that autonomy does not mean chaos. One is not advocating the creation of mutinous renegades. Teams must be disciplined. A team must have a strong leader who has the authority to choose team members. Many have argued that the team leader ought *not* to have the authority to hire and fire because the role of the team leader is that of facilitator or supervisor. The team leader must be responsible for the outcome, and as such must have full control over the project. Naturally, it is a question of placing the right person in the job.

If the objective is to construct a team that works, with the right skilled and disciplined people to do the job, there must not be any ambiguity about the objective and job goals. Each team member must understand what is required. The parameters must be articulated clearly.

How would innovation occur? How would people challenge each other if conflict did not exist? These were two questions asked of me by a CEO who almost preferred a mish-mash of people fighting it out. Drama gives the CEO something to attend to, thereby making the CEO feel useful.

If innovation is what you want, have two teams competing against each other, but they must not be dependent upon each other. The former is within the spirit of competition while the latter is akin to warfare, and this is destructive.

The rules of assembling a team apply to any team. So, when it comes to extended teams, specialist teams, crack teams, virtual teams, and task forces, one must be able to hand-pick the players and have every freedom to hire and fire. This might be unrealistic in many bureaucratic organisations. If this is true, it is also unrealistic to expect teams to function. Anything less than the prescribed formula is merely a group of people working on a project.

ONLY TEAM PLAYERS NEED APPLY

Take a look at employment advertisements and notice that the majority of them ask for candidates who are "team players". What does this mean? I suspect that such a requirement is not well thought through, and one that the advertiser puts there out of obligation or tradition.

Apart from the generally pompous manner in which many job advertisements are written, the term "team player" could send conflicting signals. Does the advertiser want someone who can work well with others? If so, why have I never seen an advertisement that seeks someone who does *not* work well with others? Are common decency, tact, and professionalism not attributes that ought to be assumed? After all, other attributes (such as honesty) are assumed.

The moment that you start to issue certificates and trophies to one person and not another you are signalling something very dangerous. You either operate as a team, or you do not.

Is the advertisement calling for someone who is prepared to listen to other people's opinions? Is this to say that they want someone who will merely co-ordinate points of view, not one who can hold an independent and professional conviction? Or does the advertiser really want someone who can keep the group happy — thus a person who ought not to make any of the tough decisions?

Whatever the case, it had better be spelt out. Skirting around the subject with clichés does not aid in explicit and clear communication. To say that one must be a "team player" is ambiguous. Furthermore, candidates might not find the courage to challenge this notion, yet it strikes at the heart of the matter. It can make or break the chosen candidate who might very well have accepted a position without understanding the dynamics of the new environment.

If by "team player" the employer really wants a happy-go-lucky "it'll be right" kind of manager, such an objective would better be put as "someone who will not take a stand on any issue that is likely to upset the group". Unfortunately, such advertisements often call for the team player to also be a *leader* — a sorry state of affairs indeed.

A WORD ABOUT THE TEAM LEADER

If you are the leader of a team, you need to have the patience to see other people's point of view. You need the grace to tolerate those who think in different ways from you. You need the energy to keep going until you reach your destination. Above all, you need the courage to pounce on anything that resembles mutiny or unrest. Any sign of manipulation needs to be confronted with all the opposition you can muster.

The best way to keep a team happy is to ensure that only experts are hired. Experts respond well to other experts. However, they feel frustrated when they have to put up with people who know very little about the subject on which they are supposed to advise the rest of the team. Make sure that the lines of authority are clear. Everyone must know what they are hired to do and what their scope of authority is.

Most job ads ask for candidates who are "team players". What does this mean?

Treat everyone in the same way, albeit you may need to compensate for personalities and preferences for work environments. Those who speak loudly over the telephone might infuriate those who prefer to work within a quiet environment. Those who smoke might smell of tobacco and disturb their non-smoking colleagues. Do not expect these people to work side by side. It is up to you to create the right environment, so that each of them can have the space to work comfortably.

As for rewards and recognition, do all of this in private. The moment that you start to issue certificates and trophies to one person and not another you are signalling something very dangerous. You either operate as a team, or you do not. For the team to work, it must consider itself a team at all times. Singling out a few people starts to create rivalry and jealousy.

Finally, as group leader, it is your job to either shield the team from bureaucracy, or to allow it the complete freedom to fight bureaucracy in any way that it sees fit. It is one way or the other, so you take your pick. If you choose the latter, you need to stand behind your team and stand up for its cause. Your job is to protect your people from parasites. If internal trouble brews you must not rest until you find the cause and the offender. If it amounts to a misunderstanding, it is your fault, and you must leave no stone unturned to find a way to be explicit in your direction.

Teamwork is about synergy. It often deals with intangibles that can bring a team to victory or to its knees. The outcome rests with the leader. **E**

CHAPTER 11

IT'S NOT
WHAT YOU GIVE,
BUT WHAT YOU
take away

POWER TO THE PEOPLE

T HE AMAZING THING ABOUT empowerment is that managers seem to expect a hug or a round of applause when they announce that they wish to empower their staff. Empowerment is incorrectly looked upon as a "gift" that can be given to employees. This is a foolish approach.

Empowerment is not a procedure nor a method of operation. It is a basic principle of life and a principle of success. Offering to empower people erroneously suggests that this is within the gift of the manager. Empowerment is as much a basic ingredient of a person as self-confidence, honesty, alertness, and wisdom. It is not related to authority, nor to the giving of permission.

Empowerment, in the context of employers and employees, relates to the *tolerance* that one gives to a person (never to a group) to exercise freedom of thought and freedom of expression. However, the moment that any stipulation is made, freedom is challenged. And once challenged, it signals to the individual that the level of tolerance is regulated. And a *regulated* level of tolerance is called a "procedure" not empowerment.

Be very careful to understand what empowerment really means. Take extra caution then to ensure that you understand what you are doing when you seek to empower people. For a start, you cannot empower people. You might be able to give them the authority to act, or the budget to spend, or the ability to employ and dismiss, but this does not mean that you are empowering your people. There is a big difference between empowerment and authority. You can give someone the authority, but you cannot empower them.

Empowerment works not by what you give, but by what you take away. Therefore, if you wish your staff to be empowered, you need not be concerned with what *they* do, but with what *you* do. It might come as a surprise that empowerment cannot be *given*. It can only surface after what you *take away*. For example, consider the question of confidence. Can you send a memorandum to your staff declaring that you hereby grant each of them ten doses of confidence? Is this something that can be *given*? No. Confidence is a vital personal ingredient that must germinate within each person. The best that you can do is to remove the burdens that might suppress the germination of confidence — such as intimidation, harsh judgement, confusing signals of displeasure, and psychological innuendoes that hinder and torment.

Often the announcement of mass empowerment comes as a desperate measure by managers who are crying for help. Their desire to empower their people has touches of abdication associated with it. They realise that the task ahead is likely to be more daunting than the task at hand, so they panic and bestow a royal decree in every direction, hoping that the front-liners will take up arms and fight the good fight.

Like many things in life, empowerment cannot be built when it is needed. The dilemma is that empowerment is rarely thought to be needed at a time when it is not needed, yet the best time to build empowerment is when you least need it. This frustrating rule is governed by the *law of timing*. For example, it applies to advertising. When you least need to advertise is when you ought to advertise. Waiting until a crisis emerges is not the ideal time to plan an advertising campaign. The same can be said for personal health and exercise. The best time to undertake an exercise program is when you are healthy. Waiting until an ailment sets in is hardly the time to go to the gym for a solid workout.

Empowerment works not by what you give, but by what you take away

Now comes the test of character. Why should a manager encourage empowerment at a time when there is no apparent need to empower the team? After all, empowerment of others might be misconstrued as diminishing your own power. Allowing others to operate independently might put into question your own worth. This is scary for most managers who are insecure at best. Furthermore, considering the rate of job change and turnover, who in their right mind would risk an innovation that might jeopardise the short-term gain in favour of a long-term result — especially when the manager is unlikely to be around to reap the rewards in the long term? In addition, short-term measures are considered to be far more important than other measures because careers are made and lost as a direct consequence of the short term.

POWER TO THE PEOPLE

Another misunderstanding arises when managers assume that empowerment means giving power to the "masses". First, empowerment has nothing to do with power, and, second, it is unwise to assume that empowerment is something that can be bestowed upon the "masses".

Empowerment and power, as two words, might resemble each other. However, their similarity ends with their spelling and pronunciation, not with their meaning.

What is power? In organisational terms power is relative — meaning that power is only important when those who have power stand over those who *lack* power. It is a philosophical question about opposites similar to the notion of direction. What is "up" if "down" does not exist? What is "happiness" if "sadness" does not exist? What is "left" in the absence of "right"? This relativity makes power something that cannot be given to all employees because, the moment that they *all* have it, it loses its advantage. In this context, power is governed by the law of saturation — when everyone has access to something (such as power or technology) it loses its advantage. (See Chapter 20, "Prosperity in the modern world".)

Empowerment can mean to accept freedom of thought and freedom of expression. It encourages and tolerates employees as *people,* not as *robots.* At its most supreme, empowerment still demands that employees acknowledge the limits of their duties. Furthermore, it does not tolerate rules being broken or any form of rebellion. Empower-ment is respectful and dutiful, yet it serves one important purpose — to allow everyone, no matter the rank, to express their feelings (if they choose to do so). Empower-ment allows all employees to react without the constraints of organisational politics, so that they can work and inter-act without fear of retribution.

From this, we can see that empowerment demands maturity and courage. These attributes cannot be given from one to the other. Rather, what can be regulated is the way in which a person's reactions are tolerated in the work environment. Although tolerance can be regulated, it is inadvisable to do so because regulating intangibles is a messy business. For the leader, the best course of action is to ensure that those with the power to intimidate are stripped of it when they practise intimidation against another employee. Those with the power to block honest conversation must be demoted when they abuse their power. Those with the power to obstruct the expression of thought must be taken out of their comfort zone the moment that they do obstruct others. Finally, trouble-makers ought to be made an example of and be stripped of their rank — no matter the rank.

WHAT IS THE DIFFERENCE BETWEEN FREEDOM AND DIVERSITY?

Encouraging freedom of thought is not the same as encour-aging diversity of thought. In a work environment, staff members must be free to express their feelings, thoughts, and ideas. However, to tolerate diversity is asking for trouble. Although diversity makes life colourful and interesting, it must not be allowed to over-rule the establishment.

Playing by the rules is important for teamwork. Playing to one tune is just as vital. Beware the team whose diverse views do not match the organisation's ethics or values. People must be free to think and to say what they feel is professionally relevant. However, they should not be given the leeway to exercise their diversity without the approval of the project manager.

MORE ON DIVERSITY

Diversity has nothing to do with equality. People are not equal. Their strengths and skills are not equal, but are diverse. Their thresholds vary. Their levels of maturity differ. Equality is impossible in human terms. It can only be possible in regulatory terms thereby making it artificial and awkward to manage. The important aspect is to face life, which means facing reality.

If equality is desired, that desire must be born from within the person who must first accept and understand the limitations of life, and set about to build on that which they seek to improve

Empowerment and power, as two words, might resemble each other. However, their similarity ends with their spelling and pronunciation, not with their meaning.

through hard work and self-sacrifice. When people are not equal, they must not set about creating a false sense of equality through regulatory means, nor seek equality by trying to drag people down to the lowest common denominator.

Often, people who seek universal equality are anxiously trying to remove *discrimination*. The latter is the more noble and reasonable of causes if it seeks to remove *unhealthy* discrimination. On the whole, discrimination is a natural and necessary human quality. It is when discrimination is exercised on the basis of *ignorance* that it becomes unwholesome and destructive. In line with this, unhealthy diversity can be just as destructive as negative discrimination. Unfortunately, in the work environment, diversity has come to mean "accepting certain *different* people as equals". These could be women, people of a different skin colour, or those who see the world in a different way. This is unacceptable. For example, appointing women into senior roles for the sake of meeting a quota, or to prove some public point, is neither diversity nor equality. It is tokenism.

Diversity in the workplace ought to focus on the removal of unhealthy discrimination — not on the appointment of women or people with disabilities to senior positions. Granted, there are men in business who do not believe that women can perform as well as men. Brave chief executive officers (CEOs) who abhor such attitudes would be doing everyone a great service if they sought to expel such officers from positions of power and influence. Setting a quota might rectify a gender or ethnicity imbalance, but it does not solve the root problem. The newly appointed woman would have to work extremely hard to battle the subtle two-faced nature of someone with whom she is supposed to interact and with whom she is told she is "equal".

The only way that women can overcome opposition in the workplace is to surround themselves with other women, thereby building their own small discriminatory empire. This is a game for the insane, and the leader is to blame.

EMPOWER IN SILENCE

The term "suffer in silence" is a curious one. A friend of mine gave me this advice when I objected to some of her ways. She said it lovingly, but I now feel that there was a lot of wisdom behind her advice. Her motive was to stop me from complaining. Her approach to life was to "do" rather than "say". If she disliked something, she took action. She was not one to sit back and whinge about the world. She advised me to keep my suffering to myself, and do something constructive with my energy to change what needed to be changed. I am reminded of this when I give advice to CEOs about the process of empowerment. It is best done in silence. If you truly want to create a work environment where people can be free to live, enjoy life, contribute their skills, and participate in their industry and in their organisation, then you must set about constructing this environment secretly and silently.

The construction of a framework for empowerment is invisible. However, the *destruction* of the obstacles must be loud and ostentatious. The CEO must show that those who strip others of their creativity, or their freedom of expression, or their freedom of thought would be ruthlessly removed from the organisation. By dealing with the problems at their root, a message would be received that says clearly that such behaviour will not be tolerated. Never mind the memoranda and workshops, or those condescending posters and patronising slogans. Have the valour to do what needs to be done. Take action.

By activating everyone's senses to detect evil, and by showing them what will become of self-righteous troublemakers, you will see that words need not be uttered about the right way to treat people. There will be no need to articulate the meaning of justice. All these things will spring up from silence — without mission statements and speeches.

ADVICE TO THE CEO (LEADER)

If you do not know who your vexatious perpetrators are, you are in serious trouble. Furthermore, if you suspect the troublemakers to be those about whom most people complain, think again.

Your role as CEO is to free yourself to become part of the breath of your organisation. You need to feel the pulse. You need to measure the rhythm. Only when you function this way can you be of any value. If you are far too busy orchestrating the management team while your back is turned to your staff, here is some advice.

The CEO is an operator who has a flexible and fluid diary. If you are the CEO of an organisation, your role is to be as free as a bird. You do not accept back-to-back meetings. You do not have fixed and perpetually recurring meetings. You do not have any major deadlines that keep you focused on any one project. The CEO must not have a "job" as such. You must be one of the very few people in the organisation who have no specific function, because the moment that you become focused you lose sight of the big picture.

Your responsibility is to delegate everything that is humanly possible, and go out into your organisation, and to your customers, and to your suppliers, and do this in a relaxed and casual manner. You need to live and breathe your organisation's ebb and fervour. And you need to know your industry and your customers. Opening ceremonies and major keynote speeches can be delegated, but

Fun
is the turbo-booster
that helps to
ignite purpose.
Purpose
creates unity.
Unity
creates power.
Power
energises the group.

remember that delegation does not mean to shift a burden from you to someone else. Delegation must be planned, and it must form part of another person's job specification for which that person was originally hired. Do not dump jobs on other people who were not employed specifically for the task.

Do not fill your diary with commitments to roadshows and product launches. Why should you be doing such time-consuming things? (If they are not time-consuming then you are not doing them well enough.) If it is a matter of status, surely there are more appropriate people in your organisation who deserve the limelight for their efforts. If it is a matter of public image, this can be delegated to a trusted person who can act as your company's spokesperson. If it is a matter of press and public relations, groom knowledgeable and qualified spokespeople to represent your organisation. It is the CEOs who like the front line who are in the wrong job, doing the wrong thing. Frontline glamour and action is for front-line staff.

Although CEOs might report to a board of directors, their chief priority is to take care of their staff, not in a nurturing sense but in a professional sense. It is the CEOs who are responsible for the generation of synergy. Their job is to make sure that their employees are well trained, well educated, well managed, and well directed. This means that when it comes to the CEO choosing between meeting a customer or meeting a staff member, the staff member must take priority because one staff member can lose many customers. All CEOs must learn that their roles are to deploy a group of people to run the business. This group must have the authority, the capability, and the integrity to conduct the business in such a way as to make the CEO proud.

OH NO, NOT A CEO ON THE LOOSE!

Now that as a CEO you have time on your hands, walk through your organisation unannounced. Do not tell anyone where you are going. You do not want to be *expected* at any location. You do not want to be greeted by location managers. And under no circumstances are you to be escorted by senior officials. For example, if you are visiting the manufacturing plant, officials from that plant must not go with you. They are not to be forewarned of your visit either. My goodness, a CEO on the loose! Whatever would staff members think if you were able to understand their daily drama? How would front-line staff feel if they have access to the previously unknown and unseen CEO whom they admired, but never had the opportunity to know?

If you can sit and chat with your workers, and caringly watch over their shoulders as they fight it out each day trying to battle through all that near-criminal red tape, you will start to learn about your organisation's body and soul. By becoming a roaming, listening, and observing CEO, you will start to see things that excite you, anger you, infuriate you, and motivate you. You might begin to see that your worst enemy is your own infrastructure, and that your biggest and most ferocious competitor comes from within the organisation.

Go to lunch with the junior mailroom clerk, and pick some boxes with warehouse personnel. You might find gems of opportunities that your senior staff had never been able to uncover — not because they were incapable, but because you had them so focused on the end-of-month results that you transformed efficient professionals into short-sighted detailists.

By the way, while you are doing all these things, your other important (now delegated) duties need to be executed with perfection and accuracy. This can be achieved if you assemble a slick team of mature executives whose egos are stable, and whose loyalty is unwavering. If you do not feel that you can find a handful of people to manage your affairs at the "top", you need to seriously question your ability to take responsibility for hundreds or thousands of workers who are managed by a handful of people who manage your affairs at the "bottom".

Your random daily involvement must not become a ritual. Dress appropriately for each visit and hand out business cards with contact details of your senior executive assistants who can respond to each and every inquiry. Your assistants need to have the power of your authority to direct the business on your behalf. Train them well, and they will act in your best interest. Your ability to reach (and communicate with) the ranks does not mean that staff members can go over their manager's head. Your efforts ought to be about *communication,* not *interference.*

Take special secretaries with you and make sure that they can assist you to follow up on your action plans.

This has nothing to do with "management by wandering around". Your tours and infiltration are not to be seen as quick-fix measures. Nor are they to be portrayed as staff-relations exercises. They are not even complaints sessions. They are there for *you* to learn about your bottleneck, your cancerous and crippling policies, and unfathomable bureaucracy that feeds on itself and suppresses anyone who tries to improve the system.

Make decisions through the right channels. Consult with your managers, but also challenge them. Do not tolerate delaying tactics. Take action about anyone who so much as hints at power games.

What has been described so far points to a CEO (leader) who *listens*. Of course, there are times for the leader to *speak*. These are important occasions during which the leader must uplift the team members' spirits and generate excitement. The leader needs to speak with compassion and conviction to communicate the direction that the organisation is taking, and the strategy that will be used to propel the group.

When it comes to the CEO choosing between meeting a customer or meeting a staff member, the staff member must take priority

Note also that a leader must take time to think, to dream, to plan, perchance to be creative — to create new futures, to create new power, to create an environment that nurtures the desired culture and exterminates the troublemakers. The leader must create a framework in which everyone is treated equally, and in which each person's dignity is protected. Within this environment, fun starts to creep in. Fun is the turbo-booster that helps to ignite purpose. Purpose creates unity. Unity creates power. Power energises the group. Energy is the ultimate resource. If unleashed internally, it can destroy the organisation. If unleashed externally, it can obliterate the opponent. It is the leader's responsibility to ensure that everyone is aiming for the right targets. If the targets are not clear, then random campaigns will dissipate the energy and, in so doing, drain the organisation.

If you can sit and chat with your workers, as they battle through all that near-criminal red tape, you will start to learn about your organisation's body and soul

WHERE DOES EMPOWERMENT COME IN?

When the leader understands that *empowerment* is vital for a healthy organisation, the immediate, urgent, and merciless removal of power-hungry staff and out-of-date policies paves the way for empowerment.

Empowerment, like confidence, takes time to blossom, so give it time. Keep your hand at the pruning, and you will see what wonders empowerment can contribute.

Be careful not to hesitate. Only justify your actions to yourself. If you, as leader, cannot cut through the red tape, what hope does a staff member fifty layers below you have? Can you live with yourself? Or are you thinking of retiring soon, and cannot see what difference it makes, so long as your share prices are okay? If, as leader, you monitor the share prices for your own personal wealth, there is only one honourable course open to you — and it is an unfortunate one that involves your immediate withdrawal.

And one more thing. If you are thinking that a survey or two might be a good way to find out what is happening in your organisation, you have missed the whole point, and you are back to square one. What a shame. ▣

CHAPTER 12

COME DO THE
nanomation
WITH ME

HOW TO
SWALLOW YOUR MARKET WHOLE

WHAT IS THE SINGLE MOST important function of technology? Think about it and you will realise that its most important function is to create an advantage. It is the notion of advantage that has perplexed many chief executive officers (CEOs) who have been promised a *competitive advantage* if only they would sign the requisition for that expensive computer with custom-built software.

In the networked world, there is no such thing as a *competitive* advantage through technology. Not even so much as a *comparative* advantage. Perhaps a *convoluted* advantage, but no more.

In the public sector, the best that technology can do is reduce wastage. In the business environment it can, at best, reduce operating expenses; not create an advantage. No competitive advantage can be created with technology unless it is exclusive, powerful, and absolute — yet, can you name a technological device or system that can deliver all three? I know of only one. The only technology that is exclusive, powerful, and absolute is the nuclear bomb. This technological marvel is exclusive in that it is regulated and expensive, putting it out of reach of all except the licensed or the outlaws. It is unquestionably powerful. Its devastation is absolute — meaning that once it has made its impact, there is nothing that can be done to reverse its effects.

Leaders need to realise that distractions emanating from stupendous technological, mechanical, and electronic development tend to lead us to suspect, erroneously, that promises of supremacy come from physical weaponry. That may be so in situations where brute force is all that matters. In the networked world, the scary thing to face is that power does not come from the physical. Excellence needs to be present before it can be enhanced with equipment. Although a carpenter's craft can be refined with better tools, no amount of technology can substitute the essence of carpentry — just as no amount of money can buy love. The technology within our reach can be used to duplicate skill, but not to replace it. It can be used to refine processes, but not to invent them.

In the networked world, those looking for a competitive advantage need to understand that it does not come from anything that is tangible. Even the most tangible and flexible of all assets (cash) is no hero on the business front. Cash is useful, but it cannot help because it has no charter. Cash is in itself helpless. It sits there until it is expended. The outcome is determined by *how* it is used, not by the fact that it *is* used.

Owning computers or sponsoring the push for office automation does not offer an advantage. In the networked world, the laws of nature reign supreme. The law that governs advantage is the law of annihilation.

THE LAW OF ANNIHILATION

The law of annihilation states that anything that offers a supposed advantage to one organisation can offer the same supposed advantage to its competitor. Any qualified executive that one group employs can be matched by the other group. Any discount that one goon offers can be topped by another fool's. This law resonates well with the saying, "Anything you can do, I can do better."

These days the window of opportunity is more like a door that slams shut very quickly. Taking advantage of market opportunities requires speed. However, organisations have become so complicated and bureaucratic that speed is now faintly known in concept, not in deed. Furthermore, opportunities that are generated by external tangible devices (such as technology) are easily annihilated because the competitor can copy your every acquisition and follow closely in your footsteps.

At this point, some of you might suspect that competitive advantage comes from those things that cannot be bought by the competitor such as goodwill, patents, and copyright, including brilliant technologies or intellectual property that no-one can legally copy. If only this were true. Sadly, the S-Class can be matched by the 7-Series; Reebok by Nike; Apple by Compaq; and Chanel by Armani. These things are surrounded by an air of intangible qualities that are encapsulated by their respective formidable brand. Ultimately such intangible brand values manifest themselves into tangible goods that exhibit the final qualities that impress the customer. Therefore, these intangibles cannot reign supreme because the qualities of their physical manifestations can be copied easily. So, as you can see, this is not what is meant by supremacy through intangibles.

CREATING AN ADVANTAGE THROUGH INTANGIBLES

If traditional intangibles no longer cut it in the rude and brutal marketplace, where could a competitive advantage come from? The secret of competitive advantage exists within the intangibles known as *atmosphere* and *attitude*. These two intangibles are stubborn, merciless, and shy compounds that are magical — not in the mushy sense, but in the ruthless sense. If your compounds are good, they will always be magical. If they are bad, they will always be ruthless. There is no middle ground.

Atmosphere and attitude disappear without warning the moment that one articulates them. They evaporate the instant that they are put on display. They explode into smithereens the moment that they are captured in some company mission statement. In the Academy-Award winning movie, *Life is Beautiful*, the main character meets a man who loves mental puzzles. One of the puzzles goes along the following lines: what disappears the moment you mention its name? The answer is "silence". Once its name is uttered, silence no longer exists. This puzzle can help to describe the phenomenon of atmosphere and attitude. These two intangibles will haunt any company that dares to describe their character. Yet, these two intangibles form the organisation's arsenal for victory in the networked world.

Atmosphere and attitude are non-negotiable. They either exist on their own terms or they do not exist at all. You cannot compromise them. They operate in two stubborn states — good or bad; right or wrong; on or off. Nothing could be simpler. Nothing could be as potent.

Each organisation has its fair share of atmosphere and attitude. Each department and every office might have a different set, but the corridors and boardrooms will foster the *worst* that exists within an organisation to the point where the ugliest, left to brood, will proliferate to contaminate everything in sight.

These days the window of opportunity is more like a door that slams shut very quickly

Tangibles and intangibles work in opposition. In the tangible world, uniting the weak and the strong creates synergy. For example, if a physically weak person and a physically strong person join forces, together they can lift an item heavier than either of them could have managed on their own. Conversely, in the intangible world, when the weak and the strong collide, they sink to the lowest denominator — meaning that when life and death challenge each other, death always wins. In the intangible world, the weak overpowers the strong while evil triumphs over good. This can be likened to a jar full of clear water. Take one drop of black ink and mix it in. In no time, the single drop of ink will contaminate the thousand drops of water.

Note that the *acceptable* is not *perceptible* — meaning that whatever is accepted as part of the normal way of life becomes invisible. Invisibility brings tolerability.

Unfortunately, tolerance is often flexible. Flexibility allows things to creep in and cause damage while unnoticed. This makes it difficult for people to know when to detect incongruent activities, and harder still to know when to raise the alarm. For those whose threshold is refined, their ability to detect undesirable intangibles is sharper than their colleagues' ability. Sadly, very few heed their warning, making it frustrating and lonely for the visionary. An appreciation of this phenomenon supplies clues about the mysteries surrounding the powers of atmosphere and attitude. These mighty intangibles can be harnessed for sweet victory. However, left unchecked, they would destroy an organisation by stealth. Therefore, the leader must find the secrets that lead to conquest.

So what is it that will create an advantage? The answer does not lie in technology, and it does not have anything to do with information technology, but it has everything to do with *nanomation* technology — using atmosphere and attitude within the realm of nanomation.

WHAT IS NANOMATION TECHNOLOGY?

Nanomation refers to the ability of an organisation to act on information that comes so "thick and fast" that the speeds reach a nanosecond (10^{-9} seconds). This means that every member of the team has the capability to react to situations and to make decisions at lightning speed.

Nanomation technology operates on the premise that anyone who has the time also has the authority. It only works if everyone in the organisation has the freedom to make or to break any rule, provided that they all understand the implications of such decisions. They must also know that any mess created as a result of such bravery will need to be cleaned up. Their understanding and knowledge must go beyond a list of guidelines. Those who engage in nanomation must always be disciplined. The moment that they wander away, they signal their intention to jeopardise the intangibles. If they operate outside the realms of integrity and honour, they must detach themselves (or be dismissed and mercilessly excluded) from the group.

Nanomation is the combination of technology, responsibility, and authority working within a framework of good atmosphere and attitude. Within such an infrastructure, nanomation can work wonders by providing competitive advantage that can escape the law of annihilation.

DOING IT IN REAL TIME

For a long time consumers have been demanding information in real time. They want to know everything, immediately. They need prices, data, delivery schedules, and other information at a second's notice. Organisations respond by putting systems in place to help their staff to supply such information. The networked world suffers from the "now" syndrome. However, despite computerisation, most organisations are ill equipped to cope with this syndrome.

What every manager must strive to do is put systems in place that enable staff members to not only find information in real time, but to be able to "think" in real time. After this major breakthrough is achieved, the next phase requires systems that enable staff members to "act" in real time. But where do these systems exist? How can the leader afford such grand technology? The answer is that such technology does not exist physically, but it does exist intangibly. Would you believe that nanomation technology can do all these things through atmosphere and attitude?

LIBERATED BUREAUCRACY

How many times have you been in situations where you knew what needed to be done, but were unable to get on with the job until you satisfied the bureaucratic manager who wanted to go about the whole thing in such a way as to stifle any sense of creativity? I have been in many frustrating situations where everyone knew that exciting opportunities were ripe, but we had to stand and watch our energy dissipate and our opportunity vanish as we waded through the muddy waters in search of the non-existent. The most amazing thing was that everyone knew that we were taking the long route. Even the taskmaster knew this.

Beware the deluded (and supposedly liberated) modern bureaucrat who permits you to make *any* decision provided that (for the record and to cover one's rear) sufficient evidence can be reverse-engineered to show that ". . . three alternatives were well evaluated and carefully considered before the preferred course of action was taken after due deliberation and consultation". Can you believe it? What a waste of life! We often delude ourselves while we conform to what the "system" demands of us. Despite this obvious sickness, every manager will still vote for bigger, faster, and better *systems*. But why is this so? It is so because the political atmosphere and point-the-finger attitude demand that all people cover their backsides. Remember that systems are only tools. They are there to serve the worker, not the other way around. Beware the organisation whose infrastructure paralyses its people. Any leader who cannot associate with this is skating on thin ice. Unless you are certain that your bureaucracy is not slowly and invisibly killing your people, you could be harbouring a ticking time bomb.

Nanomation technology operates on the premise that anyone who has the time also has the authority

Pray tell, what is this system? What is its function? Who controls the switch to its power supply? Having been affected and stifled by this fascinating phantom, I took it upon myself to study its every move. I spent years observing the "system" and how it works. I have tempted it, played with it, interrogated it, and been defeated by it on every occasion. I tried being the silent observer. I tried being the bull at the gate. I tried to chase it and to out-manoeuvre it. I became a bureaucrat, a friend, a subordinate, a shadow, but never could I get close enough to its neck to strangle it. Many a time I told colleagues that if I were able to locate its place of rest, I would sneak up in the middle of the night and put my hands around its jugular, knowing full well that I would be executed for my crime. This was one suicide mission I was prepared to take. Not just for the benefit of my colleagues, but to quench my now insane curiosity about what this system really is.

Some of my colleagues would have happily joined me, but we were disgusted by our inability to scratch this phantom. We were fighting a losing battle. We did not know the enemy, and we had the unconquerable forces of nature to contend with. Never fight the laws of nature. If you can *use* nature's marvellous power, your competitors' jibes and attempts to disarm you would be feeble. After many years of battle and hundreds of covert and overt endeavours, I finally understood what I was dealing with. Although battered and bruised, I was finally able to unmask the enemy.

Unfortunately, nobody has control over the phantom that we call the "system" because it is not a system. It is atmosphere and attitude at their very worst. I dare say that atmosphere and attitude, if rotten, cannot improve. Their movement on the scale (from bad to good) cannot be gradual because they would never reach the midpoint because of the forces acting against them. Remember what I said about the nature of intangible forces. Evil will triumph over good. A negative system can never evolve into a positive one. A putrid atmosphere cannot blossom. An obstructive attitude cannot gradually swing towards the constructive.

DROP THE BOMB

In the opening scene of the film *Outbreak* we see senior military personnel discussing their next manoeuvre. They are very much on edge because their next target, though easy to strike, poses the most difficult challenge they have had to face. They communicate with helicopter pilots who are also nervous and uneasy about their mission. The task at hand is to drop a bomb. Nothing unusual. It is a simple conventional device that could easily hit the target with surgical precision. On the ground, army officers encircle the zone to ensure that no-one gets in and no-one escapes. They, too, are praying for strength. It is the simplest of tasks. However, the nerve-racking aspect of this is the target itself — a township of fellow citizens comprising hundreds of men, women, and children who are not enemies, but family and friends. They have done

Bureaucracy proliferates automatically; solid, positive management does not

nothing wrong. They are not guilty of any crime. Their only misfortune is that they are harbouring a foreign agent. The commander finally gives the signal, and the bombs are in position. These innocent people have to die because they harbour a disease. True to name, the film is about an outbreak of a deadly contagious airborne disease. The highest priority is to destroy the carriers and raze the township lest any more widespread contamination should occur.

A chilling opening indeed. What must be done, has to be done. In disease management, the single most important and urgent response is to prevent the spread of the deadly invisible enemy. Communicable diseases can wreak havoc. Attention to prevention must come before the cure. Sad, but true.

If your organisation is spreading an epidemic through atmosphere and attitude, you need to destroy the carriers. Bringing in new blood, fresh ideas, new people (no matter how exceptional) will not generate a competitive advantage because they will become affected and/or infected faster than they care to realise. You need to destroy the silent, intangible, and merciless enemy. Only you hold the key. Your decision to destroy the offending entities such as people, systems, and processes might be the hardest thing that you have had to face. Like the military personnel who found it difficult to carry out their duty, you too might need to wipe your brow, bite the bullet, and drop the bomb. Unfortunately, there is no other way.

After the dust settles, you can start afresh. This time

be sure to quarantine new passengers. Be sure to immunise the gatekeepers, and at all cost refuse to entertain, not even for a nanosecond, anyone who is a carrier. Now that you have removed the enemy, and restored the environment for *positive* atmosphere and attitude to flourish, it will become evident that your organisation was never lacking information. Nor was it necessarily lacking technology. It's just that your troops were unable to shoot a bullet without having to run up the hill to seek permission from the sergeant while justifying themselves to death through all the red tape. Bureaucracy proliferates automatically; solid, positive management does not.

A tennis player could not possibly stop the game to conduct a situational impact study as to why a backhand would be optimal, because everything happens in nanoseconds — as it does in business. Yet, despite this obvious framework, and the endless analogies between sport and business, bureaucrats still cripple the organisation with insatiable appetites for reports, white papers, and research data.

The first organisation whose positive atmosphere and attitude encourage the use of nanomation technology will be the first organisation to swallow its market whole.

Notice that nowhere throughout this chapter did I use the word "empowerment", nor should you. (For information on the role of empowerment, see Chapter 11, "It's not what you give, but what you take away".) ■

CUT ACROSS THE *dotted* LINE

MATRIX MANAGEMENT IS YOUR TICKET TO HELL

THERE WAS A PLAQUE ON a wall in one of my managers' office. It made reference to a then famous book. I was asked my opinion of the author's comments, so I spoke my mind. I knew at the time that such vocal bravery would be unwise from a career point of view, but I gave my honest opinion just the same. As a result, I was ripped to shreds for my beliefs.

Many years later I was proven correct. Even the author eventually apologised to his readers in a subsequent book and spoke of the error of his ways.

I wonder if my old manager now realises that I had valid reasons to criticise the book. I'll never know. It doesn't matter anyway. What does matter now is that I am about to stick my neck out again and say something that my politically aware mind says I ought not to express.

Matrix management gets to the point where no-one has the authority to make basic business decisions

If you are a chief executive officer (CEO) who endorses the practice of "matrix management", I suspect that you will not like to hear my views. Furthermore, you might even become furious — as I know many have been when I have expressed my thoughts about this subject. Regardless, time will tell.

What I wish to do is ring the alarm bells and say that matrix management is the stupidest corporate structure that I can imagine. It is the most destructive, unworkable, and soul-destroying management configuration.

Naturally, different management structures suit different organisations. However, my warning is applicable to CEOs who promote creativity, endorse harmonious interchange, demand excellence, and push the boundaries for innovation, growth, and infrastructural soundness. That's my qualifier. If that's the kind of CEO you are, I advise you to stay away from matrix management structures because, even with the best of intentions, they become handcuffs.

On paper, matrix management sounds plausible — just like communism sounds good in theory. Some organisations might argue that matrix management does work for them. Yes, there might be exceptions. However, do not be deluded by such rare cases.

WHAT IS MATRIX MANAGEMENT?

To describe this set of handcuffs, I'll give you a real example of how matrix management interconnects people.

Imagine a chocolate manufacturer that designs and manufactures a broad range of products. Its headquarters is in the UK, with offices around the world.

The Asia–Pacific headquarters for the White Chocolate Division is in Japan. The Cooking Chocolate Division has its Asia–Pacific regional headquarters in Singapore. The Catering Chocolate Division has its regional headquarters in Australia.

The head of the Australian "country" operation reports to a vice-president (VP) in the UK, but has dotted-line reporting to Singapore.

Reporting to the Australian head are several VPs. One is responsible for the consumer division, one for sales into schools, one for retailing accounts, another is in charge of large accounts, yet another is in charge of government contracts. In addition, there are different VPs in charge of Family Packs, Gift Boxes, Sugar-Free Products, and Party Packs, respectively. Quality control is run by a different VP, as are Human Resources, Operations, and Finance. The advertising functions are headed by *two* different managers.

The Party Packs VP is responsible for her bottom-line results, but she has no authority for design, manufacturing, distribution, channel management, or other vital functions. Everything to do with advertising must be approved via the Communications Manager who, although reporting to the Australian head, has to take advertising direction from the USA. If the promotions campaign includes direct marketing and print advertising, the Direct-Marketing Manager, plus two different external agencies, need to be engaged — but they cannot make decisions unless they check with their respective headquarters overseas.

If the sales promotion involves direct mail that targets a retail store, the Retail VP must be involved. If the retail store falls within the category of a large account, the Large Account VP must be involved.

If the large retail outlet is inside a university campus, the Education VP must have a say. If it is housed inside a government complex, the Government VP must approve the offer. In addition, it so happens that the building is in Sydney, so the Sydney Branch Manager needs to be engaged. Would you believe, at the end of this vicious chainsaw is a salesperson trying to sell chocolate, but no-one from this matrix bothered to seek the advice of the salesperson.

I have painted a simplified picture of the matrix management scenario. I have seen much, much worse. Matrix management gets to the point where no-one has the authority to make basic business decisions. But that's not the full extent of the scenario.

The VP responsible for retail has a marketing manager who is assisting in the execution. The Marketing Manager reports to the Retail VP — but not really because all functional direction comes from the Chief of Retail in Singapore who reports to a counterpart in Japan. The Marketing Manager is located at a remote site and thus has a "Location" Manager as well.

In any case, this month the Retail Marketing Manager is rewarded on gross profit (GP). So his mortgage payment rides on his ability to attain a set GP figure. His colleague, the Product Manager, reports to the Head of Product Managers in Japan who has a different boss and whose direction comes from the USA. The Product Manager's success hinges on his ability to ensure that stock in the warehouse is halved to make way for new models.

Already with conflicting objectives, the colleagues have been pitted against each other — one keen on keeping the GP high while the other is focused on clearing the stock, even if at below cost price. To top this off, neither knows of the other's hidden objectives for the month. Under such circumstances, teamwork is an impossibility.

Huge organisations have tumbled under the weight of their stupidity

Imagine if the final offer included sugar-free products and required a response to a government tender. There are then two more departments that would have to step in. And there's more.

The client in question is a division of an institution that is run out of Germany. The German group has just signed a world-wide agreement with the confectionery company in the UK, and all sales now must comply with world-wide pricing that must be approved in Japan. To tell you more, you might not believe me, but there is more.

Add to this matrix different dimensions such as who has respect for whom? Who is in charge of what? How does the client comprehend the barrage of questions? How do the teams understand their scope of authority? Who cares to push which barrow, and what hidden agendas are there, and whose are they? The list goes on.

Ultimately, very few managers would be interested in pursuing this opportunity because they would not get to show the revenue on *their* books. Only one division can report the revenue, making it unattractive for teams to co-operate when not all can share in the victory should a sale eventuate. Vice-presidents delegate to managers who forward the request to front-line staff via e-mails that simply say, "Please look into this." It is hardly what co-operation is all about.

Those who take the game of matrix management seriously will be reprimanded either officially or unofficially. This kind of drama is designed to pull them into line. These manoeuvres are considered fun because they expose seniority and give "hopeless nobodies with fancy business cards" an opportunity to flash their obscure title on a conference call. Such chest-beating and posturing gives purpose and justifies the executives' monthly salaries and company cars. Sadly, it reminds everyone that no-one is in a position to make a decision, not even the VPs who use well-chosen words wrapped in sheets of diplomacy delivered with false courtesies.

Granted, large organisations are complex creatures. They have different needs and are faced with unique challenges. Yes. So what?

Apart from its stakeholders, its people, and its clients, a large organisation must also consider its competitors.

The competitor in this scenario has some of the finest chocolates in the world. It has a Marketing Manager who can make *all* the decisions, and can call on her suppliers of choice. She does not have to put up with food fights between the UK-appointed agencies. She knows her limits and can make a decision within two minutes — without deputations. She does not have to plead for co-operation from others, and she does not have to suffer endless unproductive and politically charged e-mails.

Huge organisations have tumbled under the weight of their stupidity. Justify it any which way you like, but in this scenario the competitor has the edge. Unless of course the larger organisation discounts the product to incredibly low levels in order to win the deal on price — as I have seen happen. The salesperson who liquidated the profits just to win this deal happened to be rewarded through commission that was calculated on revenue, not profit. So he took home a hero's trophy and a fat commission cheque. He was anointed and quickly promoted to Singapore (working from Sydney) while his colleague, the Marketing Manager (who failed to maintain the gross profit because he had no say in the matter) could not afford the home-loan payment that month.

A little later, the truth came out, but it fell on deaf ears because one-third of the people who were involved had left the company. It was later realised that the contract was deficient, resulting in massive abuse and losses, causing the legal department to step in to clean up the mess.

A third of those involved had changed jobs within the company, and the rest who remembered the deal bumped into each other at the staff canteen and looked to the heavens as they sighed in disbelief at the farce. But the subject was not discussed for long because there were other debacles on the lunch-time gossip agenda.

THE PRODUCTION-LINE MENTALITY

Generally, time-and-motion studies prove that speed at production lines can be improved if the manufacturing process is broken down into small, sometimes single, tasks. By delegating the smallest of tasks to different operators on the line, speed can be increased to the point where ten people working together can produce 100 items through synergy. Conversely, working alone to produce the product from start to finish, ten people would hardly be able to assemble one product each. As explained in Chapter 12, "Come do the nanomation with me", the tangible world allows synergy to emerge when the weak and the strong work together for a common outcome.

Conversely, the *intangible* world does not enjoy such luxuries. The joining of the weak with the strong dilutes the outcome to the lowest level. Herein lies the secret to the sorry state of matrix management. Management is intangible. It cannot be enhanced if it is broken down into its smallest components and spread across a group of people who handle each decision via a production-line mentality.

When no-one sees the big picture, no-one can improve it

In an attempt to break down the large organisation into smaller components, the CEO has created a black hole where synergy cannot withstand the burden of ambiguity, the lack of definition, and, above all, the absence of one big picture in the mind of the "director" — the one person who *directs* the picture.

In the same way that kryptonite cripples Superman, matrix management destroys the fabric of an organisation. When people with vision cannot execute anything to their specification because not every step is under their control nor within their scope of supervision, they are rendered ineffectual. Those with power are disarmed. The troops cannot follow because there is now more than one beat pounding from more than one drum — cacophony at its most deafening. Those capable of innovation have their minds dulled by brick walls that surround them. These bureaucratic barriers are erected by megalomaniacs armed with an endless supply of red tape.

THE MORTGAGE MANAGER

When two people have to negotiate, the one who has the power to say "no" holds the greater power

Who can withstand the force of matrix management? It can't be done. No single person can overcome the inertia. When no-one sees the big picture, no-one can improve it. When staff members are concerned only with their own little empires, they cannot know or care about neighbouring castles. Those who realise that their senses are becoming numbed have the choice to leave, but they soon remember that they have a mortgage, a family, and other commitments. They become frightened to leave the organisation because they truly believe that they do not have the ability to obtain another job. They are intrinsically doubtful of their skill and capability, and they fear humiliation should they fail a test on a broader scale than their systematic production-line task has trained them for.

Mortgage Managers, once tripped, fall in the groove. They soon become insensitive to the Animal Farm that pays their bills. Adults return to their school-day blues and recall the sense of comfort in following the school's timetable, governed by the bell. Only now their timetable is an endless workflow. The more complicated their task appears to co-workers, the greater their sense of contribution. Looking busy and being busy is vital because it bolsters their egos in an environment where "triumphs" are no longer real at the human level, but are recorded only within the annual report — if they have a good year. This syndrome would be almost impossible for the CEO to detect and quash because very few would dare to admit to their own lack of importance on the production line. Besides, they all know that no-one holds the key to anything in matrix management. That's part of its attraction. By breaking down the organisation into bite-sized chunks, no-one can challenge another group, no-one can stand up to the CEO, and, what is worse, no-one can combat a competitor on anything other than price or on that which the founders of the organisation managed to amass for them before matrix management — things such as patents, brand values, goodwill, or cash. In matrix management, each group is kept on its knees begging for some activity to make it feel useful.

The environment surrounding a matrix management structure breeds amiable masses depleted of energy and stripped of any ability or desire to fight. Anyone who tries ends up rocking the boat for all, and thus the masses soon step in to trample on the audacious. No republicanism is tolerated in a "communist" matrix structure. It is communist because the structure revolves around a commune where services become centralised as dependencies become entrenched.

WHAT PART OF "NO" DON'T YOU UNDERSTAND?

The corporate commune becomes reliant on itself as divisions begin to need other divisions. Not in the hope of building on ideas and moving to greater heights, but in the fear that the links in the chain might exercise their one and only authority — the authority to say "no".

When co-operation is faked and common courtesies are begrudgingly exchanged, the players are not hedging for approval but hoping for the absence of disapproval. Divisions do not care what their downstream colleagues have to say or what they think, but they do want to avoid a red light.

When two people have to negotiate, the one who has the power to say "no" holds the greater power. Herein lies the gridlock. In matrix management, everyone has the power to disagree, stall, delay, discuss, study, and seek clarification in the interest of avoiding that which they cannot easily arrive at — the "yes" which is far too risky. No-one can count on sufficient support to break away. Those who innovate within this territory soon realise that their colleagues' jealousy and fear combine to create hell. In all, matrix management is *your* ticket to hell.

WHERE TO GO FROM HELL

The only way out is out. Do not bother trying to compromise. If you are a CEO who is horrified to think what your organisation might resemble, you can fix it. However, your only way to effect change is to do it immediately and thoroughly.

If you wish to, you can maintain your business units but each must be autonomous. To see champions in action you must give them the scope. This does not mean that they can run riot. Challenge them to produce the results that you specify, but do not burden them with other people's incompetence and fear.

Some CEOs worry that such freedom might result in divisional managers going against the direction of the company. However, once trained, managers can use their intellectual capacity to follow the corporate guidelines. An ability to stay within the corporate ethics is not the monopoly of the mind-guards. Others can follow the standards too. Which would you rather: to place a police officer at every street corner to catch all those who litter, or to launch a public campaign to encourage all people to keep their environment beautiful?

Employ experts who can operate ethically. Teach them what the guidelines are, tell them what you need, outline their parameters, and leave them alone. Create an environment that allows them to paint their own big picture, supporting them as they set about executing their vision. However you structure this, do not infuriate experts by expecting them to negotiate with inexperienced people who hold authority. There is nothing more bewildering than the feeling of contradiction that befalls an expert moments after some buffoon perks up in a meeting and says, "I'm no expert but . . . I'm your boss."

Do not expect that everyone can see the big picture. This is not always possible. Furthermore, sharing the vision is one thing, but justifying it beyond reasonable boardroom measures saps the director's energy. Remember, vision comprises millions of ideas interwoven in a special language of the brain. Such "brain-speak" cannot be easily articulated in English "tongue speak". (For more on brain-speak, see Chapter 7, "Can you speak another colour?")

WHEN PUSH COMES TO SHOVE

In marketing circles, when professionals speak of "push" and "pull" strategies, they are referring to marketing activities that either *push* the product (from the factory through the channel to the retailer who actively sells the product to the end user) or to efforts that have the end user *pull* the product (by going into the retailer and demanding a specific product, forcing the retailer to stock it).

For management structures there is another "push" and "pull" philosophy that must be decided. The CEO must commit to only one model. In the "push" method the organisation is said to be "factory-driven" — when the factory decides which products it wants to manufacture, which markets it wants to pursue, and the pricing policies.

Those with the ability to refuse passage ought to become passengers themselves. Instead of watching people queuing up, they will have to wait in line themselves. When they become part of inactivity, they will have a different perspective on the meaning of "progress".

The "pull" method relies on the marketing division to instruct the factory about what is required to meet the market's needs. In a "market-driven" organisation, the factory takes instructions from the field.

Both "push" and "pull" methods have advantages and disadvantages. However, this ought to be another binary decision for the CEO who must structure a company that is driven from one engine or the other. A combination of the two does not work in the long term because matrix management would raise its ugly head.

So many people carry on about what the customer

needs, as if to suggest that they operate a market-driven company when, in truth, the factory is in control. There is nothing wrong with a factory-driven organisation. But it is folly to espouse one thing and do another.

CAPTAINS, MY CAPTAINS

The absence of matrix management enables the CEO to ensure that every employee can be afforded the right to only one manager. No employee, contractor, or agent ought to be burdened with more than one line of reporting. In dynamic organisations that expect speed and brilliance, no room exists for dotted-line reporting. You must cut across the dotted line.

Go one step further and disarm your employees by confiscating their ability to say "no". Those with the ability to refuse passage ought to become passengers themselves. Instead of watching people queuing up, they will have to wait in line themselves. When they become part of inactivity, they will have a different perspective on the meaning of "progress".

Each division must be autonomous. Do not fragment responsibilities. For example, a marketing manager can only function if that manager has control of all the marketing functions. Checks and balances can be put in place, but these ought *not* to be performed by sinister mind-guards, but by helpers who themselves are passengers. Checks and balances ought to exist to strengthen and support, not to weaken and drain.

If the organisation is so large that business units and divisions are needed, each unit should be treated as a separate entity. Do not pretend that synergy can be realised by splitting job roles and expecting people to co-operate. This brings us back to rule one: do not tolerate any form of matrix management.

If central divisions are constructed so that central services can be provided with a view to achieving economies of scale, each service provider must realise that its existence is reliant upon its delivery of quality services in line with market availability. Furthermore, no manager ought to be forced to use the internal service centre. Managers must be able to do whatever they have to do to compete in the marketplace. The day that an internal service provider oversteps the mark to utter the word "no" is the day that the manager can decide to go elsewhere to obtain the service — without justification, without white papers, without excessive memoranda. Why should this be? Because

Beware the day that suppliers call themselves "partners". They are not your partners. They are in it to maximise their profits, are they not?

the business unit or division exists to operate within supposedly logical market segments. Each of these segments has its own competitors. You (from the large organisation) and the competitor (from a small specialised organisation) each have to present one face to the customer. How can you win in the face of competition when restrictions come from within your own group?

AT WHOSE SERVICE?

When appointing central agencies and suppliers, do not expect your managers to comply with your "world-wide" rulings. For example, centrally appointed advertising agencies often become an incomprehensible blob of goo that stifles the organisation.

I know all about the merits of global branding. I am not suggesting that global brand positioning and broad-based campaigns are not important. I am not criticising the merits of good advertising. I am warning against central suppliers who think that it is their God-given right to own an account. Worse still if they too operate within a matrix management structure. Watch the sparks fly.

The amount of time and money that is wasted with political innuendoes and the slapstick comedy that arises from these suppliers is a joke. All shareholders ought to be nervous about it. Beware the day that such suppliers call themselves "partners". They are not your partners. They are in it to maximise their profits, are they not? So when push comes to shove, they are there to do what is right for them.

This is not to say that agencies are bad. Or that creative people do not understand the bottom line. All I am saying is that if you need the services of an agency or a supplier, the manager who is responsible for the unit's bottom line should appoint the suppliers and service providers at a local level. Headquarters may still dictate certain rules about the brand, or the corporate image, but no more. Headquarters ought to specify the "what", not the "how". If it needs to do both, it ought to employ administrators to execute its specified tactics.

Rather than appoint a world-wide agency, large organisations would be better off if they established an information office to assist the countries with their queries and needs. The information office could work with the agencies appointed by each unit to assist them to maintain the corporate image by providing timely information and services. Note that the information office must not interfere with local decisions.

FROM TASKMASTER TO GROUP LEADER

If the CEO cares to rectify matrix management, this can be done by implementing simplified structures that remove the burden from employees and set them free. The strong will fly, the corrupt will fall, the rest will be liberated.

In the absence of matrix management, and in the presence of powerful visionaries who are ethical and competent experts in their field, things might start to happen ahead of the CEO. The role of the CEO would change from taskmaster to group leader, and this shift would put the chief on the moving train. CEOs would no longer referee from on high. They might even stop pandering to market analysts. At best, they could become invisible. My goodness! G

CHAPTER 14

fluid SHARES

How to Cause a Chain Reaction

I F YOU HAVE EVER FIRED a double-barrelled shot-gun, you will have felt the kick-back that could have easily dislocated your shoulder if you were either not ready, or not strong enough to handle the impact. This analogy serves to highlight how the ideas in this chapter, if implemented, could impact on the executive who decides to cause a chain reaction through fluid shares. As with the gun, the power not only jolts the executive but also shocks the organisation in a most powerful and definite way. And as with any weapon, fluid shares can be used to hit a target, or can cause all sorts of unfortunate destruction. However, no earnest implementation of a business solution can take place without casualties; and as with all serious solutions, the results can be exceptionally powerful.

Of all the controversial chapters in this book, this one could be the most infuriating to employers and unions. It could also prove to be invaluable for them if only they would take a moment to understand its essence, and why fluid shares is different from traditional profit-sharing schemes. This chapter must not be judged hastily. It is powerful because it examines an age-old problem — the destructive notion of management versus unions, and workers versus management. The "them-and-us" attitude has destroyed corporations and industries.

This chapter offers solutions based on the creation of magical *chain reactions* through powerful *fluid shares*. Anyone who does not grasp the importance of these concepts will not understand how this chapter can crack a problem that has stifled organisations for decades. In fact, those who do not appreciate the significance of these concepts might conclude that this chapter expresses naive recommendations.

The ideas contained in this chapter could not work in all organisations. In some industries, acts of parliament might be required if current industrial awards were to be modified. If such major reforms are required, so be it.

As for unionists, this chapter might make them furious. However, this would be a curious outcome because the ideas espoused here are beneficial to their members. Sadly, some unions have forgotten their charter.

TO BE OR NOT TO BE

There are people who amuse themselves by latching on to new concepts that spring to mind as a result of a recently expanded vocabulary. They learn a new word and are impressed by what that new word can do to their understanding of a particular concept. For example, there are managers who learn that there are differences between being "effective" and "efficient". As a result, they take it upon themselves to tell their employees that one word is more important than the other. Thereafter, they will speak about these differences at staff meetings, and if overly enthusiastic, they begin to use them in memoranda and reports. On occasion, the words will find their way into the mission statement of the month.

This chapter deals with two words that have confused employees and managers alike for a long time — "proactive" and "reactive".

These two words should not exist. What does it mean when a corporate directive requests employees to be either "proactive" or "reactive"? It would be like suggesting that people ought to either "speak" or "listen". Surely the combination of both would be ideal, and undertaking one and not the other would be as erroneous as suggesting that the flavour of the month is to breathe in, and not out.

> *What does it mean when a corporate directive requests employees to be either "proactive" or "reactive"? It would be like suggesting that people ought to either "speak" or "listen". Surely the combination of both would be ideal?*

WHAT IS PROACTIVITY?

Those who promote the concept of proactivity suggest that it is better to engage in tasks that have been decided upon as a result of taking initiative, and not as a result of a crisis. It is more akin to being on the *offensive,* rather than being on the *defensive.* Clearly, it is better to attack and keep the enemy at bay, than to be attacked — where the latter consumes more time, energy, and resources. When proactivity refers to customer service, it involves a level of educated guesswork that can keep the organisation one step ahead of the customer, saving time and money, and creating a perception that the company cares about its customers so much that it is thinking about their needs and taking action without being prompted, or before it is too late. (For more on customer service, see Chapter 17, "Customer service — my foot!")

WHAT IS REACTIVITY?

In the 1980s and 1990s, it was most unfashionable, and definitely unpopular, to endorse reactive behaviour. To be reactive was associated with images of people not having a plan of action, and moving from one crisis to the next. When this school of thought clashed with the newfound wisdom that customer service relies heavily upon the need to react to customers' demands, a new word was substituted, "responsiveness". This meant that organisations were allowed to be *responsive,* but not *reactive.* Being reactive is a vital part of any business. Being reactive not only encompasses responsiveness but also demands that people be alert, amiable, and aware of the customers' and the environment's changing needs.

Why is it that, despite the most elaborate of incentives, corporate results are still lacklustre?

WHAT IS THE ROOT CAUSE?

What was it that started managers talking about proactivity and reactivity? Why was there a need to articulate behaviour? The root cause was the realisation that employees were confused. They had been brain-washed into providing excellent customer service to external *and* internal customers, thereby creating a burden within the organisation. Priorities were convoluted even further when the mission statement espoused "making the customer happy" while internal measurement systems focused on the "bottom line". This over-eagerness by staff members to be "reactive" led managers to insist that "proactivity" ought to be just as effective, and much more efficient. At this point, people became utterly dumbfounded, to the point of inactivity.

The root need is to ensure that every board member and every staff member operates at the same level of urgency and diligence. With this realisation managers are better served to implement a system that utilises a chain reaction.

WHAT IS A CHAIN REACTION?

Scientifically speaking, a chain reaction refers to a nuclear or chemical process that, once started, continuously releases energy. This means that after only one trigger, a process will continue to occur without any further need for input.

In the context of this chapter, a chain reaction refers to a series of events that occur automatically (and unaided) as a result of a preceding action.

If the root need is to engineer an environment in which staff members can act according to the best interests of the organisation, nothing beats the chain-reactive process. However, can you rely on all the players to do the right thing? How can managers rely on staff members to act with the company's best interests in mind?

Before answering these questions, consider first that most people do have the intelligence to make the right decisions. Most employees have the skills and experience to assess a situation and come up with reasonable solutions. If you believe that this is the case, ask not what can be done to promote a sensible attitude to the business. Ask instead why it is that intelligent members of the workforce are discouraged from making the *right* decisions. Ask why it is that normal people find themselves engaged in activities that are not in the best interests of the whole organisation. Why is it that, despite the most elaborate of incentives, corporate results are still lacklustre? Why is wastage so severe in organisations? Furthermore, ask not what staff members can do to improve the situation; rather look at what it is that causes rivalry and hatred within and among divisions. What circumstances turn ambitious or conscientious people into irrational, ineffective opponents? The solution to these problems has nothing to do with "empowerment".

If you work in an organisation where managers and staff find it normal and acceptable to embark upon a spending spree at the end of the financial year in order to spend all the budget for fear of a reduction in the forthcoming allocation, your team is in desperate need of a chain-reactive process.

If you have seen people waste money by undertaking projects and campaigns simply because it is important to "spend the money" lest their rivals accuse them of inactivity, you can confidently prescribe a chain-reactive process.

If you have seen storerooms full of products, brochures, and other tools and resources that are only to be discarded in due course, such wastage can be cured with a chain-reactive process.

The worst scenario of all is if you have witnessed experts arguing about headcount, advertising budgets, marketing expenses, and capital expenditure, while employing schoolyard bully tactics as a result of conflict arising from incentives, bonuses, and commission schemes. Nothing will resolve the difficulties better than a chain-reactive process.

WHAT IS A CHAIN-REACTIVE PROCESS?

I coined the term "chain-reactive" to describe a process that puts into place systems that work not on computerised schemes and spreadsheets, but on emotional, logical, and measurable systems that automatically cause everyone in the organisation to act with one vision and one voice. A chain-reactive process will silence anyone who works against the betterment of the team, removing the need for divisions to compete with each other, thus diminishing the desire for employees to outdo each other. Chain-reactive processes will enable the whole organisation to realise that there is no need for the notion of an "internal" customer.

Only external customers count. The concept of internal customers suits the organisation headed by a person who tries to appease everyone and satisfy no-one. And, finally, chain-reactive processes will remove the focus from internal competition to a healthy preoccupation with the external competitor.

It is vital to understand that the construction of a chain-reactive process is unsuitable for the faint-hearted. It does not tolerate compromise. It cannot be politically fine-tuned. A leader must either embrace it completely, or stay clear of it. If you believe that you need the promises outlined in the previous paragraphs, consider that the purpose of implementing a chain-reactive process is to make everyone automatically care about the things that count. With that in mind, consider that the root causes of the problems outlined above are two in number. The first is the conflicting, contradictory, and sometimes paradoxical incentives set by the leader. The second is the *lack* of unwavering standards that ought to be applied to all people and in all situations.

Many would agree that it is a noble maxim that "no-one in the organisation is to steal". Anyone who steals, no matter what their rank, should be treated in the same way. However, this level of fairness (standards) is not applied universally to other situations — for example, the maxim that says *no manager is to exceed the allocated budget*. Yet many do. Those who do not spend their entire budget are asked to relinquish the surplus and donate it to the incompetent manager who decided to break the rule and hope for the best. This example illustrates destructive behaviour. It would signal to the careful manager that careless colleagues will be bailed out, and that those who plan carefully and do not spend their funds all at once are likely to be penalised by being asked to surrender the funds that were set aside for agreed programs.

Note that chain-reactive processes ought not to be confused with reward systems. A mouse ringing a bell and being rewarded with food is not a chain-reactive process. To implement a chain-reactive process, everyone in the organisation needs to become involved in the loop. Everyone either wins together or loses together.

THE POWER OF THE CHAIN-REACTIVE PROCESS

How many products would your organisation have to sell to make one dollar of profit after all expenses and taxes have been paid? Look into this and you might be surprised.

Managers and staff who have had to endure the "them and us" syndrome can demolish it if all the people in the chain are made *part* of the chain by being rewarded in the same way. If everyone either wins or loses together, it becomes everyone's business if one staff member decides to steal. It becomes everyone's business if stock is damaged. Everyone becomes a custodian of the corporate assets. No longer would security guards outnumber the staff because all staff members take responsibility for security. Wouldn't it be desirable if everyone assumed the role of quality controller and customer-service specialist? This can be achieved without any manager ever having to speak about it. Diligence, initiative, and care would become such automatic and natural qualities that they would not even need to be mentioned in job descriptions.

Note that such teamwork is not the kind that emerges after a morale-boosting lecture. We all know that enthusiasm from such hype events is short-lived. Also, note that implementing a chain-reactive process does not detract from *authority*. It has nothing to do with the notion of communism. Chain-reactive processes, once implemented, have nothing to do with treating everyone equally. Managers remain managers. Those in authority retain their authority. Those who misbehave will still be dismissed.

If you have understood what is meant by a chain-reactive process, and have decided that you have the courage to implement it, but now need a framework, the following information relates to one solution, fluid shares.

WHAT ARE FLUID SHARES?

Organisations offer all sorts of incentives to their staff members. Some offer schemes where employees can become part-owners in the business. Some allow staff members to have share options while others offer discount programs. All of these are valid ways of rewarding employees. However, they do not change people's daily behaviour because their salaries might not be directly tied to their actions; and not all employees are in all the schemes. Besides it is of no benefit to argue about the merits of share schemes because they each have their place. Used properly, they have their advantage, but they do not impact on the *daily* operation. In contrast, every move by every staff member *does* have a dramatic impact on the business. Therefore, one ought to make *every* move important by rewarding it with fluid shares because it is the collection of little daily tasks that contributes to the bigger picture.

The "fluid" concept in the proposed share scheme focuses on the fact that everyone ought to benefit together or be disadvantaged together. This is a generous approach to rewarding staff members. Its generosity has the tendency to cause hesitant executives to become concerned about the increased payroll without giving a thought to the fact that an increased payroll under this scheme could only have occurred from increased profit.

HOW TO STRUCTURE A FLUID-SHARE PROGRAM

The following five steps comprise advice that you might find challenging, albeit rewarding. Organisations whose performance is substandard will find that fluid shares are highly potent. However, the brave will be tested.

| STEP ONE |

To structure a powerful fluid share scheme, based on the chain-reactive criteria, start out by listing the name and salary of every staff member in your organisation. Add the salaries and divide by the number of staff members. In effect, you have just determined the average salary paid in your organisation. This average figure will now become *everyone's* salary. The store person, the truck driver, the general manager, the receptionist, the typist, the engineer — everyone will now be on the same salary (being the average figure). To make matters even more interesting, everyone will be on the same benefit structure. At this point anyone who was earning more than the average will protest, and suggest that this is a preposterous idea. My suggestion for those who are infuriated is that they resign gracefully because their selfish attitude is the one that has been conflicting with the organisation for a long time. This kind of attitude however is not as bad as the fact that such reactions come from managers who either cannot *understand* the long-term power of fluid shares, or who do understand it, but do not plan to be around long enough to benefit from it.

Aligning the salaries is step one. There are several more. The alignment of salaries quickly removes any thought that some people are being rewarded more than others. There can be no more discussion about managers having to work harder because they "get paid more".

| STEP TWO |

Step two is to declare that, at the end of each month, once profits have been calculated, 10 per cent (or another reasonable and generous figure) will be set aside as a company-wide bonus that will be divided equally among everyone. This measure will show all those involved that profitability is a serious affair — the more of it that is generated, the more that everyone will benefit. If the organisation is not generating a profit, all the more reason why this scheme becomes an imperative. It focuses the group on the most important elements of running a successful business. With careful planning, and the right education, people will start to plan for a profitable turnaround.

| STEP THREE |

Step three requires that the leader embark upon an *education* campaign that will illustrate to everyone in the organisation the importance of the dollar. Everyone must be taught about the value of the dollar and what it is worth as a net-profit figure after tax. People will soon understand the effort that is required to generate one dollar of net profit after tax. For example, how many products would your

If you are starting a new production line, be sure to test its productivity before you allow uninterested workers to set your standards

organisation have to sell to make one dollar of profit after all expenses and taxes have been paid? Look into this and you might be surprised. The education program should also encompass a general awareness of typical costs associated with running the business so everyone understands.

| STEP FOUR |

Step four involves setting cost-reduction goals. Every three months select one or two major areas of expense that can be fine-tuned. Challenge the team by telling them that for every dollar saved, fifty cents will go into a pool that will be divided equally among the team. Therefore, a saving of $10 000 will result in a one-time bonus of $5000 being added to the end-of-month bonuses. This powerful incentive not only reduces an expense, it also rewards the efforts, focuses everyone on the challenge and, most importantly, sets a new *standard* for the level of expense. This kind of standard-setting exercise can be used for manufacturing production lines where output could be doubled with direct rewards being divided among the *whole* team — because it would require the co-operation of the whole team.

Finding the standard for expense or output is a vital step to success. How have you arrived at the current standards and benchmarks? I was privy to confidential information about the production schedule of a factory. Each day it was expected that a certain batch of products be produced, packed, and stacked ready for picking and delivery. This "norm" was expected each day of the week. The entire company's finances were based on this level of output. Unfortunately, the workers were nonchalant about their work. Why should they try any harder when, as far as everyone was concerned, they were working to maximum capacity?

The Logistics Manager was curious about the benchmarks, but he was powerless to reset the standards. Furthermore, he was not really sure what was possible in the way of production improvement because he was unable to test his theory. One day his chance came and he took the opportunity to set a trap. It was the day before the Easter holiday. Most of the production workers were anxious to leave work to join their families for the holiday. Seizing on their sense of urgency, the Logistics Manager told all the employees that they could go home, with full pay, the moment that they finished their regular batch of products. He displayed a sense of compassion and goodwill while deep-down he was curious about how long it would take enthusiastic workers to complete a regular eight-hour shift. Much to everyone's surprise, they finished their work, to perfection, in four hours. Such productivity could send the share prices sky-high. Imagine being able to double output.

If you are starting a new production line, be sure to test its productivity before you allow uninterested workers to set your standards. On the other hand, if you have inherited a mediocre team, use fluid shares to give them a direct benefit and a tangible reason to break down the "them and us" syndrome. The next step explains how.

| **STEP FIVE** |

In step five continue to invest in skills development so that staff members can continue to contribute. Also, announce that bonuses will be divided equally among the total staff headcount. This means that if several staff members, for whatever reason, resign (or are dismissed) and are not replaced, the bonus per person will *increase* because fewer people would be taking a share.

Sharing bonuses equally causes a most sensational chain reaction. Divisions and departments that would normally have screamed for additional headcount would now think twice about employing new people if they are not necessary for the business. Not only will employment and payroll-related expenses be avoided, other significant savings will be made, causing another chain reaction whereby all staff members help out as appropriate. In most corporations, too many incompetent people are allowed to abuse the system because the "majority" does not have the incentive to speak out against wastage or against people whose actions resemble the effects of cancer. However, with fluid shares driving the chain reaction, everyone has a vested interest in securing and defending a tight and professional organisation.

WHAT ABOUT SKILLED PERSONNEL WHO DESERVE MORE PAY?

It might be possible, during the earlier stages of implementing fluid shares, that the average salary, while high for the majority, is lower than a senior manager would require. This would only be a short-term issue that can be solved by asking the executive in question to think of the long-term health of the company. If major personal financial commitments genuinely prohibit an executive from taking a pay cut, the rule would still apply, but the company would advance the executive some funds at the executive's own risk, and later deduct the loan from the due bonuses. This should only be done in exceptional circumstances, and not abused or overlooked. There must be no compromises, favours, or creative accounting.

Under the fluid share scheme it is more than likely that talented staff would earn more than they would otherwise have commanded. The real issue that may be contested is not the amount paid to skilled employees, but the fact that unskilled employees are earning the *same* amount. This is nothing more than a selfish approach to life. Such selfishness is naive and destructive.

What difference does it make if an engineer who would normally command an $80 000 salary and who, under this scheme, is earning $100 000 earns the same as the receptionist (who would also earn $100 000)? The engineer's extra $20 000 could not have been forthcoming if it were not for the fluid-share scheme. So, why wish it upon the receptionist to earn less for no reason at all? This is a very serious obstacle that challenges the selfish and the short-sighted. The only advice that can be given to a leader is that the person in question be asked to undertake some counselling to understand the facts of life, or else resign because such attitudes are not of any value to the company.

WOULD THERE BE A DANGER OF LOSING EXPERTS WHO PROTEST?

If a highly skilled person resigns as a result of this scheme, they should not be convinced to stay on. Instead, a consultant may be employed at market rates. The team would not object to payment for expert advice from a consultant on a short-term assignment. The team would understand that the organisation needs such services, in the same way that a television station's services might be needed to place advertisements. However, it is incumbent upon the leader to ensure that this avenue is not abused. Remember the rules stated much earlier in this chapter: *No rule can be broken and no double standards can be tolerated*. No-one must be allowed to resign and then brought back as a consultant. Such actions will go against the very reasons why fluid shares were deemed desirable in the first place. Deviation will lead to destruction. Stay on track!

IN CONCLUSION

Imagine what kind of chain reaction will take place when everyone is on fluid shares. All of a sudden, pilfering and wastage will be reduced like never before — automatically. Productivity will increase — willingly. Innovation will surface — enthusiastically.

After the initial stages of adjustment, staff members will begin to see each other not as internal customers who take delight in complaining about each other, but as team-mates who are in the same boat — if it rocks, it will make everyone seasick. Staff loyalty will be improved by the chain reaction — where else could junior staff earn so much money (possibly four times the market rate)? And, where else could managers find such co-operation from their employees?

With the chain reaction being fuelled by fluid shares, what would become of the feeble notions of being pro-active or reactive? These things will become invisible, contributing to the simpatico. How delightful!

Fluid shares are not about commissions. They are not even about traditional bonuses. They are about a new form of profit-sharing. So the fluid share scheme must have an equation that relates to costs.

Fluid shares means "we win together, and we lose together". The wins have to be worthwhile. Under this scheme, everyone will be affected by good or bad results. Furthermore, no team member is more important than another. Those who have the ability to lose or gain a customer are part of the team that shares unusually generous profits. The whole scheme, although initially painful to implement, would be so worthwhile that results will show what people are really capable of. They, too, would be amazed at how easily success can be attained when they have a reason to try.

WHAT ABOUT THE NON-PROFIT SECTOR?

For some reason, the antiquated ideal is that public sector officials ought not to enjoy high salaries because their work is a service to the nation. Professionals in the public sector ought to be in a position to command fair compensation and their departmental staff ought to be treated like any other workforce. Sometimes there are perks associated with government jobs, such as exceptional retirement benefits, and a much more secure career.

The concept of "profit" seems to be shied away from, but government departments are in the business of making a profit too, not of making a loss. To avoid a loss, they must manage their funds dutifully, having the responsibility of administering public funds. A profit in the public sector means more back into the public coffers.

Once the concept of profit and fair remuneration for services rendered can be accepted, the next stage is to realise that the public sector workers are normal people who live next-door to other normal people from the private sector with the same issues of raising a family and surviving. This being the case, they too would respond favourably to rewards based on successful "outcomes". Fluid shares *can* work in government organisations. (See Chapter 18, "Lip-service".) ▪

CHAPTER 15

READY...AIM...
now WHAT?

HOW TO HIRE; WHEN TO FIRE;
AND WHAT TO DO IN BETWEEN

I ONCE HAD THE GOOD fortune of working with a self-made millionaire who headed his own international multi-billion-dollar organisation. Despite his complex advice about personnel management, his leading maxim was, "Each year, go through every division and flush out the bottom three per cent of the staff." This cleansing ritual was designed to remove hangers-on who were not contributing to the success of the company.

In thinking about such maxims, I set out to gather the best advice in relation to hiring and firing employees, and getting the most out of them. Here are the top dozen maxims most commonly used in today's corporate world.

1) Hire slowly, fire quickly.
2) People do what gets measured, so measure it, and it shall be done.
3) These days, workers should be treated like volunteers, not employees.
4) Hire people who can work while unsupervised.
5) Apart from high IQ, be sure to hire people with high emotional intelligence.
6) Teamwork is vital because none of us is as smart as all of us.
7) It is wise to adopt kaizen (continuous improvement).
8) Strive for world's best practice.
9) People don't like change.
10) It is important to allow diversity in the workplace.
11) Your people are your greatest asset.
12) Each year, flush out the bottom three per cent of your staff.

Apart from minor paraphrasing for the purposes of grammar, these quotes come from the biggest names in the business, and were distilled from a list of over 150. The ranking is not important, other than the fact that my survey participants selected these as their most preferred pearls of wisdom. Participants were asked to rank what they considered to be the twelve most useful pieces of advice for managers who hold responsibility for hiring, firing, or managing employees.

Would such a list be applicable in the networked world? Is good advice ageless and timeless? Are words of wisdom beyond reproach?

It is important to ask these questions because there is something deceptive about wisdom — it is not a cure-all ointment that heals personal and social problems.

Wisdom is the act of arriving at a decision that one knows will not trigger regret

Wisdom is not a word that refers to a particular set of advice. It does not point to anything; no more than honesty relates to anything. Honesty is a condition, a value, and a principle. It is refreshed with each situation, and refers to different things at different times. In the same way that one cannot say, "Let me give you some honesty", one cannot say, "Let me give you some wisdom". It is not a matter of pre-packaged solutions. Wisdom is the act of arriving at a decision that one knows will not trigger regret.

This list of twelve internationally recognised gems is, in fact, misleading and harmful. In the networked world, they are useless because wisdom must always be fresh. Anyone who holds these maxims up as useful advice is engaging in the oft-foolish practice of magnetic thinking. (For more information about magnetic thinking, see Chapter 21, "Characteristics of the modern world".)

Each of the items in the list will be explored in more detail to show why the networked world demands fresh wisdom. At the end of each point, I have included my suggestion for the modern version that contributes to success.

I have not set out to prove anyone wrong. I am trying to reveal the new demands of the networked world. Furthermore, the purpose of this chapter is to give twelve *examples*, not to suggest that there are only twelve important issues facing managers.

> *I am not one to be impressed with "good decision-makers". I prefer to work with "makers of good decisions".*

OLD WISDOM #1
Hire slowly, fire quickly.

My colleagues often ask me how a perfectionist like me manages to get so much done. Their first mistake is to assume that a perfectionist must be pedantic. They also assume that good decisions are those that require long bouts of deliberation. My typical response is that I am productive because I make a decision only once. I also make the point that I am not one to be impressed with "good decision-makers". I prefer to work with "makers of good decisions". This eliminates the error rate, and allows me to plough through the day with speed.

The point here is that the advice to hire "slowly" is misplaced. The speed of a good decision is irrelevant. In the networked world, hiring slowly is not at all a useful thing to do. In corporate life, anyone who does not snap up the opportunity to increase the headcount could bet that within thirty days, the rules would have changed, with headquarters putting a freeze on hiring. (Conversely, managers tend to tolerate low performers because if they let someone go during a hiring-freeze, they might not be allowed to replace that person. So they suffer incompetence merely to protect their empire.)

By firing people without fully understanding why they have performed poorly, you stand to lose the opportunity to pinpoint the bad circuitry

Incidentally, these days, talented and skilled people are being snapped up. If you take too long to make an offer, you'll find that your candidates would have accepted another offer elsewhere.

As for firing quickly, this too is a mistake. The question of speed pertains to executing your decision once you have made it, not making the decision itself quickly. Firing quickly could not only be unjust and unfair to the employee, it might also be detrimental to your organisation. By firing people without fully understanding *why* they have performed poorly, you stand to lose the opportunity to pinpoint the bad circuitry. Removing the employee might not equate to removing the problem.

NEW WISDOM #1
Don't hire if you have the slightest doubt.
Fire without the slightest hesitation.

OLD WISDOM #2
People do what gets measured, so measure it, and it shall be done.

No, this is not true. This kind of statement is as inappropriate as any of the generalisations about "men being this way, and women being that way". Dismissing an issue as one of a clash between the sexes is a superficial approach that could never lead to understating the crux of a matter. Saying that "people do what gets measured" suggests that humans are hard-wired to behave in a certain way. Don't fall into self-destructive logic loops.

Within the right environment, when people understand the bigger picture, they will act well and do what is right; not because they are *keen* to do the right thing, but because it would be *natural* to do the right thing. Employees will do what is right when they understand the business, the market, the customer, the direction, and the environment. The moment that you place stupid measurement processes, you are insisting that they throw out all their common sense, and all their intellect, and act myopically, no matter how damaging that might be for the organisation.

While matrix management is your ticket to hell, measurement systems are your membership renewals. I know that almost no employer would agree with me on this score.

Managers who disagree with me on this often say, "But how will we get people to do their job properly?" Hire mature professionals who are experts in their field, or those who are willing to learn and who possess a healthy attitude and an enquiring mind.

Your priority ought to be on making sure that everyone understands what business you are in. By that, I mean they must completely and totally understand what their contribution means to the company. This does not mean gathering everyone twice a year to listen to a bunch of managers recite the mission statement and the five priorities for the year ahead (which, incidentally, are invariably

Depleted creativity leads to intellectual shutdowns

something earth-shatteringly original and specific to the organisation, like: 1) We need to increase our revenue; 2) We need to reduce our expense; 3) We need to increase our market share; 4) we need to improve customer satisfaction; and 5) Oh by the way, let's have fun).

Don't measure people by what they do, but by how they protect and nurture your business, and by how they rationalise their decisions. Judge your people based on their intentions, their passion for life and work, their expertise, and their willingness and capability to learn. The moment that you reduce intellectual beings into robots, you will have sapped their creativity. Depleted creativity leads to intellectual shutdowns.

NEW WISDOM #2

*When you give people a common dream,
and are able to facilitate their imagination,
you will be fostering innovation.*

OLD WISDOM #3

*These days, workers should be treated like volunteers,
not employees.*

This trendy statement will no doubt take flight and crash somewhere sacred.

Don't be fooled into thinking that, these days, employees are different. Or that work conditions have changed. Don't assume that the supply and demand has shifted to the point where the candidate has the upper hand. Sure, this is contrary to the latest statistics about the supposed brain drain. Be careful not to blind yourself by staring at the symptoms. Divert your eyes and take a look at the root cause.

For example, a few decades ago, divorce rates were lower. What did that mean? Could it have been that couples were happier? I doubt it. There were issues of co-dependence, taboo, stigma, and fear on the part of one or both partners. Today, divorce rates are not higher because more people are unhappy with each other. They are higher because those who are unhappy (or selfish) can now exercise their desires within societies that provide supportive infrastructures.

The same question applies to employees. Are they less satisfied these days? No, it's just that they have the means to protest. They resign knowing full well that they can get another job elsewhere. In some sectors, they become millionaires by the age of twenty-five.

So it's not a question of pandering to employees, but one of asking what can be done to rectify the issues that have been driving employees mad for decades. Before you start treating your employees any differently, take a good look at your environment. What is it about your organisation that needs to be fixed at the roots? Why were the conditions allowed to deteriorate in the first place?

NEW WISDOM #3
Treat your employees like precious clients;
because that's exactly what they are.
You sell them your dream,
and they buy it with their services.

OLD WISDOM #4

Hire people who can work while unsupervised.

A smile sweeps across my face every time I read a job advertisement that says, "candidates must be able to work unsupervised". What is it trying to convey to the reader? Regardless of where this statement came from, it now applies to organisations whose managers are so busy that they cannot supervise their staff. They are consumed with their own distracting tasks, and are overwhelmed writing useless reports to cover their backside.

In a world that is so hung up on vision and mission statements, I would suggest that we need employees who can work *while* supervised. Supervision is a fine process of overseeing the operation to ensure that the whole team is on track. Megalomaniacs think that they can keep their finger on the pulse through monthly reports. Monitoring an organisation's health through written reports is akin to staring at the bandage, not listening to the heartbeat.

Monitoring an organisation's health through written reports is akin to staring at the bandage, not listening to the heartbeat

Recently, while watching an orchestra, my friend asked, "What's that conductor there for? None of the musicians are paying any attention to him." I tried to explain, to no avail. This made me think that perhaps the conductor, as a supervisor, is doing such a good job that his job seems superfluous.

Besides, do you think that musicians dislike being supervised by the conductor? Even though they might each be accomplished maestros, they would not think it demeaning or unnecessary to have a conductor bring the orchestra to life.

Supervision is not a bad thing. In the networked world, the pace is such that every organisation, and every division within it, requires a supervisor, much like a conductor, or an umpire, or a flight controller.

I recall a conversation I had with a CEO whose salary package exceeded $20 million. When I asked, "So, what is it you do that enables you to command such an annual income?", the reply was, "I am there to provide *adult supervision* because I am in an organisation that is being run by young geniuses who don't have business skills, so my job is to keep an eye on them."

You need to find people who *can* work under supervision. Your supervisors need to be graceful and switched-on. Supervisors need to be professionals, not someone within the group who exhibits charisma, or is the eldest, or the one least likely to move on. Tokenism is destructive.

NEW WISDOM #4

People who resist supervision are a danger to your organisation.

OLD WISDOM #5

Apart from high IQ, be sure to hire people with high emotional intelligence.

Oh, the pain of management fads. I find supposed revelations about human nature to be unsettling. All of a sudden we are told that we need to hire people who are emotionally intelligent. What's new about that?

Surely the need for emotional stability and maturity has been important for thousands of years. Surely managers worth their salt know that self-awareness, self-control, and self-confidence have always been vital ingredients. Civilisations have flourished without the need to "measure" anyone's emotional intelligence. Let's stop trying to categorise people. Let's stop pretending that we can ask sixty questions to ascertain integrity and inter-personal skills.

Human intangibles cannot be examined through a battery of written exams. Those who enjoy the exercise are not unlike those who believe in their daily horoscope reading (trick them, and read to them any one at random, and they will vouch for the accuracy of the reading). The gullible who devour such fads are usually impressed with statements like, "This is scientifically proven", or "In the past we were wrong, but now we have the answer", or "Studies show . . . " These are the same words used to sell emotional intelligence *and* hair-removal systems, thigh-toning machines, and skin cream at 3:00 am on television.

The most private essence of a person's fibre can only be measured by deed; not through written tests or sets of trivial and self-indulgent questions. If you want to really know what a potential employee is like, you will have to ask very private questions (usually illegal in most countries). You then have to find some way of knowing that the responses are completely accurate and candid. Just think, would you tell your boss or examiner the answer to *any* question whatsoever? Would you be prepared to answer probing questions about any aspect of what you do, think, and feel? Questions about your most inner secrets, your most inner desires, and your most private thoughts and opinions? Agreeing to do so would not equate to bravery but to stupidity, because what you think and feel is one thing, but how society reacts to it is something you cannot control.

What you think and feel is one thing, but how society reacts to it is something you cannot control

I once walked into the office of a human resources manager with whom I was friendly. She had a grin on her face, and was showing something to her offsider. They were poking fun at a candidate's résumé. "What's so funny?" I asked. "Look at this guy, he sends in his resume and says he is in a choir." I was disgusted to learn that she thought the man was a "pansy" for being a member of a choir. She made it perfectly clear that she had no intention of interviewing the applicant. I can still visualise the way in which she flung the resume to the corner of her desk.

Call it what you like. The fact remains that a perfectly suitable candidate applied for a job and divulged something about himself that was used against him. Yes, life is full of injustices like this. I am not suggesting that anything can be done about it. My point is that despite your bravery to answer questions, and irrespective of how comfortable you might be with your choices in life, others might not be able to cope with them. The interesting aspect of this story is that the human-resources manager is, at the time of writing this chapter, the managing director of a large and influential organisation in one of the most significant industries.

Humans do emit clues that can be detected by the astute. However, the people I worry about most are not the simpletons who answer questions honestly unaware of the response they might invoke, but the manipulators who know how to spin a web of deceit. If you really want to find out what people are like, you will have to wait for a technological breakthrough that will enable us to graph not only everyone's genetic signature, but also decrypt brain cells that hide our secrets. Furthermore, if you want to measure intelligence and emotions, I might go along with it if you can also measure creativity, integrity, humour, spirituality, valour, gallantry, bravery, audacity, courage, wisdom, acuity, and above all, perspicacity.

It is a marvellous thing that organisations are looking beyond academic achievement, and starting to value competence, maturity, mental stability, attitude, and other "soft" qualities. However, the best organisations have always valued these qualities. We are tending to forget this because these organisations have been sidetracked and tricked by IQ merchants, MBA merchants, and all sorts of other opportunists whose kitbag contains a new buzzword every day. I object to the notion of emotional intelligence because it is a buzzword that describes what every sensible manager has known about and has been using wisely for decades.

It is my opinion that this modern craze is a framework for consultants to sell training programs. I've not come across a single professional promoter of this fad who has not tried to sell me a training course. They seem to have a module for every kind of emotional condition. I would have thought that amongst us are a few loonies for whom no training course would be beneficial. In all the literature I could get my hands on, I'm yet to come across a sensible statement like, "Some people in your organisation might be so emotionally docile that you will have to let them go."

If you delve into this new movement, you will learn about emotional economy, emotional ecology, emotional leakage, emotional implosion, and emotional incontinence (where the leader at the top spills some bad vibes down onto subordinates). By the way, if you want to appear learned and well versed in this embarrassing trade, you'll need to learn how to use the term EQ alongside IQ, and drop the word "cognitive" into the conversation every now and then.

For those who do not know, emotional intelligence has been defined by the supposed experts as the capacity to recognise our feelings and those of others, and to be able to motivate ourselves, while managing emotions in ourselves and in our relationships. This type of thinking is seriously flawed. In short, I would suggest that rather than seek employees who possess emotional intelligence, we need to look for people who have intelligent emotions.

NEW WISDOM #5
*Categorising people will legitimise their
idiosyncrasies and weaknesses.
Raise your standards and
let them rise to the occasion.*

OLD WISDOM #6
*Teamwork is vital
because none of us is as smart as all of us.*

Truisms like this sound plausible, yet they tend to ignore the environment. It is not always true that "ten people can know more than one person" because that depends on who those ten people are. Ten world-class electricians might, collectively, be able to solve an electrical problem that neither one could have done on their own. However, nine butchers and one electrician could not succeed at the same challenge. Nine butchers could not know more than one seasoned electrician.

In the networked world, the weakest element will win. This means that forcing people to work together will not always yield a better result. Beware that you do not stifle innovation by pushing people to work in cross-functional teams where duties and responsibilities are tripped up by a haywire of authority that will only slow everyone down to the pace of the slowest person.

Experts work well together, and they energise each other. If you force them to work with those who do not have a clue about the subject matter, the best that you can expect is unmitigated disaster.

NEW WISDOM #6

A team is as fast as its slowest performer, and as docile as its worst bureaucracy.

OLD WISDOM #7

It is wise to adopt kaizen (continuous improvement).

The Japanese practice of *kaizen* refers to an organisation's deliberate strategy to set its sights on achievable goals. It then gradually improves its processes so as to do two things: 1) enable people to set modest targets and achieve them so as to gain a sense of satisfaction; and 2) encourage workers to slowly increase the challenge so as to improve over time.

Kaizen has been taught in the East and West. Although it sounds plausible and commendable, it is not suitable for the merciless networked world that demands excellent *now*, not later.

The endorsement of "continuous" improvement makes people lazy because it signals that imperfection can be tolerated so long as one *intends* to improve over time.

Continuous improvement might have worked for organisations that dominated their market for twenty years. It can still work for monopolies that do not feel the pressure to offer a better product or service. The networked world demands that organisations hire workers who will make an extra effort to get the job done to perfection and with a sense of urgency.

NEW WISDOM #7
Gradual improvement
leads to speedy failure.

OLD WISDOM #8
Strive for world's best practice.

Truly superior organisations do not hover around the mediocre standards of "best practice". World's best practice is mistaken to mean excellence.

Consider the world's leading airlines. Their idea of world's best practice expects economy-class passengers to squash into the cabin like sardines. According to all the studies, the minuscule space and non-existent legroom were optimised to allow the craft to maximise its load. All the spreadsheets in the world proved that the seating arrangements were the best that they could be. No-one asked the passengers for their opinion. After all, what would they know about passenger comfort? The airlines' excuse was that passengers who wanted extra space could upgrade to business class.

Regardless of whether doctors can agree about the legitimacy of the so-called, "economy-class syndrome", the conditions have been appalling for decades. Why has it taken so long for airlines to do something about it? It is because they were all hiding behind the numbing effects of "world's best practice".

NEW WISDOM #8
Don't look to the best in the world.
Look to becoming the best you can be.

OLD WISDOM #9
People don't like change.

For years, I have heard all sorts of people say this phrase. It has never sat comfortably in my mind.

The statement is very much at odds with the facts of life. The world is changing so much all the time. Who has created and embraced that change? Surely it's been the people. So how can we say that people do not like change?

I advocate that people love change. They like innovation. They enjoy variety. They appreciate improved dental procedures and they are grateful for advancements in medical science. They seek new opportunities and they devour new flavours and new music. In fact, we all seek new experiences and desire to discover information, love, and avenues that can take us closer to our dreams.

People do not like to change from something that they know works to something they can bet their bottom dollar won't work. For example, I have seen accounts personnel resist new software systems — not because they do not desire faster, better, smarter systems, but because in all their years they had never undertaken a software changeover that did not cause them heartache and irritation.

People welcome change that is for the better. It's the broken promises they dislike — along with endless rhetoric that they know, from years of experience, will not live up to expectations.

Don't subject your workforce to anything that is not thoroughly tested and completely robust. If you are forced to work with untested systems, then isolate them so that they do not spread to contaminate existing systems.

NEW WISDOM #9

People love change if it delivers on its promise.
They hate change that is unpredictable,
inconveniencing, unstable, and erratic.

OLD WISDOM #10

It is important to allow diversity in the workplace.

No thank you. Diversity would confuse every cell in the organisation to the point where undesirable compo-nents would take over. Solid organisations need stability, not diversity.

In my organisation, I do not need diversity of *values* — I will not work with cheating, conniving hounds. I do not need diversity of *ethics* — I will not work with liars and thieves. I do not need diver-sity of *culture* — I will not

> *Solid organisations need stability, not diversity*

work with people who excuse their undesirable behaviour by virtue of their culture.

The only time that I tolerate diversity is when I am deal-ing with decent people who have certain features or issues that are beyond their control. People cannot control who their parents are. They cannot control the colour of their hair, or what they look like. However, they can control whether or not they steal, lie, and intimidate and bully oth-ers. As for their sanity, that too is something they cannot control. Even though I can understand their unfortunate condition, I do not wish to be affected by it in my organisa-tion although I might assist them morally or financially).

Do not allow anyone to lower your standards on the

basis of diversity. (For more information about diversity, see Chapter 11, "It's not what you give, but what you take away".)

NEW WISDOM #10
Work with people who can
help you to diversify your understanding,
not your morals.

OLD WISDOM #11
Your people are your greatest asset.

Although employees play a major part in making or breaking an organisation, they do not "belong" to an organisation.

Managers should stop trying to employ brilliant people. Instead, they would do well to focus on injecting the winning spirit so that their existing employees can do brilliant things.

Therefore, they cannot be classified as assets.

Can the world's leading organisations lay claim to having hired the world's leading employees? Have high-performing businesses employed high-performing people? It would be easy, albeit erroneous, to agree with these statements.

Don't think that excellent organisations employ excellent people. Most of us are average people. This is not a slur on the human race. There is nothing wrong with being an average person. Managers would do well to learn how to work with average people, and resist the search for geniuses. One of their important challenges is to harness extraordinary results from ordinary people.

Managers should stop trying to employ brilliant people. Instead, they would do well to focus on injecting the winning spirit so that their existing employees can do brilliant things. Additionally, how employees interact with each other will determine the fruits of their labour. An organisation's tangible assets, such as technology and cash, are less potent than the intangible assets, such as atmosphere and attitude. (For more on atmosphere and attitude, see Chapter 12, "Come do the nanomation with me".)

NEW WISDOM #11
It's much easier to make winners than to find winners.

OLD WISDOM #12
Each year, flush out the bottom three per cent of your staff.

Corporate hygiene must not become a ritual. Flushing out low performers or misfits ought to be a daily task not an annual one. If you allow lethargic, indifferent workers to contaminate your environment, you will pay dearly for your hesitation. Leaders who want healthy organisations must not harbour ineptitude.

The concept of an "annual cleansing" has another undesirable side effect in that it encourages managers to pin shameful blunders on scapegoats. Those who are discharged are usually the sacrificial lambs — the innocent parties who neither have the power nor the inclination to fight the injustice of their dismissal. Once they are gone, corporate memory can be erased so that manipulating managers have breathing space to manoeuvre.

Leaders who want healthy organisations must not harbour ineptitude

When I encounter low performers, the first thought I have is, "Who hired this person?" When I come across intimidating, soul-destroying political animals, my first reaction is to blame the manager who allows that person to roam the office and menace others.

Therefore, I am never impressed with managers who see their round of musical chairs as the solution to poor performers. It's interesting that we categorise performers as those who are: 1) conscious incompetents; 2) unconscious incompetents; 3) conscious competents; and 4) unconscious competents.

I would prefer to examine managers' intentions for how they hire and fire based on those who: 1) know but don't care; 2) don't know and don't care; 3) don't know but care; and 4) know and care — where the latter is the more desirable trait.

NEW WISDOM #12
There's no smoke without fire,
and no bad employee without a dubious manager.

READY . . . AIM . . . FIRE

Hiring and firing are not at all important in their own right. The reason we engage in them is to ensure that what happens in the middle of these processes works well (to transact with employees who add value to the organisation).

Although the process of firing employees sometimes verges on being abusive, I've observed more abuse associated with the *hiring* process.

For example, I see the abuse when a job advertisement does not disclose the name of the company. How can advertisers expect us to divulge the fact that we are looking for a job, and risk our existing employer finding out, when they do not have the decency to tell us who *they* are. Sometimes they don't even give us a name, and expect us to write to "The Manager" at a mysterious PO Box address.

Ethical organisations will divulge to a candidate everything they can before they ask for anything in return. A civilised approach to hiring is to have a Web page that contains all the information about the job, including the salary, a photo of the office or desk, a photo of the canteen and car park, and other information that can allow candidates to decide if it is worthwhile for them to send in a resume, or even trek into town for an interview. Job hunting can be draining both emotionally and physically, and if done well, expensive and inconvenient. It would save so much time if candidates could see a short video on-line, and maybe hear a message from the manager to whom one would have to report.

Besides, good candidates would want to customise their resume after they have understood what the company is looking for. How can people put their best foot forward if they are forced to send a generic resume about an unknown challenge?

Beyond the resume is the interview itself. My suggestion is for you to find five experts whom you could call upon to assist you with the interview process. Individually they could meet with the candidate and give you their perspective on the candidate's suitability. For example, some might do this over dinner, some over lunch, some at their home, or even the candidate's home. Each of my experts would focus on a specific angle. Some would help me to assess the candidate's sense of humour, or level of expertise in finance or marketing, or perspective on life and other important facets of a person's wholesomeness.

After an extensive interview process, I would organise a few meetings with that candidate's future colleagues. Then I would invite a select group to a social outing to see how well everyone interacts. In the past, I have even taken some candidates to an amusement arcade to see how well they can play and enjoy themselves.

Once candidates have been appointed, you can welcome them by having everything ready when they arrive. Don't just give them a desk and expect them to find their way. You need a comprehensive training and induction program that leans towards the luxurious and indulgent. It must be informal, insightful, and customised. If you do not have the time to spend with your people, then you are the one who needs to have your professionalism examined. By the way, this level of attention ought not be reserved for senior appointments. It applies equally to any job, from forklift driver to receptionist. My rule is that any member of staff who has the ability to *lose* a customer is as important as anyone who can sign up a *new* customer. In my experience, forklift drivers who are not switched on to your needs can make life difficult for everyone depending on them, particularly when they need to meet deadlines and promises on a wet Friday afternoon.

If you do not have the time to spend with your people, then you are the one who needs to have your professionalism examined

On the question of firing, I expect managers to treat staff with dignity and respect. Nothing is too much trouble for me when I have to let someone go. If employees have outgrown their job, or have lost interest in the company, or are unable to rise to the new challenges, I work with them to make the termination as smooth and as pleasant as possible.

All of my staff members have known that it is never a taboo to seek employment elsewhere. In fact I often say to them, "Don't try to tell me that you are going to a dental appointment to cover up for a job interview that you are attending. Just tell me the truth, have the day off, let me know what I can do to help you." Many have taken me up on this offer, and I have

When it comes to extricating manipulative political animals from an organisation, I suggest that you do this in the loudest most ostentatious manner possible within the law

helped them improve their resume, and given them tips and ideas about their application, and assisted them as I would assist any friend in need of support. There ought to be no shame in supporting people who explore greener pastures. Who amongst us has not changed jobs? So why make it difficult for others to do so?

When it comes to extricating manipulative political animals from an organisation, I suggest that you do this in the loudest most ostentatious manner possible within the law. You need to live and enact your set of values. And when your code of conduct says, "We in this company will not tolerate anyone who tries to destroy our soul," then you had better take arms and fight a bloody battle so that everyone will know that certain behaviours will not be tolerated.

And before you take off the armour, go in search of the person who was responsible for making that appointment, and make sure that they do not have the very disease that you have just eradicated.

I LIKE TO BANG MY HEAD
BECAUSE IT FEELS GOOD WHEN I STOP

I know that many organisations are guilty when it comes to human abuse. I also know that those companies would convince investigators that they care about their people. Exams and tests would show that the reigning managers possess all the competencies. The quandary is, why are they not doing what they know has to be done? Why do they keep hitting their heads against a brick wall?

Apart from the damaging effects of matrix management (explained in Chapter 13), I submit that managers are not managers at all. If we take a close look at what it should mean to be "a manager", you might agree that the majority of people who have that title do not deserve it. If I were to incite a revolution in business, it would be to relieve workers of their managerial title, and to restore the essence of what it means to be a manager.

A manager is someone who has all the necessary "hard" and "soft" skills and loiters on the safe side of sanity. Managers must never carry the title unless they have the supporting tools of control, power, authority, and responsibility. By the way, if you like this idea, and find reason to strip people of their title, do not downgrade them to the level of a supervisor. In my organisation, a <u>super</u>visor is more senior than a manager! ∎

PART THREE

SURVIVING IN THE *modern* WORLD

IT USED TO BE THAT
IF YOU WANTED SOMETHING
DONE, YOU GAVE IT
TO A BUSY PERSON.
THESE DAYS, IF YOU WANT
SOMETHING DONE,
DO IT *yourself.*

CHAPTER 16

MANAGEMENT STYLES ARE OUT OF *fashion*

EVERYTHING IS DIFFERENT, BUT NOTHING HAS CHANGED

A YOUNG STUDENT IN HIS FINAL year at a private high school decided to wear a small diamond-stud earring. His teachers harassed him to remove it, stating that it was against the school's policy to allow boys to wear jewellery. The student refused to remove it, and for that year there was conflict.

The student's argument was that if girls were allowed to decorate their ears, why not boys? He had contacted the Anti-Discrimination Board which advised him that, had the school been a public school, it would be acting illegally. Alas, it was a private school whose code of dress did not allow boys to wear earrings.

This student was no ordinary boy. He was a model student who had shown academic excellence at school and held an important role at his city council.

Because of the earring, teachers threatened the student with all sorts of penalties, such as withholding his graduation certificates, refusing him entry to the graduation ball, and threatening to deprive him of a school reference — a serious threat that could have jeopardised his job prospects.

Indeed, everything is different, but nothing has changed

As the situation unfolded, its most fascinating element was the unbelievable discrimination and victimisation the boy suffered. He became outraged, not so much by the school's insistence that its archaic rule be followed as by his treatment at the hands of his teachers.

The student soon lost interest in the earring and its value as a fashion object. He was now pursuing something that showed him how discrimination works. He observed his teachers intently (some of them he had thought of as his friends) and noted how they began to exhibit unpleasant, frightening behaviour.

The looming showdown finally took place. Out of respect for his teachers, the student removed the earring to avoid the now-unbearable pressure. He was humiliated, upset, and defeated. However, one teacher insisted that he hand over the earring. When he refused to part with his expensive jewellery, the teacher reached her ultimate position and suspended him for one week for insubordination — a mean-spirited technicality.

During the final week of school, there was a film on television called *The Crucible*. The student was familiar with it because he had read the book and knew that it showed the vicious side of victimisation and social intolerance. While reading a newspaper advertisement promoting the film, he looked up at me and said, "I don't think that anything has changed."

Indeed, everything is different, but nothing has changed.

STANDING ON THE GIANT'S SHOULDER

The student, soon to turn eighteen, decided to take it upon himself and call the press. One by one he telephoned editors to voice his concerns. Not so much about his desire to wear the diamond stud — for he had finished his schooling and had nothing more to gain. He wanted to remove a stumbling stone for others less confident, less vocal, and unable to stand up for their rights.

I attended the student's graduation ceremony where once more he was badgered backstage to remove the ear-ring or risk not being allowed to appear on stage to receive his certificates in front of several thousand invited guests.

The guest of honour and guest speaker for the night, much to my surprise, was an old school principal of mine who had bucked the system by leaving the Brotherhood to marry the light of his life. The well-spoken ex-principal gave an uplifting speech about the school's history and shared his memories of old. He spoke of a middle-of-the-road student who was not academically bright, but whose hard efforts enabled him to find a job in the local area. He recounted what the exuberant student had told him: "I showed the boss my school reference, and he took one look at the school crest and was impressed that I was a student of the school. The boss said, 'If you went to that school, then that's good enough for me, you've got the job.'" It was at this point that the hall erupted with proud applause — the only such spontaneity.

My ex-principal then concluded his speech by telling the students that they could benefit from the school's for-midable reputation by standing on the shoulders of the giants who went before them. That brought a shiver to the back of my neck.

Who were these giants? The footballers and athletes whose trophies made the school proud? The academics who scored full marks in their examinations? No, these were not the giants. My definition of social giants is *those who, in their time, make an important contribution to the advancement of a cause.* However, such folk, in their day, were better known as troublemakers — not giants.

It is the so-called troublemakers who pave the way. They carve new paths, find new solutions, and break down the barriers in search of the truth — like the student with his earring. How humiliating it was for him to walk on stage, shaken, emotionally battered, harassed, to stand in front of so many people who knew him as the troublemaker. I wonder who had the grace to know that he was, in fact, a giant?

My definition of social giants is those who, in their time, make an important contribution to the advancement of a cause. However, such folk, in their day, were better known as troublemakers — not giants.

This story is relevant to this chapter because it highlights two important elements. The first is that things have not changed. The second is that those who push back the boundaries are often perceived as troublemakers.

On the subject of management styles, management trends, and management fads, the astute will see that nothing has changed. The fact that certain management styles are out of fashion brings no relief to giants because the unpopular nature of management fads is, in itself, a fashion trend. The root causes of fads being easily adopted or just as readily rejected remain the same root causes. When the majority rejects a fad, this does not mean that most people have seen the light. Nor does it mean they have understood the situation. Most of them are still unaware of the truth. Their rejection of the now-worn fad is caused by the same fear or excitement that led them to accept the trend in the first place. So, nothing has changed. The fickle managers are none the wiser for choosing the new fad. They remain vulnerable to the next wave.

No-one needs another book about the pros and cons of different management styles. There is no value in regurgitating the same data and re-packaging it in modern wrapping paper. No-one needs a book that merely criticises management styles or fads. It is not that an idea is bad. The crime is not in thinking up bad ideas, nor in adopting a bad idea. It is the fact that other people's ideas are revered. They seem to replace all else. Furthermore, the concern is that even good ideas are not implemented properly. So, when they fail, they are dubbed "cons". The implementers never consider that it was the way in which they executed the idea that might have been at fault.

WHY DO FADS EXIST?

Fads appear for several reasons. They are generally introduced by an author, consultant, or academic, who has never worked in a corporation, or by those with a hidden agenda. Ill-equipped and easily influenced managers quickly adopt such ideas, not because they seem to be brilliant but because the new ideas offer managers an opportunity to move on. New ideas enable managers to buy time while they try to figure out how to dissociate themselves from the failed methods. Meanwhile, chief executive officers (CEOs) ponder their team's incompetence while the giants are aghast at the team's lack of direction.

> *Invisibility means acceptance. Acceptance is that which is permissible. And it is permissibility that infuriates me.*

ADVICE FOR LEADERS

To make it clear and to avoid any ambiguity, it is hereby stated that management fads and management trends of all sorts ought to be dismissed, disowned, and disregarded. It would be politically correct for me to suggest that certain fads, implemented in certain ways, could yield certain results. This is a manipulative statement that does not offer firm direction. Let's not tempt the weak. Let's not create uncertainty. Leaders in the modern world ought to make it clear to those they lead that management styles, new revelations, and new methods should be discussed only if such ideas emanated from the heart and mind of the person initiating the discussion. This means that ideas adopted as a result of reading about a new fad (or attending a seminar) are more likely to lead to hollow time-wasting concepts.

To suggest that you operate within a "style" is, in itself, the problem. "Management" is management. "Leadership" is leadership. There is no such thing as good management or bad leadership. Just as there is no such thing as fake leather. Leather is leather. It cannot be fake. Any other material conveniently called "leather" is not leather. Similarly, management is management. There is no such thing as bad management. Anything that is not management is not management. Management cannot be bad. Those who carry on through incompetence cannot be called bad managers. They are simply not managers to begin with. Therefore, it stands to reason that you cannot speak of *styles of management*. One could speak of *styles of behaviour* if that behaviour is engineered, if that behaviour is consciously chosen and adopted. But to speak of styles of management or styles of leadership shows a gross misunderstanding of each role.

Managers do react differently in different situations. They respond appropriately to certain issues. But that's all part of management, not a style. If an executive chooses to be polite or intolerant or indignant, that is the choice of the person, not a function of management. Therefore, those who speak of management styles are displaying a misunderstanding of the function of management.

At all costs, resist new fads, new waves, new styles, and new solutions hailed by supposed experts. You would do well to understand what it is that drives so many people and so many organisations to the new wave. At the root of all management fads is hope. An organisation might be in desperate need of direction, but its own inertia prevents it from carving its own path.

Like management trends, fashion trends also offer a safe haven. Fashion norms sweep the world offering solutions, ever so subtly, packaged behind brand names. Yet, take a look at the fashion trends of old. The styles, patterns, and colours seem embarrassing now. Those hairstyles and accessories look hideous through today's eyes. But were they so odd at the time? No, they were invisible, just as today's fashion is invisible. In time to come, observers will look back at this era and laugh at what we are wearing and how we style our hair. They might feel embarrassed at the things we are doing — until future generations become enamoured of our tastes and copy us in the name of fashion.

INVISIBLE AND PERMISSIBLE

The key point here is that of *invisibility*. And it is this invisibility that drives so many leaders to frustration. When leaders can see something that others can't, they stand alone and lonely. Invisibility means *acceptance*. Acceptance is that which is *permissible*. And it is permissibility that infuriates me.

You can observe permissibility when you next attend a party of any kind. Take a look at the dance floor which is usually a separate area made from square wooden panels affixed to the floor. When the band begins to play, the brave few will lead the way onto the dance floor. But notice that they begin to dance *within* the parameters of the dance floor. As more groovy movers fancy a body-wobble, they too get on the floor. They dance only on the wooden panels that make up the dance floor, not *near* the panels. Take a good sober look at this and you will notice, as I have hundreds of times, that the small dance area might become congested with many couples, yet none has the courage to boogie off to the side. I have seen people struggling at the edge, hanging on for dear life as if the edge of the dance floor represented the edge of a cliff. They know that dancing seems to be a strange animal-like behaviour, and they are embarrassed to do it anywhere else. They would never do it in the lift, or in the middle of the supermarket, or in the boardroom, but they find it permissible to do it within the four sides of the token designated area called a dance floor — until of course they consume copious amounts of alcohol (or other substances) to blur the edges.

The lack of corporate memory is a major element that contributes to the proliferation of management fads

Permissibility makes people comfortable. This is why it is easier to adopt someone else's idea than to generate a home-grown solution.

The greatest difficulty is not in coming up with an idea or a solution, but in obtaining support from colleagues and managers who cannot see the big picture or who do not understand how to create things that did not exist — whether these be the creation of products, opportunities, or situations.

When we think of pioneers, we often think of scientific excellence, and the like. However, who was the first person to clap hands to show favour? Who thought that applause denotes approval? This might be a trivial question, but how is it that clapping has become a universal expression when it is a strange, almost unnatural, human act? And when the masses applaud a performer, what is it they are trying to do? Is it the sound they are aiming for, or is it the action itself, or is it what the action represents (a way for some members of the audience to show appreciation)? What of party-goers who hold a glass of wine in one hand and pound their other hand against their thigh as a sign of applause? What is that trying to achieve? As you can see, the masses are prepared to do things, inexplicable things, but ask them to support a new direction, and you would need to be prepared to stand alone.

There are many inexplicable things in life. For instance, why do car manufacturers that make motor vehicles for right-hand drive countries still install windscreen wipers that wipe from left to right? In times of heavy rain, the driver's side receives the bulk of the water because the wipers take the water from the left and swish it to the right, making it difficult for the driver to see the road through the thick wash.

There is the question of scratchy, uncomfortable labels affixed to the inside of shirts. Their positioning seems to be universal, yet their irritation is well known. So which shirt manufacturer is going to be the first to re-position these labels? And why is it that such labels (which have no real function) are almost impossible to remove, while the buttons that form a vital part of the garment seem to come loose of their own accord? This does not make sense. We all know that it is a ridiculous situation, but manufacturers still follow questionable traditions in the same way that many organisations follow inexplicable practices. Well, it's about time that things were rectified. However, the only one who can permit any form of rectification is the leader.

THE ROLE OF THE LEADER

It is the leader's role to ensure that the environment exists for fresh ideas to surface. The important element is to structure the environment for this to take place. It is not important for everyone in the team to agree or approve, but to support the one who proposes a new structure, or a new product, or a new path. It is the leader's responsibility to provide unwavering support.

It stands to reason that in the absence of direction, any direction will do. In the absence of truth, any lie will do. In the absence of justice, injustice takes its place. In the absence of love, hate creeps in.

The next step is to ensure that there is complete clarity about people's boundaries, responsibilities, and authority. By clarity, I am referring to unequivocal "in-your-face" definitions.

And, finally, the leader must ensure that the person carving the path is an expert in the field — with the ability to perform all the peripheral tasks such as people management, financial management, and project management.

CORPORATE MEMORY

The lack of corporate memory is another major element that contributes to the proliferation of management fads. High staff turnover diminishes the team's collective memory to the point where "learning from one's mistakes" is no longer an option. It is for this reason that leaders are encouraged to conduct an audit of their staff turnover, not just by checking to see how many people have left the organisation, but how many people have changed job roles, divisions, and focus. This lack of continuity in staffing has deprived companies of corporate memory whereby cumulative knowledge cannot be exercised.

Leaders would do well to ensure that stability is restored. The slash-and-burn approach to departmental adjustments and right-sizing is out of hand. The notion of organisational flexibility and elasticity has been misunderstood thereby creating untold damage to the enterprise. It stemmed from a 1970s fad that promoted the idea of "crack teams". These are quickly assembled and instantly dismantled, all in the guise of speed and reactivity to market pressures.

Such ideas cannot work unless you look at the reason behind the motive. Crack teams sprang up because the internal bureaucracy could not cope with creativity. The administrative burden and the can't-do attitude stifled innovation, so independent autonomous structures were required. However, it would have been better to loosen the bureaucracy and the stranglehold once and for all.

If fluid structures are needed, they should be assembled on solid foundations. Breaking away from bureaucratic foundations through the use of crack teams does not solve the problems. It is a leader's role to fix the issues at their root. Only the leader can fix this. Anyone who insists that it is up to the "team" to rectify the problems ought to burn the book from whence that advice came.

THE FOUNTAIN OF TRUTH

The only fountain of truth is you. Do not believe what you read about other corporate environments. It amazes me that writers who interview CEOs about their respective organisations actually expect to receive sincere answers. For a start, many writers undertake this exercise so that they can get closer to the CEO with a view to abusing the relationship in some way, such as by selling services to the interviewee at a later stage. Even if the intention is wholesome, who really expects a CEO to divulge raw information? I suspect that loaded questions are met with hygienically cleansed responses that must gain the approval of the public relations department and legal fraternity.

I have read statements published in journals by some of my former managers, only to stand in disbelief with some of my colleagues. We were perplexed and bemused at the utter nonsense. We were insiders who knew the truth. It was disconcerting to read public fodder. The private stuff was much saucier, but who was to know any better? The average reader would have been impressed, as I know many were — if the number of unsolicited job applications to our organisation was any indication.

FILLING THE VACUUM

When we drink after a period of thirst, we feel satisfied. The thirst is quenched — for the time being. The thirst is never extinguished. It is only temporarily relieved. However, you can maintain a healthy fluid intake that pushes back the thirst. This does not mean that the thirst vanishes. At its core, the body needs the water. And so long as the fluid is forthcoming, thirst is held at bay.

A runaway train is not exactly the epitome of organisational direction

When an organisation lacks a leader, it lacks direction. This corporate thirst is best likened to a vacuum. Given the opportunity, a vacuum will suck the surrounding air to satisfy itself. Hence, corporate vacuums draw pseudo-solutions to them so that they can fill the void. It stands to reason that in the absence of direction, any direction will do. In the absence of truth, any lie will do. In the absence of justice, injustice takes its place. In the absence of love, hate creeps in. This is why it is not advisable to exert your energy to hold back the tide. You cannot hold back thirst. You cannot hold back a trend. Instead you ought to remove the triggers.

In the same way that you can remove the feeling of thirst, but not the need for fluids, you can remove the corporate void by carving or finding a direction. But how can you find a direction amid the surrounding pressures? How can the lure of another management panacea be fought off? It can't. By trusting the cure-all, one falls in the trap because there is no such thing as a timeless all-encompassing solution.

THE DIFFERENCE BETWEEN FOCUS AND AWARENESS

This is where an understanding of "focus" and "awareness" is needed. There is a big difference between the two. When focused, you need to be aware lest the competitor sneaks in. Focus does not mean blindness to the surrounding environment. Attention to one thing does not mean neglect of another. Solving the issue of corporate thirst is only temporary. That's the trick to the whole puzzle — and the dilemma as well.

The solution lies in the realisation that there are no ultimate answers. There are only solid foundations that support fluid infrastructures that provide temporary solutions. An organisation needs to be able to grow. But it cannot grow in bursts. It cannot grow in huge punctuated breaths marked by the annual ritual of musical chairs. It can only develop like every other living organism develops — through daily expansion via daily doses of nourishment such as the rewarding of sound judgement and the prevention of ill health through a relentless pursuit to weed out the dead cells. Organisational hygiene ought not to be a ritual, but a daily routine.

When the leader combines organisational excellence with organisational memory and organisational conscience, the leader has the seeds of hope. Hope is what paints the picture. Hope is what fuels the engine. Beware the fuel that starts to dictate the engine's direction. A runaway train is not exactly the epitome of organisational direction. Your fuel forms your substance. Beware the hope that fuels your organisation.

Have you checked your intake lately? ▣

CHAPTER 17

CUSTOMER *service* — MY FOOT!

NEVER MIND THE "WOW", JUST GET RID OF THE "ARRRH"

IT IS A FACT OF corporate life that no enterprise is in the business of "service". Despite initial denials, no-one can dispute this shock–horror. Corporations are not there to serve anybody. At best, they sometimes operate under a clear mission — but serving people is not one of them. Motherhood statements are a dime-a-dozen. Chief executive officers (CEOs) still kid themselves, espousing customer-care or customer-delight or service excellence. They believe that they are out to put the "wow" into customer satisfaction. Well, never mind the "wow", just get rid of the "arrrh". (For ideas about improving customer service in the non-profit or government sectors, refer to Chapter 18, "Lip-service".)

At your next dinner party, start a conversation about customer service and watch as guests eagerly share their hair-raising experiences. From heart-stopping airport sagas to shopping soap operas, there is no shortage of drama when it comes to service.

My friends delight in my unfortunate stories about "service" and plead with me to retell them because they find the detail fascinating, interesting and, above all, entertaining. The more traumatic the experience, the more laughter I encounter over a late-night gathering. My misfortunes are now in high demand. I collect memorabilia associated with most of my conflicts and

> *If a person is honest only some of the time, that person is not honest at all. Integrity is not something that can be applied selectively. One is either honourable all the time or none of the time.*

show these at lectures and public debates. My multimedia presentations have audiences in stitches, gasping for air, as I tell them about the funny things that happened to me on the way to the forum. At times I feel that the audience would have every right to suspect that I am spinning a yarn or stretching the truth. My struggles often sound so unreal that I worry about coming across as incredible.

For years, I have been saying that service in most industries is so atrocious, it brings me to the point of having to invent violent words merely to come close to exclaiming my dissatisfaction with any degree of accuracy.

This chapter is not about countless anecdotes or mushy customer-service stories. I don't care to hear any more about who did what to whom at that famous department store, or what happened on Flight 42. There is no place for such page-fillers in a serious book like this.

ARE YOU READY FOR A SEX CHANGE?

What is it that customer service hinges on? The single most important element is "speed". However, before an organisation decides to engage in customer service, it must treat the decision with all the due diligence that one would afford to the notion of a sex change.

If, after exhaustive deliberation, an organisation decides that service is the way to go, it must then make it clear to all concerned that "customer service" means doing for the customer *whatever* the customer wants. It does not matter what this is — for such is the burden of "missionary" work.

In doing for the customer whatever the customer demands, speed must be the key factor. Within this framework, an organisation is promising to invent new systems and processes within a matter of seconds — and this sounds unrealistic for most bureaucracies. Therefore, it might pay for honest organisations to own up and call it like it is. We would then no longer suffer false promises such as those expounded in advertisements, showing a half-naked traveller clutching a telephone outside a village café in Timbuktu, recounting his sad plight to some sympathetic operator who manages to replace his debit card within twenty-four hours,

> *Before an organisation decides to engage in customer service, it must treat the decision with all the due diligence that one would afford to the notion of a sex change*

find him a local neurosurgeon, and set him up in some swanky hotel with a cash advance and a new Armani wardrobe — delivered pressed, with starch; on a hanger, please.

Instead of grand promises, we will begin to see some self-truths in advertising, with body copy that reads, "You might have to wait more than five minutes in our bank queue, but at least you know that our low overheads will mean lower interest rates on your home loan." The decent might say, "Our airport service stinks, but we put all our money in safer aeroplanes."

The day that frequent-flyer programs, economy-class travel, and gold memberships disappear, we might see the end of the "regular-customer" epidemic.

Businesses fail when they set out to treat *regular* customers differently from *irregular* ones. In essence, this action eventually translates into treating irregular customers *less well* than the regular ones. Besides, in large organisations, not all staff members would be able to distinguish between the two. It amounts to asking staff to differentiate between groups, and to treat each group differently. This intangible process fails because, in the intangible world, the weakest element dominates. (For more on tangibles and intangibles, see Chapter 12, "Come do the nanomation with me".)

If a person is honest only *some* of the time, that person is not honest at all. Integrity is not something that can be applied selectively. One is either honourable *all* the time or *none* of the time. Similarly, staff members need to be courteous all the time. They need to excel in everything they do. They must capture every opportunity to win a customer. With this in mind, serving "gold" or "platinum" members goes against the grain.

Those who construct loyalty programs through frequent-flyer points, and the like, are merely trying to trap the customer. Loyalty must come naturally, not via points and schemes. If your customers are loyal to you as a result of such programs, they are *not* loyal. Such schemes are tangible, and tangible things are susceptible to the law of annihilation. Anything that you do can be matched by your competitor. Frequent-flyer points have become a serious financial burden to airlines. However, which airline dares to be the first to cancel its scheme? Having the scheme no longer provides a competitive advantage, but *not* having the scheme would create an unattractive deficiency — unless something of perceived equal value takes its place. In short, this makes the scheme more of a *burden* to the organisation than it is a *benefit* to the customer.

Customer loyalty is intangible — meaning that it must come from the heart. In business, matters of the heart come from *atmosphere* and *attitude*. Do you have the atmosphere and attitude within your organisation to win the heart of each customer? Only then can you count on loyalty. (For more on atmosphere and attitude, see Chapter 12, "Come do the nanomation with me".)

YOU CAN'T SERVE TWO BOSSES

It is too difficult to operate a profit-seeking business and have *two* bosses. The customer cannot be your boss when the shareholders are your first priority. Therefore, the customer cannot come first — meaning that you are *not* in the business of serving the customer. You are in the business of supplying goods and/or services to the specifications that were agreed upon. Your obligation is to be truthful and honourable. Beyond that, you need not put up with customers' demands that do not comply with your corporate objectives; nor should you raise expectations about things you cannot deliver.

For your own sake, reel in those advertisements and read every one of them. Watch your television hype then scrutinise your brochures and media releases. You might begin to understand why unsuspecting customers appear to be too demanding. Examine the statistics that show how frequently you targeted a certain group with over-exaggerated statements about your service, your quality, and your supposed responsiveness. Can you blame customers for thinking that they deserve better than what you give them?

Although customers know what they personally want, do not expect them to work out what they want from you

Furthermore, when you hear of a complaint, do you delegate it to the very group of people whom your customers are warning you about? Senior executives who receive letters and have them redirected to someone else for action ought to be ashamed. When it suits them, they are happy to have their photographs in the newspaper, along with some caption about their dedication to the community. However, when customers reach the end of their tether and do the only thing left, short of legal action or a brick through the window, executives hide because they cannot stand up and deliver.

One CEO told me that if he or his senior executives had to interrupt their day to look into customer complaints, they would never get their jobs done. I shook my head as I choked on my pasta. "Can't you see that if you have so many complaints, it's a sign that something is wrong?" I said. He subconsciously reached for the BMW keys on the dinner table and touched them as if they were the source of his inner strength and replied, "Yes, but at this stage it's cheaper to put up with nagging customers." I said no more.

When I say that your customer is not your boss, this does not mean that you abandon courtesy to new customers or to customers with whom you have developed a long-term relationship or a friendship.

FORGET ABOUT CUSTOMER SERVICE

The customer-service craze has its roots in one thing — making more money. If this be the aim, let's get to the point. Forget about ways to "serve the customer" and find ways to "sell to the customer" so that you *can* make more money.

There is a big difference between "serving the customer" and "selling to the customer". The former implies activity designed to make the customer happy. The latter is a sales process that makes your shareholders ecstatic.

The naive will call this "semantics". The astute will realise that a simple shift would focus the group on the fundamentals of the business — profits. The pedantic would say that without happy customers you would not have profits. The point is that if profits are what you are trying to generate, set out to generate them. When you start with the end goal in mind and work back to reverse-engineer a solution, you will find that customers are important because they *buy* things. Therefore, it stands to reason to find ways for your customers to buy *more* things. The emphasis ought to be on "selling", not "serving".

There are ethical ways of capturing extra business to make extra profits. It would be a delight to enter a store and see a plaque on the wall that reads, "We are in the business of making a profit. If you know of additional ways that we can do this, please let us know." Customers would be delighted to respond to such honesty because they would be happy to spend more money with one supplier in return for a predictable and satisfactory outcome. Organisations know this, but they say that they would be willing to oblige if only they knew what customers want. This is a mistake. Never mind what the customers want. Go in search of what the customer will pay for.

Many CEOs have complained to me that customers are unreasonable. They say that not many customers express their needs, and fewer take the time to complete the questionnaires and surveys sent to them. In fact, it is only when a prize is offered that many survey forms are returned; but one should question the accuracy of the data under such circumstances. Those CEOs who rely on surveys are out of the picture. (For more on statistics and surveys, see Chapter 19, "You can only lie if you know the truth".)

If you truly wish to generate more profits in the networked world, there are three things that you need to understand. The first is that customers do not always know what they want. The second is that most of an organisation's preoccupation with customer service stems from complaints about faulty goods and broken promises. The third is that most organisations have all the data that they need to capture more profits from their customers. These three aspects are explained below.

If companies would stop that insatiable urge to survey everything that moves, and stop manufacturing faulty products, life would slow down sufficiently for them to realise that opportunities abound

CUSTOMERS DO NOT KNOW WHAT THEY WANT

Although customers know what *they* personally want, do not expect them to work out what they want from *you*. Do not expect customers to come up with breakthroughs for you because they would not understand the inner workings of your organisation, nor would they have a clue about your managerial capabilities.

When it comes to innovation, you can engage customers in focus groups for weeks, but they will still not come up with the concept of Nike, Ray Ban, or Tommy.

Customers did not ask for anti-lock braking, nor for CD–ROM drives in personal computers, nor for automatic telling machines. Customers did not ask their petrol station to sell flowers, nor did they come up with the Internet. Although there are things that customers now insist upon, they were not what customers wanted at the time of their introduction.

| CUSTOMER COMPLAINTS |

There is an element to customer service that focuses on complaints resulting from faulty or incompatible goods and/or broken promises. Chief executive officers must carefully study why certain issues arise. If organisations do not manufacture robust products, or if they send out service technicians who perform half-hearted tasks, the organisation deserves to be out of business. Chief executive officers whose production lines still pump out substandard products do not deserve one moment's rest. Senior executives cannot ethically command a salary so long as they cheat the customer by taking good money only to deliver rubbish, frustrations, and broken promises in return. Furthermore, profits are lost every time an error is made or a faulty product is replaced. Therefore, such floundering is a disservice to shareholders — and what could be more irresponsible than that?

Many organisations fail to realise that once customers have paid for their goods or services, they have exchanged money for whatever was given in return. Money is predictable. It works every time. It does not need service calls, nor is it ever faulty. The exchange is a very safe bet (notwithstanding fraud). Whether it be exchanged for bananas or a new computer, fault-free money is given in good faith.

Imagine if money were as susceptible to faults as the product for which it was exchanged, thereby "inheriting" the qualities of the product. This would mean that every time the operating system on your computer froze, the money you paid for it would freeze in the bank or wherever it is at the time.

A person who has never worn a man's business shirt should not be allowed to iron one. A person who dislikes desserts should not be allowed to cook them.

What if every time your toaster failed to work, or you bought apples that tasted like chalk, the money that you used to buy these items also failed or perished? What if there were some metaphysical link associated with each transaction? What would become of certain rich people who have amassed their wealth through lies and deceit? How successful would some organisations be today if they were accountable through a "law of inheritance"? This would be a scary notion indeed. As the networked world develops, more of this kind of accountability will befall organisations that can least afford it. Financial "ancestry" would prohibit corporations from building their empires on money taken from customers who were given shoddy products.

There is also the issue of "unfair exchange". Any organisation that seeks to make a profit from its goods or services ought to come to terms with the fact that it is not doing the customer any favours.

When a customer exchanges money for a new chair, the customer is the one doing the company a favour. In exchange for one chair, the customer is paying the retailer for the chair's original cost, *plus* a little extra to help pay for expenses and overheads, *plus* more free money for the retailer's personal bank account.

| ORGANISATIONS HAVE ALL THE DATA THEY NEED |

Most organisations have an enormous amount of data that they can use to generate extra profit. If they would stop copying the competitor for a moment, and stop that insatiable urge to survey everything that moves, and stop manufacturing faulty products, and stop promising things they can't deliver, life would slow down sufficiently for them to realise that opportunities abound. In Chapter 16, "Management styles are out of fashion", I highlight the problems arising out of waning "corporate memory". Let us now look to the opportunities that exist within "corporate observation".

DON'T SERVE, OBSERVE

When I was a lad studying science, I was taught the *Table of Elements*. You know the one: hydrogen, helium, lithium, beryllium . . . and so on. I loved science, and thereafter became fascinated with astronomy — the stars, the moons, and the sky.

Whenever my friends and I heard about a discovery of a new galaxy, gas, or metal, I was unable to enjoy the celebrations because I felt that we were being disrespectful. To cheer and clap was well and good, but I could not help feeling we were insulting nature. The human race did not *find* anything. That which we had the effrontery to put a new name to was there, and had been there for millions of years. Who were we to suggest that *we* found it?

I suspect that there are still millions of undiscovered things in this world. As we learn about them, we ought to be humble in the knowledge that they have been there even though we were blind to their existence.

Many organisations are blind to what is going on in *their* environment, unaware of what is happening around them. When it comes to customers, they might have many opportunities to make extra money, but they fail to see them.

When their competitor finds a new way of making money, they seem to think that something *new* has emerged for them to act on. Very often what they think is new is not new at all. Opportunities to make money exist at many levels.

Corporate observation is about observing the customer and searching for ways to make extra money. For example, hotels would find it difficult to make a profit if they had to rely on revenue from room bookings alone. They depend on additional revenue from restaurants, laundry, and incidentals. That being the case, why don't they try to maximise profits from things such as the in-room refrigerator?

I travel extensively and stay at all sorts of hotels. Those I stay at more frequently could easily study my buying habits and realise that I do not drink alcohol. My mini-bar purchases *never* include alcohol. Therefore, they could do themselves a favour and replace the miniatures in my room with more of the things I do consume, such as chocolates and nuts. They could wheel in a different "non-drinker's" bar, stacked with fruit juices and tempting delicacies. However, no hotel I have stayed at has ever picked up on this lucrative idea. They even find it a struggle to keep their commitment. They lodge me on the "smoking" floor, despite their assurance to the contrary at the time they agreed to accept the booking.

If there is a business that could use its existing data to learn more about my personal life, it is the bank that provides me with my credit card. The data that it captured about me before my card was issued would be sufficient to compile a comprehensive dossier. Even more revealing is the current data about my purchases. The issuing bank has the capability to learn about my every move — where I go, what I buy, my preferred store, and the time of day I make each purchase. However, despite this potential, my bank still sends wine offers to me. I have been a customer for more than ten years, and every month I am sent, with my statement, a wine or spirits offer. When will they stop their senseless mass marketing and start to *observe* that I have never responded to any of their offers. Furthermore, if they examined how I spent the thousands of dollars per month, they would realise that I have *never* bought alcohol from *any* retailer.

Never mind the fact that I am beginning to find their offers insulting, what about the many opportunities they have to make extra money if they observed what I do buy, and structured offers based on my preferences. The same can be said of retailers in general.

There are many ways that organisations can make more money. All they have to do is stop fussing about customer service, and start selling via clever, targeted offers. There is much to be said about up-selling, cross-selling, and on-selling. They have all the data to double their business, but they do not know what to do with it — which makes one wonder why they amass so much data in the first place.

EAT YOUR OWN PUDDING

We have heard it said that the best way to find out about your level of service is to become your own customer for a day. However, there are some things that can be improved simply by *thinking* through the process. Yet, it still baffles me to see how organisations operate.

Why can't managers *think* about a process before they engage in it? For example, whose bright idea was it to deliver the newspaper outside hotel rooms during the early hours of the morning? Obviously newspapers are not delivered to the hotel until after midnight, but if they have to be dropped off outside each guest's door, why must they be plopped with force? I am not a light sleeper but I always wake when the noisy bell-hop slaps down that newspaper time and again along the corridor. Does it take too many brain cells to work this out? And when the "do not disturb" sign is on the door, what makes hotel staff think that telephoning the room to ask an unimportant question is not another way of disturbing your rest? "Oh, Mr Nader," says the voice, "you have your 'do not disturb' sign on the door so I'm calling to see if you would like your sheets turned down for the night." How disturbing. "No, thanks," I exclaim tersely. "I was asleep already!"

Is it too hard to ask for a shirt to be ironed well enough for a business meeting without it looking like some sheet of cardboard with arbitrary creases? What does a person have to do, and what language would that person need to speak, to convince the laundry to refrain from placing that embarrassing double track along the length of a pair of trousers? Who was the brain behind those small highly adhesive laundry tags that ruin anything they are affixed to?

What it comes to is one of two things. Either a comprehensive training program must be instigated to stipulate precisely how things should be done, or people should not be allowed to engage in any activity if they do not understand the full process. A person who has never worn a man's business shirt should not be allowed to iron one. A person who dislikes desserts should not be allowed to cook them. If the objective is to get the customer to spend more money, get real!

These discussion points are not mentioned for the purpose of making the customer *happy*. You need not concern yourself with making the customer happy. Instead, concern yourself with removing the things that make the customer *unhappy*. This assists in customer retention. The next stage would be to find ways to sell *more* to the *same* customer. You know how this can be done. So, as the song goes, *do it, dear Henry!*

(For ideas about getting your staff members to put their shoulders to the wheel, see Chapter 14, "Fluid shares".) 🆄

CHAPTER 18

Lip-SERVICE

SERVICE IN NON-PROFIT
AND GOVERNMENT ORGANISATIONS

IN MOST COUNTRIES MUCH OF the economy is delivered via non-profit organisations. In many cases, these institutions were set up to deliver a service to the community, or to provide a system of administration for the purpose of a smooth-running public network — whether it be health services, law and order, education, and/or transportation.

The framework, tradition, and nature of non-profit organisations have tended to diminish the importance of customer satisfaction. In some cases, customer retention is not even a consideration, especially where government monopolies exist. However, with privatisation looming over many infrastructures, and since the emergence of competition either directly or indirectly (through shifting emphasis within the networked world) the question of customer service has been gaining importance.

Going to elections every few years is hardly what democracy is about

To improve the levels of customer service and to create an environment whereby service providers truly care about the quality of their service delivery, major reforms are required at the top. Those in charge need to be given the autonomy to act, unencumbered by red tape and bureaucracy. The best way to remove the bureaucratic stranglehold is to make the process of government accountable. This innovation could occur through a novel scheme called "democracy". Within the networked world it is possible to give the public a real and regular say about how things ought to be run.

WHO NEEDS TO BE GOVERNED?

In a democratic networked world, people do not need to be governed, therefore they do not need a *government*. Instead, they need an *administration* — that is, a reliable and professional team of experts who can "administer" the policies voted for by the people.

Unfortunately, people have very little say in how their country is run. Going to elections every few years is hardly what democracy is about. We are all playing one big and costly game of politics that stirs most citizens to anger.

Citizens are asked to elect a new government every few years, based on a convoluted combination of promises. When we vote, we are asked to distinguish between good and evil amid mud-slinging and insults. We are expected to swing one way or another, based on a few headline-grabbing ideals that do nothing more than confuse and distract the voters from the real issues of a changing world.

We are told of "polls" that go up and down like a yo-yo. Forget what the polls say. Let us put a simple system in place that allows all voters to have a real say on a regular basis. Citizens need to begin to insist on a *real* say. If countries start to plan for the democracy they desire, it would be possible to plan for, and to introduce, computerised regular voting on issues that affect the constituents.

Such a proposal could use simple telephone and/or computer technology to connect all voters to a central system that can log their votes. Important public issues would still undergo rigorous investigation and public debate, but the final say could be made by the voters through their telephone or public computer net-work (or any other reasonable method to suit the environment). This is more than a new style of ref-erendum or plebiscite. This is a new way of involving the public in life-changing decisions. Such a system would extend to dozens or hundreds of issues whereby the voters would be able to vote on specific policies, rather than vote for one or two people who promise things that they might not be able to deliver. This does not mean that you should destabilise the country. It does not mean that the parliamentary systems should be abandoned. It does not mean that local or state represen-tation should be abolished, but it does mean that we would hear less of the political innuendoes and lies, and less speculation about what voters really want because the computerised system would record each voter's wishes. As times change and situations force us to make new decisions, voters would be given the opportunity to make new selections.

The single most important function of any Opposition is to tear the Government down so that it can get into power. This is destructive!

If voters do not want to cast a vote on some or all of the issues, they can opt to give their vote to their local member of parliament (MP) who will represent them in the best way possible. Furthermore, their MP would be one that they have voted for based on competence, not on geography — meaning that people ought to be able to vote for their preferred candidate, not the one who happens to be standing for election in their district.

When a corporation is looking to employ a senior executive, it does not limit itself to applicants of a particular locale. Instead, it conducts a wide-ranging search to find the best person for the job. In the same way, citizens should be given the ability to vote for any MP, no matter the region.

Only when we can elect our MP of choice will we start to see an improvement in the calibre of members. We would no longer be forced to select "the best from a bad bunch". Instead, we could start to select "the best from the most qualified". Unfortunately, the current system encourages mediocrity by forcing voters to select from a limited choice. Under this proposal, the function of MPs would become more important because they could be entrusted with more votes than the one they carry in parliament. MPs currently have one voice, and one voice only. Whether they represent one town or twenty, whether they represent 10 000 people or one million, they have just one vote in parliament. However, under this proposal, MPs could end up the custodians of hundreds or millions of votes. And each vote would carry real weight.

Converting "Opposition" to "Competition"

I have been a long-time critic of the concept of an "Opposition". When you think it through, you will realise that the single most important function of any Opposition is to tear the Government down so that it can get into power. This is destructive! The Opposition (no matter the party) seems to think that it has a duty to oppose, obstruct, and obfuscate every move. Citizens ought to demand maturity, innovation, and co-operation — not opposition.

In the past, the Opposition of the day helped to keep the Government on its toes. But times have changed. We now need a co-operative process that will enable the minority party to act as a *competitor* — not one that *opposes*. Let us see some real competition, based on better ideas and better proposals. Within this framework, if the Administration were to suggest a new tax reform package, it would be the competitor's job to offer a *better* solution or additional ideas — not to confuse the public and damage the credibility of the Administration. Then, both packages could be put up for scrutiny and debate, and voters would have the opportunity to select their preferred option. Beyond that, the general majority principle would still apply. But we would not be bound nor hijacked by one or two Independents. Why should one Independent with the balance-of-power determine our course? Let the voters decide!

The technology is now available to enable people to

become involved in how their country is run. Many people are interested in local and national affairs. They try
desperately to make their views felt. However, they are
often frustrated because they cannot influence important
decisions.

The technology now exists to enable the public to
cast a vote on a number of issues. Naturally, not everything needs to go to a public vote, and not all voters have
the expertise to understand all the issues. This is where
their elected representatives need to be experts in their
field. They would need expertise in such areas as analysis,
managing projects, solving problems, commerce, planning, and negotiating. Voters would be asked to choose
one of several options. The competition may also put forward a proposal. If theirs were chosen, they (the
competition) would be given the budget to implement it.
This system respects the will of the people. The better
party will continue to win the contracts. Each party
would be seeking to build its own credibility by proving
its capabilities — not by discrediting the other.

*When the public
is part of the
decision-making
process, it is less
likely to blame
the party in power*

Elections would still continue
according to a democratic country's
traditional system, but it would be
plausible to increase the term so that
an Administration could focus on
long-term issues. Elections of this
nature would focus on *people* and
their *expertise,* not on one major issue that clouds every
other. No longer would a government get into power on

one popular issue and then assume it has a mandate to enact all its policies.

It is folly to argue that the public does not have the knowledge to vote on important issues. If that is the case, how then is it that under the current arrangement the public has the knowledge to vote for one party or another every few years?

This proposal requires hard work. Naturally, many will try to find fault with it. However, citizens are urged to consider the bigger picture and work with their elected MPs to put long-term plans in place to make this work. This proposal is all about *democracy*. It is about citizens taking responsibility for their future. When the public is part of the decision-making process, it is less likely to blame the party in power. For this idea to progress, it requires much debate centred on how to make it work.It would take many years to put the computer and administrative systems in place, but it is possible if all parties agree to engage in this democratic process. This proposal would stop the bickering between parties because their job would be to design programs and to sell their ideas to their constituents. This would be a vast improvement on the current counterproductive and crippling nature of inter- and intra-party wrangling.

IMPROVING THE LEVEL OF PUBLIC SERVICE

With the introduction of reforms to the political system, it is possible to improve the level of service to the public.

The *level* of service would be something that the citizens have set. Measurement systems would keep track of their success or otherwise, and the results could be compared with the initial promises and worldwide benchmarks. However, until this major reform takes place, improvements in service could be achieved if competition were encouraged. By the way, competition need not come from external entities. It is possible to generate competition within one's own infrastructure. Although this would be unusual, it is certainly plausible for many service organisations. By setting up competing interests, members of the public would decide which provider they wished to use. Staff could be paid bonuses on the basis of customer retention or customer acquisition.

Most public service professionals know what it would take to improve their level of service. However, they can only act in accordance with their measurement system and within the constraints of their bureaucracy. To change either may require innovative attention at the *root* of these barriers. One of the roots is *motivation*. To change an outcome requires that a person changes behaviour. To change behaviour, a person needs to examine the motives. (For more on motivation, see Chapter 3, "The secret destroyer".)

> *To change
> an outcome
> requires that
> a person
> changes behaviour.
> To change
> behaviour,
> a person
> needs to examine
> the motives.*

Political will is very strong. Where it surfaces, it creates enormous change. When it does not exist, the constituents will tolerate all sorts of inferior outcomes without so much as writing a letter of complaint to those in office. At best, they will complain to their friends, and this is nothing more than whingeing — not taking action.

Much of the frustration that arises from inadequate service in the public sector is caused by a lack of courtesy. This lack is brought about by excessive delegation of responsibility so that each task is divided up to the point where no-one can see the full picture. Without a clear understanding of the whole transaction, the best that a service provider can do is feel sorry for the customer. No other action is possible because nothing else can be done within the jurisdiction. This problem is akin to the matrix management structure that plagues corporations. (For information about matrix management, see Chapter 13, "Cut across the dotted line".) ◼

CHAPTER 19

YOU CAN ONLY LIE
IF YOU *know* THE TRUTH

BEWARE THE STATISTICIANS

ONCE RESEARCH IS PASSED DOWN the line to the workers, it becomes *fact*. Once fact is known to cost millions in fees, it becomes *gospel*. Once gospel is branded with a consultancy firm's logo, it becomes *direction*. Once direction is disseminated by the regional headquarters, it becomes *policy*. Dare you challenge policy!

There are very few instances where research is used to help run an organisation better. Research is often a political tool that is used to cover one's rear. I have seen organisations spend millions of dollars amassing data that is never used. I have seen statistics being engineered to support an idea that could be almost criminal. Furthermore, and what is even more frustrating, in some organisations, as with some sacred establishments, it is unthinkable to question the "data". It is unheard of to question the findings, and it would be professional suicide to go against them.

Data on its own cannot point the way. That thing we call "gut feel" or "intuition" is still the primary ingredient that must be used in decision making.

First, survey results are often presented by a consultant or doctorate fellow who finds it necessary to make the exercise much more complex than it needs to be in order to justify the huge invoice. Second, it is well known that there is an art to structuring a questionnaire to yield the desired answers. By the way, conduct an audit (a real audit) into the money spent on all forms of research in your organisation, and then try to justify that level of expenditure. I doubt that you could.

To avoid any misunderstanding, I must make the following four statements up front: 1) An inquisitive mind is a healthy mind; 2) The search for innovation and improvement ought to be applauded; 3) A constant evaluation of one's position is vital for survival; 4) Research offers much value when it forms part of an expert's everyday life.

This chapter warns about research that is employed as part of a "ritual" or something that must be performed for political or bureaucratic reasons. This kind of research becomes a waste of resources and is a distracting force that commands more attention than is healthy or reasonable.

It is shocking to observe the existence of managers who *do* need research data to run their day-to-day operation. Managers who need to *rely* on data to know where to take the next step are doomed to fail.

SHOW ME THE WAY SO THAT I CAN LEAD

The word "research" means to "look again", not to "go and find out". In business and in life, to research a subject first requires some appreciation of the subject at hand.

Managers of every persuasion are put in charge of projects they know very little about. They commission research in order to glean some ideas about the direction forward, yet they are in no position to be making decisions. They know this, so they let the data point the way. However, data on its own cannot point the way. That thing we call "gut feel" or "intuition" is still the primary ingredient that must be used in decision making. If a solid feeling of "rightness" does not precede a decision, failure then creeps in with unrestricted access. Alas, how can you show "gut feel" on a chart for the committee's approval?

In modern worklife, *people* rarely matter because *systems* and *processes* seem to have taken over. These days it is rare to hear a thought or an idea being attributed to a *person*. Instead, managers speak of what the "research" says. They hide behind it as if it had an unshakeable personality of its own.

If you strip a manager of intuitive decision making, you stifle creativity and pave the way for departmental disharmony

I have worked with people who knew exactly how to manipulate the research to suit their needs. They knew how to deluge the board of directors with more data and charts than would be reasonable for anyone to digest. Yes, this is laughable. As are the cases where statistics are manipulated to show the preconceived desired results. What is deadly serious is the authority with which research is used to beat people over the head. "What do you mean you don't agree!" shouts a troubled manager. "The research bears this out. Do you dare go against the truth presented here? Are you a fool to be so courageous?"

What fascinates me is how people shrug off responsibility for the past. I am flabbergasted every time I hear managers say, "We need to change direction because we now have *new* data showing that we are not on track with our current campaign." That is what they said about the *last* campaign, and the one before that, and the one prior. So who says that *this* campaign will not be denounced by the new regime in twelve months' time? It baffles me how managers can declare they have discovered the path to nirvana with every new direction they point to.

HERDING ALL SHEEP

I once attended a meeting that was graced by senior managers from all over the world. One of the items on the agenda was a presentation by the head of the research division. The passion with which the academic researcher believed that certain market segments existed was surprising. In a world of billions of people, the research department managed to slice the globe into five groups. My goodness, that must have taken some herding.

It was a very serious meeting because people knew that the "tablets" were being presented from on high. I could not believe what I was hearing.

In the meeting, it was explained that the research would set the direction for every division — what the engineers invented, what the designers crafted, what the advertisers projected, and what the salespeople eventually sold. No question about it. Once our group of 2000 people started to sculpt the product, there was no turning back. This was the most serious meeting of the year. A sign on the wall read: *"Speak now or forever hold your peace."* No-one dared to speak. The research does not lie. This is what our market wants. Who has the temerity to go against what customers want!

My offsider knew me well. With every irritating chart he looked at me, desperate for a reaction. Half-way through the meeting he gave me one of those looks that burst my balloon. I could not take it any longer. My patience had evaporated. I was in the middle of vivid colourful thinking using *brain-speak*. (Brain-speak is explained in Chapter 7, "Can you speak another colour?")

Beware the one who speaks in statistics, paints pictures with probabilities, and presents assurances in percentages; and, worse still, fear the one who cannot discern the differences between them

Strangely, when engaged in brain-speak I am unable to utter the *words* because I do not *think* in words. So, unintentionally and inadvertently I burst into the biggest, heartiest, most uncontrollable laughter that my body was able to expel — short of bursting a blood vessel.

It took several minutes to regain my composure. Others started to laugh at me, and that spread the contagious situation to all. Still, that outburst went a long way towards cementing my colleagues' unfounded opinion that I was crazy.

I tracked that campaign every step of the way. Twelve months later I nearly fell off my chair, gasping for air, when I read the official memorandum advising that "we got it wrong" — meaning that "the *previous* manager got it wrong, but he has been promoted to another division". Apparently the target market could not be divided into five groups, and our products would have to change to reflect the new findings. They would not listen. That was not the first time. Unbelievable!

DO YOU KNOW THE TRUTH?

In most organisations, auditors are not the same people as the controllers and accountants. This is not a bad thing. They cannot be from the same company for fear of collusion. Keeping an independent eye on financial matters is a fair approach to financial integrity. This model is often erroneously used in research whereby the research group is headed by a different manager or an external organisation that has no pecuniary interest and no ties to the project owner. For example, the research group that measures consumer feedback to an advertising campaign is independent of the advertising agency itself. This practice is *wrong* on two counts.

First, the company that measures consumer response to an advertising campaign must not differ from the creators of the campaign. Oh, now sparks will fly. What I mean is that if you wish to check on how well your advertising is doing, call this an "audit", not "research". Furthermore, if you wish to conduct an audit, be clear about what you are trying to find out, and how you will measure or assess the results. And, the advertising agency and project manager need to have been informed of the parameters and measures before they begin the campaign. By the way, there is nothing wrong with audits. Go audit all you like. I am merely differentiating between researching and auditing.

Second, it is wrong to conduct research via an independent group that does not ultimately report to the project manager. If you strip the project manager of all the elements that contribute to effective intuitive decision making, you stifle creativity and pave the way for departmental disharmony.

Another adventurous meeting I once attended was one that was supposed to have been a fact-finding mission. Creative directors and account directors from the advertising agency's headquarters, along with support and administration staff, flew in to visit my "geography". Also on tour were head honchos from the independent research firm. To keep everything to protocol, the bigwigs from my regional headquarters also flew in, along with their local equivalents, and little old me.

Throwing a die and having it land on a specified number may be, according to mathematics, five to one, but in reality it could be 500 to one

The purpose of the meeting was to ensure that the advertising campaign devised for my group would meet local needs. There we sat to discuss the creative execution. No matter what I said, the agency disagreed. To my surprise and delight, my local colleagues agreed with me. But the difficulties arose because I was under the misapprehension that everyone in the room was on the same team, trying to find the best solution for the geography, and trying to ensure that the millions of dollars we were about to commit would be used wisely and in the best interests of our shareholders.

It was a futile meeting. There we were, each in charge of our own little group, but no-one in charge of *us*. Not that the one in charge of us was not there. It was that there was no such person in the hierarchy. I know it sounds unbelievable, but our matrix management structure, as complex as it was, had these little loopholes in it. It was a hostile meeting full of diplomacy, but nothing more substantial than that. (For more on matrix management, see Chapter 13, "Cut across the dotted line".)

I put up a good fight, but short of a tantrum there was nothing more I could say to convince the agency to customise the campaign for our region. That evening we conducted two focus groups. Many of the issues my colleagues and I had raised surfaced during the focus groups. In a way, we had smiles on our faces because our "public" was reacting in ways we had predicted. However, the advertising and research agencies could not see what we needed. It seemed to me that they did not *want* to see it because they had flown in not to research, but to massage the figures so that they could say, "We surveyed all the major countries, and conducted focus groups, and now we are as enlightened as can be, therefore our decision must be as good as any decision can get." The writing was on the wall.

A hot debate ensued well into the night, until I bowed out, saying that I had another engagement to attend to. It was an appointment with life. I had better things to do than sit there and beat my head against a brick wall for shareholders who want integrity, professionalism, *and* blood!

One of the agency people walked me out. "Oh, before you go," he called out from the foyer, "I just wanted to make sure that you realise my position. I totally agree with everything you said in that meeting."

"Well, why didn't you say that upstairs?" I exclaimed. "Well," he said, "as you can appreciate, we have to defend our position. But, frankly, it stinks. We know that you guys are right, but there is nothing we can do about it. There is no way we'd get the changes approved back home. Besides, *your* people at headquarters can't make up their minds either. We get conflicting briefs from the corporate teams and the brand teams, and then we come here, and we just don't know how to work this thing."

He then confided in me that he was thinking of leaving the agency and going to do something different. Something with more "sanity". Well, I appreciated his comments, but could not help feeling that I was speaking with an enemy who showed predispositions to defection. Except in his case, he just wanted to get out, not swap sides.

Exactly six months later a report landed on my desk. It was written by the same independent research company that had been in that stormy room. The findings about the campaign showed exactly, almost to the sentence, what I had cautioned them about. So, why did it take six months and millions of dollars (and lost market opportunities while competitors advanced) to arrive at findings that were evident to all at the meeting? (By the way, at the time, I did bring this issue to my manager's attention, but I was told that nothing could be done. I could not take this any further because I subscribe to the school of thought that prohibits me from going over my manager's head.)

This chapter does not suggest that research is bad or of no value. I am just suggesting that the head of a project ought also to be the head of the research program at hand. Also, I suggest that those who have to *rely* on research findings in order to make a decision tend to fly blindly. Get them out of their position! Finally, managers who use research to reverse-engineer decisions in order to cover their rear ought to be dismissed from the company — but, before you do that, be sure first to dismiss the person who drives them to such actions.

BEWARE THOSE WHO SPEAK IN STATISTICS

Arresting incompetent managers who duck accountability ought to be the responsibility of every staff member. However, it is the leader's role to ensure that the framework exists to expel such incompetence. If you are the leader, beware the one who speaks in statistics, paints pictures with probabilities, and presents assurances in percentages; and, worse still, fear the one who cannot discern the differences between them.

How many times have we heard that "we have a *fifty-fifty* chance of winning a deal", or "there is a *high probability* that the project will be finished on time", or someone is "*99 per cent* certain of success"? Why do we let such elusive promises go unchallenged?

What is a fifty-fifty chance, and what is meant by it? Consider the following terms and stir yourself to anger and action when next you are exposed to such nonsense.

| FIFTY–FIFTY |

In the first instance, fifty-fifty implies that there is as much a possibility for failure as there is for success — and such odds hardly justify anyone's salary.

| 50 PER CENT |

For anyone working on unique projects, the term "50 per cent" is meaningless because it only applies to situations that can be simulated at least ten times, and preferably more than 100 times. Without such controls, no-one can ever say that a project has a 50 per cent chance of succeeding.

| 99 PER CENT |

The term "99 per cent" is often used by people who cannot argue the point or justify their position, avoiding heavy-duty scrutiny. However, on behalf of your shareholders, it is imperative that you retrieve the missing percentage point. What is 99 per cent, and why does it leave a loophole through which it can exonerate itself? This is unacceptable.

| HIGH PROBABILITY |

"High probability" says nothing, means nothing, and promises nothing. Probabilities are unpredictable. Therefore, anything with a high probability would be highly unpredictable.

Why is it that around the boardroom table we hear of probabilities in terms of "possibilities", yet around the gambling tables we hear of probabilities as odds *against* a successful outcome? When throwing a die, we do not say that the probability of it landing on a specified number is one in six. Rather, we say that the odds are five to one *against* it. Furthermore, outside of academic circles, do not take comfort in such probabilities because they are subject to the laws of permutations and combinations. To suggest that a project or sale has a high probability of succeeding is tantamount to admitting that its likelihood of success is as remote as mathematics will tolerate. Besides, throwing a die and having it land on a specified number may be, according to mathematics, five to one, but in reality it could be 500 to one.

CHANCE WOULD BE A FINE THING

If you do not understand the essence of the warnings highlighted in this chapter, please take note of how many times people try to hide behind percentages, probabilities, and statistics. Remember that mathematics ought to *support* language, not *quash* it.

And pray tell, from where do folk acquire their irreverent cerebral patterns? Thankfully, I am afforded a measure of tolerance having witnessed the frivolity that surrounded the mathematical subjects at college. Topics other than algebra and trigonometry were treated with contempt — and now we pay the price. By the way, when lecturers spoke of the ability to lie with statistics they were not encouraging us to make it a habit. Nonetheless, we are spared because one can only lie when one knows the truth; and this is hardly the case with incompetent managers. ■

CHAPTER 20

prosperity **IN THE MODERN WORLD**

LUCK HAS NOTHING TO DO WITH IT

TO EVADE POVERTY IN THE modern networked world, you must understand its dynamics in relation to prosperity — in the same way that you understand the current dynamics between the rich and the poor. Although wealth is now conveniently measured in dollars, this does not reflect where we have come from, or point to where we are heading.

In bygone eras, and at the macro level, the rich were those who possessed a title. A person was blessed by birth or election with the title of pharaoh, king, queen, duke, or duchess, and so on. Such titles were reserved for the privileged few, and could only be acquired by those who were born into a "great house" or were elected. Over time, conquerors gave themselves grand titles (sometimes taken from those they defeated), and later it became customary to reward loyal subjects with honours befitting their heroic deeds.

Justice has little value in complex court cases where those with superior information could challenge even the most logical of arguments to the point of destroying the notion of "right and wrong"

In time, wealth became dependent upon those who appropriated the greatest mass of land. Rich nations were those who extracted the fruits and resources of the lands they conquered, and the people therein. For example, it was said that the sun never set on the British Empire, meaning that at every point around the world, no matter where the sun happened to shine, its rays hit a landmass owned by the empire.

From land we moved to military supremacy. To defend the land, great armies had to be assembled. In no time, superpowers were formed until the Cold War standoff became obvious, and military supremacy became a game of psychology.

In trying to keep nations productive, energy became the next major measure as reliance on crude oil and other natural resources mounted. Eventually, these became commodities that were bartered or bought with money. Everyone could play the money game because money could be exchanged in the smallest of amounts, and it was easy to understand, store, count, and compare.

The Internet is not about communication — any more than a motor vehicle is about communication. It is not about entertainment — any more than a telephone is about entertainment. It is not about liberation — any more than a book is about liberation. The Internet is everything — yet it is nothing.

As populations boomed, the focus turned to access. Prosperity became dependent upon societies having *access* to credit, medical services, legal assistance, and general social services. Coping with a consuming world required technology. This fuelled the race toward technological wealth. All sorts of barriers emerged to protect the technologically affluent from the technologically hungry.

Legal frameworks, patents, and trade secrets depend on information. In no time, information became the focal point where espionage, theft, and trade found customers who were eager to stock up on vital information. Justice had little value in complex court cases where those with superior information could challenge even the most logical of arguments to the point of destroying the notion of right and wrong in light of quality information.

Whether on a personal, organisational, or social front, nature always wins

At such a pace, time became the next differentiator. Nations that had time could (and still do) use it to produce material through clever use of labour. Others saw time not as a resource that could be turned into output, but one that could be isolated in the form of leisure. Very often, the materially rich were also time-poor.

With such a string of tangible and intangible wealth indicators, the question arises: "What will be the next wave?" Nations, organisations, and individuals who can pre-empt the next major wave, and learn about the forthcoming dip-stick of wealth, stand to gain from the networked world.

BRACE YOURSELF FOR THE NEXT WAVE

The next major wave is one of "infrastructure". The strangest feature of this wave is that infrastructure requires equilibrium between the rich and the poor. Infrastructure, the very thing that will determine who is rich and who is not, has to be accessible by all. A facsimile machine is only useful if the party to be contacted has one as well. One telephone is useless until a second one is produced for the person at the other end of the line.

The whole purpose of technology is to create an advantage. However, if you put technology in the hands of all people, it loses its value.

Understanding the truism does not mean that you can rush into constructing an infrastructure because often the biggest obstacle to developing a new or better infrastructure is the *existing* infrastructure. Existing barriers hinder development because current infrastructures might force technologies to plateau. There are many examples of plateauing technologies — where things cannot be improved upon owing to limitations of the current system, the existing law, the modern taboo, or the status quo. Improvement becomes as challenging as trying to change an aeroplane's jet engines and electrical wiring while the aircraft is in flight — hardly a plausible proposal. From these revelations springs the question of the Internet and its role within a technological infrastructure.

THE INTERNET IS EVERYTHING — YET IT IS NOTHING

Gurus of the networked world have placed extra emphasis on the Internet and its peripheral technologies.

Although many new opportunities have surfaced, and much confusion surrounds them, the basic elements of information technology have not changed.

People's fascination with the Internet is a weird one. Perhaps it is the mysterious nature of the technology that makes it so intriguing for so many. The point is that the Internet (and all the technologies that surround it) ought not to be the focus. This is the toaster/toast challenge posed in Characteristic 10 of Chapter 21, "Characteristics of the modern world".

In time to come, people will use the Internet without knowing it — just like they use electricity. Today, when they reach for milk, they don't stress that it was in the refrigerator, much less that the refrigerator was powered by electricity. When they receive a letter, they don't mention who delivered it and how. When they go to a film, they don't emphasise how they drove there, or the fact that their car was fuelled by petrol. The important item of focus is the *content* of the subject at hand, not the *medium* through which an activity takes place.

The Internet is not about communication — any more than a motor vehicle is about communication. It is not about entertainment — any more than a telephone is about entertainment. It is not about liberation — any more than a book is about liberation. The Internet is everything — yet it is nothing.

The Internet gives technologists their biggest opportunity to redeem themselves by allowing them to justify the horrible things that they have done to this Earth and our environment. In very tangible ways, the Internet can help us to work on important issues such as pollution and traffic. Through invisible means, we can use the Internet to alter many strange and wasteful habits. The Internet is no different to the wheel, or to the invention of gears and light bulbs. How it develops and the use to which it is put will sort out the weak from the strong, the meek from the courageous, and the followers from the leaders.

The Internet is only a tool — yet it offers a mysterious dichotomy. Once applied, it has as much constructive power as it does destructive — and that is a healthy trend for a change. Unlike many of yesteryear's technologies, its forces for good are as strong as its forces for evil — and that is a tip in the right direction. Furthermore, the Internet's ability to facilitate is as grand as its ability to obfuscate — and such a promise is better than many previous technologies.

Bases of influence and power will become vacant once more. They can be captured only by those who understand that the Internet is not ammunition for another boring technological war. Instead, it refuels the marketing wars by shattering current paradigms, breaking existing value chains, and collapsing once solid and lucrative life cycles and frameworks.

Power bases will be useless in the future until it is understood that prosperous nations and organisations will be those that realise that wealth and poverty may be unevenly divided, but that the technological infrastructure must be evenly distributed. We stand before a future that demands technological equilibrium between those who *have* and those who *have not*. Selfishness on the part of the infrastructure-rich will be self-destructive. Within this secret lies new forces for new potential. Technological equilibrium in the networked world refers to an infrastructure that serves both rich and poor. For example, it would be pointless if the roads were improved for the benefit of the rich, if the same roads could not be used by the workers who need to drive their vehicles to and from the markets to supply food to both rich and poor. Another example is the electronic mail system. It is pointless for the rich to have access to electronic mail if the poor cannot access the same system to retrieve messages posted by the rich who need to obtain services from the poor.

WHAT ERA ARE WE CURRENTLY IN?

The rain falls lovingly on both rich and poor. The educated and uneducated are blessed with the same golden sunshine. Whether suffering ailments at an early age, or propped up by scientific intervention, the body expires just the same and rots in the ground without fear or favour. This even-handed approach sounds ominous, but it does play a role in the networked world, in that the ruling era is important because it torments all the players without prejudice.

Whenever I ask an audience to tell me which era we are in, most speak of the information age or the technological age. Neither is correct. We are currently at the mercy of the "era of law", meaning both the law in relation to litigation and courts, and the law in relation to nature. The issues about litigation are broad and fascinating. We are seeing, and will continue to see, a rapid increase in the number of laws being introduced to cope with the networked world. What is overwhelming is the speed at which new, unfathomable issues are arising to challenge the legal system. These include ambiguities and difficulties about jurisdiction, interpretation, and applicability about a wide range of issues including ownership, copyright, intellectual property, and intent. For example, the traditional laws about the production of counterfeit money impose severe and harsh penalties. But how can a court sentence a child of fifteen to fifty years' imprisonment for counterfeiting a small amount of pocket money? The laws were written before the invention of home scanners and home colour printers, at a time when anyone who managed to produce fake banknotes would have had to engage in serious planning. The notion of premeditated crime was an important element in the setting of severe penalties and punishment.

There is the question of the wider implication of petty crime, especially in the area of digital cash. A petty criminal who scans a twenty-dollar note and then prints it out on the home colour printer could still be caught and dealt with. Even if never caught, the fake notes could eventually be proved to be fake. The dilemma with digital cash is that there would be no such thing as "fake currency" because an electronic dollar looks the same no matter how it is generated, and no matter who generates it.

At what point would a country's monetary system collapse if most people started to trade in digital cash that was born as a result of tampering with computer code, rather than from commerce? Take a simple taxi ride. If a passenger paid the taxi fare using a smart card on which was stored digital cash, how is the taxidriver to know where and how the funds were generated, if in fact the funds were fraudulently made by the passenger using a home computer and an illegal software program? Money is money. If the taxidriver were none the wiser, and accepted the digital cash, where's the problem? If the taxidriver happened to be a computer whiz too and engaged in similar illegal tampering so as to pay for fuel using digital cash that was created at home illegally, would the garage know, would it care, and would it be affected? How could the garage be disadvantaged if it received apparently perfect digital cash?

The year 2000 computer issue will look like a peanut next to a skyscraper when compared with the devastation of undetectable and untraceable fraud — soon to become known as U2F

It seems that as long as no-one admits to the crime of counterfeiting, and no-one asks any questions, and everyone pretends the problem does not exist, the economy would boom. Conversely, if the truth were to leak out, entire nations could collapse. Although these scenarios are simplified, they do illustrate the burdens that law and the legal fraternity have to cope with.

337

Regardless of the difficulties and challenges, it is the *laws of nature* that would force themselves upon the rich and poor in more profound ways. Foolish is the one who tries to meddle with the laws of nature. Fighting them would be futile. The best that we can do is to understand and respect nature's way.

It is important to understand the stronghold that nature still has on us. Whether on a personal, organisational, or social front, nature always wins. The three main laws of nature that apply to the networked world are: the law of *saturation;* the law of *propensity;* and the law of *annihilation.* We would do well to comprehend their character. These are explained below.

| THE LAW OF SATURATION |

My colleague and I had been travelling in an aircraft for more than four hours. Upon reaching our destination we waited eagerly for our luggage, keen to make our way to the hotel where we were to present a series of lectures about technology in business. As we stared at the conveyor belt we were hopeful that our luggage would be among the first to appear because we were both frequent flyers and members of the "club" that secured for us an orange priority tag on each of our bags.

Diplomacy is a waste of time. There can be no argument about it.

The conveyor belt started to fill with bags of all shapes and sizes. Strangely, after ten minutes, our luggage was still nowhere to be seen. At that point, another impatient passenger exclaimed to his colleague, "What's the point of having a priority tag when *everyone* on this flight has a priority tag?" This was true. It seemed that all the passengers on that predominantly business flight belonged to the same club. We were all endowed with those tags. The law of saturation liquidated our priority the moment that everyone's luggage was treated with the same (worthless) priority.

The law of saturation was in full swing. When everyone has what you have, its value is diminished if you expect it to position you ahead of them. The law of saturation puts you at the mercy of the law of numbers — chance and luck. Despite the technological marvels of the motor vehicle, it too is susceptible to the law of saturation. What good is a fine motor vehicle during peak-hour traffic? Those on foot might steal the advantage.

The whole purpose of technology is to create an advantage. However, if you put technology in the hands of everyone, it loses its value through the law of saturation. This is the blessing and the curse of innovation in the networked world.

THE LAW OF PROPENSITY

The law of propensity tricks the hopeful. It states that what is likely to happen *will* happen. For example, at the casino, where the propensity is to lose, it seems laughable to play for any other reason than the experience. Playing to win against the odds, and engaging in false hope, is a sign of disrespect to this law of nature. When the law of propensity is in charge, the only way to beat it would be to understand its every parameter and be prepared to collide with it head-on, knowing that at worst everything you gamble could be lost. The only way to challenge this law is from a position of well-calculated risks. However, if you pit yourself to the point where you could lose everything, the chances are you *will* lose everything. Do not enter if you would be devastated by such an outcome.

In business, as in life, many play with the law of propensity. Yes, it could be lucrative, but nature has the upper hand and the better record. It would be wise to team up with nature, not play against it. The networked world is full of opportunities where such partnerships can flourish. However, it is only through leadership that one would dare to attempt such a partnership.

| THE LAW OF ANNIHILATION |

The law of annihilation is the equaliser. It states that anything that you can do can also be done by your competitor. It is explained in more detail in Chapter 12, "Come do the nanomation with me".

On the whole, an advantage can be annihilated by those who have access to the same solution, technology, or infrastructure. In the networked world, finding an advantage requires a concerted effort.

The law of annihilation does not assist you in finding an advantage, but it does serve its purpose when a competitor dashes ahead with an innovation that you had not previously contemplated. You can learn from your competitor and use the law of annihilation to your advantage.

If you wish to risk it all, you can try to find an *exclusive* advantage by trying to trick this powerful law of nature. However, it might obliterate you. It is merciless in its retort.

STABILITY AND INVISIBILITY

When we understand nature's forces and can operate within the framework of the networked world, we must only enter its sanctum if what is done is *invisible,* and what is established is *stable.* Invisibility refers to things that are so well accepted that their presence is not noticed. For example, light bulbs in your house do a marvellous job, yet you do not notice them. Stability refers to things that work superbly well, with minimal fuss. For example, the television is a product that requires very little attention. Unlike personal computers, it works without the need for constant programming and rebooting.

For humans, time steals life with every tick of the clock. We are helpless.

Upon reflection, it might seem to you that such wisdom is not new. Indeed it is old, for wisdom is timeless. The peculiarities of the new networked world seem to provide us with a new level of consciousness at another plane through a different dimension. It seems to require of us a whole new level of awareness. It is important to note that the networked world does not belong to us, but we to it.

LIFE AFTER Y2KABOOM!

If people fear the consequences of the year 2000 computer issue, they ought to ponder what the next major international challenge will be. The dangers of *undetectable* and *untraceable* fraud will hit much harder and impact more people in more communities and in more countries. In fact, the year 2000 computer issue will look like a peanut next to a skyscraper when compared with the devastation of undetectable and untraceable fraud — which might become known as U2F. ∎

CHAPTER 21

CHARACTERISTICS OF THE
modern WORLD

APART FROM SUDDEN DEATH,
NATURE IS GENERALLY FAIR

THERE ARE MANY NETWORKS OPERATING around the globe. We have social, monetary, political, and military networks, as well as corporate, infrastructural, and religious ones. Although some are larger than others, their characteristics are similar. We are at a stage where networks form the *backbone* of an organisation or system. Hence, understanding their characteristics has become a matter of survival.

During some of my lectures I ask participants to name the single *biggest* issue facing organisations that compete in the modern networked world. Very often participants vote "technology" as the biggest issue. Some say that an organisation's success hinges on its ability to effectively implement and use computer technology. After all, almost everything in the new networked world is computerised in one form or another.

As a Post-Tentative Virtual Surrealist, I beg to differ. I have been an avid technologist for two decades, and I have observed organisations of all shapes and sizes. During this time, it has become apparent that technology, although important, is not the most vital or the biggest issue facing organisations. From my observations and studies, I rank "the lack of leadership" as the biggest issue facing organisations in the networked world. Those who do not engage in leadership will find that no amount of technology can give them the advantages they seek.

Next we must ask: "What is the most important issue facing *leadership*?" Again, the answer is not technology.

The biggest issue is that of nurturing *wisdom* in managers. Wisdom cannot be bought nor borrowed. When born, we have no wisdom. During life and through maturity, we learn how to acquire it. Sadly, upon death, wisdom cannot be bequeathed. It stands to reason that leaders ought to focus on nurturing wisdom in the people around them, especially their managers.

If we follow this train of thought to examine the biggest issue facing *managers,* we see that "time-wasters" are the most challenging. Although technology plays a big part in sound management, it ranks lower than the need to eliminate both genuine and artificial emergencies that drain managers. Time-wasters include extraneous meetings, politically induced reports, deputations, explanations, and office gossip.

What is the biggest issue affecting *time-wasters?* What is it that overrides our better judgement and commandeers precious time? The single biggest issue is that of "diplomacy". Diplomacy is a waste of time. There can be no argument about it. I am not suggesting that we ought to discard the art of diplomacy. Whether it is necessary or not does not alter the fact that diplomacy devours precious time. At its worst, diplomacy becomes "politics", and political machinations soon become "backstabbing". Such behaviour eventually seeps into every project and every action. Disrespect becomes the norm and its roots are difficult to trace because it emanates from a "corporate cancer" that lurks invisibly and permeates quietly. Its removal becomes as difficult as catching the elusive. This turns the spotlight on the single most important factor in allowing diplomacy to permeate: *lack of leadership*. With this we have travelled full circle. We are back to square one. Better technology cannot mend this problem. Leadership in the networked world cannot flourish when it is besieged by corporate cancer. The only way to break this vicious cycle is to arrest it with big doses of *audacity*. (For information about audacity and leadership, see Chapter 9, "Leadership".)

UNDERSTANDING THE TOP TEN CHARACTERISTICS

Through the years I have conducted hundreds of lectures, workshops, and focus groups, and have engaged in overt and covert research and studies. From these, together with my professional observations, I have arrived at what *others* believe to be the ten main characteristics of the networked world — namely, the networked world: is fast; lacks time; is changing; demands information in real time; is complex; is linked; places emphasis on tangibles and intangibles; catapults an operator from the "marketplace" to the "marketspace"; relies on information; and seeks growth through convergent technologies.

Although many executives agree with the top-line results, they do not always realise that there are more profound findings at deeper layers. My pertinent finding behind each of these characteristics is outlined below.

| CHARACTERISTIC 1 • SPEED |

To say that the networked world moves very quickly does not seem to be of much value because, upon closer scrutiny, we find that, throughout the ages, every generation has experienced a pace that could be said to be *faster* than the one before. Naturally, things today occur at a much faster pace, but the most important element to surface from this is not the speed but the *acceleration*. To say that this period is "fast" does not really explain the main issue. If it were a case of things happening quickly then organisations need only determine the speed, communicate this to their staff, and put systems in place to gear up for that speed. However, upon reaching that desired speed, the organisation would find that things have changed once more. The exercise would have been futile because by the time an organisation manages to reach the speed in question (which others loosely call "fast") the speed would have increased yet again. This is why we must comprehend the nature of acceleration.

The concept of acceleration brings with it a whole new set of requirements. To gear up for a particular speed is much easier than to build an engine that can constantly grow to cope with the energy required for perpetual acceleration. Furthermore, the rate of acceleration must be flexible, so that both minor and major bursts can be accommodated.

It is no longer true to say that "we live in fast times" because it is now a matter of living in "accelerating times".

To prepare for acceleration requires much smoother operating procedures that allow things to happen when they *need* to happen, not when they are *approved* by a committee. The networked world does not wait for you. It has its own agenda and follows its own rhythm. Within such a framework, it is true to say that, when we blink, we are likely to miss something; and definitely appropriate to warn the weary that, when we sleep, we automatically fall behind. This is a tough road indeed.

> *If the suggested path is being applauded, stay away from it. If a rumoured change is hated, investigate it. If an innovation is being laughed at, invest in it.*

CHARACTERISTIC 2 • TIME

The perception of time seems to have acquired new dimensions through the years. Some people find microwave ovens too slow. Despite the marvels of flight, many still complain about a long journey, oblivious of the time when the same trek would have taken months instead of hours.

As children, we are taught that "time is precious". Time is all that we have. It cannot be bottled nor bought. Wasting time in the networked world is tantamount to crime. True, for humans, time steals life with every tick of the clock. We are helpless. However, despite this grim reality, there is another natural law that is just as powerful, working in our favour. Apart from life itself, time is the most precious and the most loyal resource (for societies who accept its abstract form and use it). Furthermore, time is *not* the scarcest of resources. In the networked world, time is the only resource that is dependable, predictable, and self-replenishing. It is generous and, best of all, it is free. When viewed in this way, we can see that time does not work *against* the modern organisation, because time has been consistent in its performance. It has never promised us any more of itself, nor detracted from its generosity. If we choose to expect more from time, we only have ourselves to blame for being unreasonable.

When we choose to waste time, we must not expect it to bail us out. Our ability to waste time has been increasing during the years. It is much more sensible to look at ways of reducing (and preferably eliminating) the things that waste time, rather than attempting to overcome the futile habit of trying to *find* more time.

As a mark of respect, we must never utter untruths such as "time is against us" or "we have no time". Such irreverence does more damage to our reality because it tricks us into blaming the loyal resource that cannot be changed. Complaining about something that cannot be changed leads to a warped sense of expectation. Instead of saying "I do not have time to complete the report by the due date", the office environment ought to allow people to say "I believe that your insistence on this report will waste my valuable time, so please alter your requirements". I knew a managing director whose company's annual revenue was $200 million. He would preface each management meeting with, "I have a $200 million business to run, so every hour you take from me during this management meeting is worth $100 000, so you had better be keeping me here with a view to providing me with more value than this amount." This straightforward announcement generally made everyone think about the value of the meeting — notwithstanding the other items on the agenda (such as golf) which some executives estimated to have greater value. By the way, these quarterly off-site management meetings usually consumed seven days (including preparation and flight times). By his estimate, seven days would represent $5 600 000 of revenue, for which the executive was ultimately responsible.

We fail when we confuse "complexity" with "complication". To messy minds, complicated things are much easier to construct than complex orderly structures.

| CHARACTERISTIC 3 • CHANGE |

To suggest that things are changing hardly points to anything new. Things change daily. Change is not something new to have emerged within the networked world. Change is not exclusive to an accelerating environment. The important factor about change is that we need to be able to understand the differences between "lasting change" and "temporary change". The ability to discriminate quickly between the two will differentiate between the winners and losers.

It has been said that long-lasting change is the kind that improves upon the things that do not change — such as love, emotions, human nature, greed, and the laws of nature, including our entrenched systems such as existing technological infrastructure, monetary agreements, and legal boundaries. Another element that must be considered is that change in the networked world should be introduced only if it satisfies the WOW Factor. WOW stands for "worth-or-wealth". Anyone who wants to implement change should be able to specify the outcome by worth and/or by wealth.

When I first coined the term "worth-or-wealth", I defined it as the added value that a new system or process would create as a result of its implementation. When an organisation implements a system for the purpose of creating an advantage, or reducing costs or wastage, the question of its *value* must be raised. A system is said to be of value if it helps to create worth or wealth (whether financial or otherwise). For example, when water and gas pipes became common features in the home, they offered a high degree of WOW because they brought with them a very high level of convenience. The WOW factor can be used to help estimate whether an innovation would be permanently adopted by those whom it is trying to serve or attract.

Gas pipes to the home were considered worthwhile because they eliminated the need to go to the store to fill heavy gas bottles. In this example, the worth could be measured in convenience, time-saving, and the ability to have an endless supply of gas for all-night heating and uninterrupted cooking and bathing.

The WOW factor must be assessed in light of the changing environment. For example, when the introduction of water pipes was first considered, its worth was compared with the environment of the day. Back then, people had to walk to the well or the dam to fetch buckets of water. Pipes improved on this situation. However, when water supplies became contaminated, people resorted to the older method and fetched water once more, except this time the well was replaced by a supermarket, and the bucket was replaced by plastic bottles.

Another important element to consider in the networked world is that of the "Backslash Syndrome". I define this as the introduction of a product or service that, when announced, is superior within its market but, over time, as the environment surrounding the innovation (including competitive pressures) becomes more complex, the benefit starts to decline. I use this term because the line on the graph resembles the backslash character "\" on a computer keyboard, and it is a play on the word "backlash".

When both theories are combined, we can see that, even if an innovation generates a high level of WOW, it is susceptible to the Backslash Syndrome — the more complex an innovation becomes, the more difficult it is to maintain the WOW at its founding level. For example, life insurance was once a very simple service. When the policyholder died, a payment was made. This offered a high degree of WOW. However, competitive pressures have made life insurance a very complex service with hundreds of variations on the same theme. If the insurer does not innovate in line with market pressures, and does not continue to improve its services, its original WOW might not look so attractive against the myriad of modern offerings. Once the original WOW becomes affected by the Backslash Syndrome its value is dwarfed in the face of newer offerings that provide a higher level of worth or wealth.

Change in any organisation needs to be assessed so that we can consider if, in fact, it is offering worth or wealth above what is generally available. In the networked world your organisation will find it a challenge to maintain a high level of WOW because the complexity of innovations drags your worth and/or wealth down.

Although change is neither good nor bad, it is either long-lasting or fleeting. If it is an idea, system, or innovation that is likely to offer worth and/or wealth, and one that can withstand or adapt to competitive pressures, change must be embraced. If it does not pass these simple tests, it is unlikely that you would need to embrace it.

If we do not have the foresight to assess these things, fear of change is likely to surface. This fear is often spurred by ignorance or myopia, not by the change itself.

It is easy for us to laugh at the naivety of bygone sceptics who ridiculed Galileo, Pythagoras, and Alexander Graham Bell. It is only now, decades after their deaths, that these visionaries are appreciated. Given that society has not changed, who now dares to speak of the future? Who now has the ears to listen to a futurist? Who has the vision to see what so many cannot see or refuse to accept? Who has the audacity to embrace the beckoning change?

Change is about the future. To develop a keen sense of what the future is likely to hold, we must discard all inhibitors and stand in defence of the incomprehensible. We must defend things that cannot be comprehended at this juncture and within the existing framework. The ability to defend what does not make sense cannot be realised through knowledge and intelligence alone because our reasoning and logic are naturally limited by what we know today. Such barriers can only be broken with doses of audacity. If we fail to believe the unbelievable, we could be in for a surprise.

When leaders ask me to advise them about the future, I say, "Do not worry about the future, let the future come to you, as it no doubt will, whether you like it or not. The future will do unto you what it will. Are you ready for that? Do you want to stand and be subjected to the future's indiscriminate forces, or . . . would you rather engineer your own future?"

What are *you* doing to engineer your own future? Apart from sudden death, nature is generally fair and will allow you to engineer your future so long as you understand nature and its laws. Sadly, many who gaze into the future do not see anything. To them, waiting for change is like watching a kettle boil. Luckily, despite nature's mischief, nature's tremors give clues to the astute.

Many of today's changes are engineered by board-room zealots who no longer believe necessity to be the mother of invention. To them, opportunity is the driver of innovation. The dilemma is that, although they can innovate, they are unable to see where their innovation will lead. Usually, they cannot capture the full complement of rewards. For example, the inventors of the automatic telling machine (ATM) that now adorns most street corners had no idea of the impact their technology would have on society. Even the banks that adopted ATMs had no idea that their customers would use them to such a degree. In fact, early studies showed that people would rather deal with humans than machines. What banks failed to do was assess the WOW factor. Users saw a lot of *worth* in not having to wait in long bank queues to be intimidated by indiscreet and unpleasant tellers. They also saw value in being able to withdraw cash at their convenience — even on weekends. The WOW did not come because people loved ATMs. It came because people had the option to turn away from the older, inconvenient set of offerings.

Finally, about change, I remind leaders that if the suggested path is being applauded, stay away from it. If a rumoured change is hated, investigate it. If an innovation is being laughed at, invest in it.

| **CHARACTERISTIC 4 • REAL TIME** |

In the networked world, people want immediate answers to their questions. Customers want information, prices, data, and delivery dates, and they want them at once. We have seen this level of expectation rise slowly over the years. With the advent of real-time computer processing, it became reasonable to ask for *immediate* information.

Today's markets demand the ability to: accelerate without warning; implement and cope with change; operate and think in real time... and have the flexibility to sway between tangible and intangible frameworks — all at a pace dictated by the market

The winners in the networked world will be those who not only *process* data in real time, but those who train and enable their staff to *think* in real time.

It is ludicrous to raise customers' expectations for immediate answers from computers when instant answers are not forthcoming from humans. It is bewildering to see employees who cannot think in real time, and bemusing to see them engaged in *magnetic thinking*.

In the networked world, magnetic thinking poses a paradox in that it is both vital and stifling. Magnetic thinking is important because it enables people to arrive at seemingly foregone conclusions within nanoseconds. Unlike intuition which involves heuristics (rules of thumb), experience, guesswork, and some risk, magnetic thinking is not so calculating. It relies on historical programming — something that has happened many times before is likely to happen again. There is much assumption in magnetic thinking. It is like an auto-pilot mode for the brain that uses a look-up table of previous actions without interrogation.

The problem with magnetic thinking is that it becomes a trap for those who cannot *think* in real time. It is like the child who cannot add basic numbers without the aid of a calculator. Remove the calculator, and the ability to add numbers is also removed. Not having the ability to think in real time, or make decisions in real time, puts the organisation at risk. Magnetic thinking must only be contemplated by those who also have the ability to think in real time.

In some cases the development and promotion of real-time thinking requires the fostering of an environment that allows people to take risks, to access information, to engage in some guesswork, and to make decisions *independently*. Thinking needs to be an independent act. Therefore, systems must be put in place, including the extension of authority, to allow individuals to act immediately and independently. Failure to structure such a framework might maintain greater control, but it is also the supreme form of obfuscation. You cannot play in the networked world by *your* rules. If you do, it will be at your peril.

| **CHARACTERISTIC 5 • COMPLEXITY** |

A complex world is what we are familiar with. Complexity is normal. It is something we have grown to respect. We stand in awe of nature's complexity, from the function of the human body to the incomprehensible marvels of microscopic particles. This reverence for complexity has led us to develop our own complex machinery and intricate social support structures.

We fail when we confuse "complexity" with "complication". To messy minds, complicated things are much easier to construct than complex orderly structures. As a result, we suffer bureaucracies that once offered hope, but now offer complicated webs of inexplicable, interdependent structures that follow no rhyme nor reason. Their only defence is their dominance and interrelated reliance. When no-one is able to crack the codes, no-one is in a position to decide which element of the codes can be discarded.

The winners in the networked world are those who insist that complex structures, systems, or procedures must never harbour the "complicated". In addition, the test of compliance should be applied to elements that threaten to join with *complex* systems. Compliance requires any new element to fit the existing structure without it necessitating a change to that structure. Apply this rigid test to the next bright idea that comes your way and see if it passes this logic. If it fails, you would be advised to isolate it until its full implications are understood, costed, and planned for. If this requirement seems arduous, imagine how much more unpleasant it would be if it began to demand of you the things that *you* failed to demand of *it*.

| CHARACTERISTIC 6 • LINKAGE |

Survey your colleagues about the networked world and they are likely to tell you that one of its characteristics is the way in which things are linked — computers, telephones, facsimiles, the Internet, international agreements, banks, and educational institutions.

Take what you do best and ignite it (not smother it) with technology

Being linked might be a characteristic, but it is not the *linking* that offers the advantage. Everyone with a telephone is linked to every florist and bakery in the world. What good is that? Being linked is not, in itself, an advantage. The important element is that of connectivity. Being *connected* is the vital goal.

If all the spectators at a football stadium joined hands they would be linked. However, what good is such a link? Joining hands does not offer any value because the people would still have very little in common. They would not know about the strengths and weaknesses of the people with whom they are linked, or know how to tap into each other's resources.

In the networked world, the aim is to be *connected* with customers, suppliers, partners, friends, banks, governments, influencers, and resources. Current unobtrusive connectivity between you and the electricity company is a good example. You have electricity on demand. You pay your bills with minimum effort, and your electricity is provided without qualification — in other words your supplier does not dictate to you which appliances can or cannot be connected to the wall socket. Furthermore, you need not concern yourself with the daily challenges associated with the running of the power station.

The need for physical connections in the networked world can be illustrated by the following incident which involved a bank and several ATMs inside shopping centres. Traditionally, ATMs were always connected directly to the bank, so that all transactions could be recorded and accounted for. One bank decided to offer its customers the convenience of its ATMs inside several shopping centres. Unfortunately, those ATMs were not connected to the bank until midnight, when the records were updated. However, connection once in twenty-four hours was not convenient for customers whose records could not be updated as regularly as was desired.

One customer decided to take advantage of this by going to nine different branches and opening a savings account in each branch. The bank clerks were not suspicious of him because he deposited $1000 every time he opened an account. He waited until midnight for the ATMs in the shopping centres to be updated. This meant that every ATM was aware of the fact that he was owed $1000. The next day, the customer went to the first shopping centre and proceeded to withdraw $1000 from each of his nine accounts. This meant that, from one shopping centre, he walked out with $9000 — money he rightfully owned, albeit placed in nine different accounts under different fictitious names.

The customer then went to the second shopping centre and did the same thing. The ATMs there were not updated. As far as their records were concerned, he still had funds in the bank. His previous withdrawal would only be noted at midnight when the ATMs were connected once more to the bank's central computer. From the second shopping centre he withdrew another $9000. He managed to visit ten such shopping centres. That gave him $90 000. He then topped it off by going to the ATM attached to the bank, and withdrew another $9000. This time, the computer was updated, and everything seemed to be in order until midnight, when all the ATMs tried to replicate and reconcile the accounts. This lack of connectivity taught the bank a lesson it was too embarrassed to publicise for fear of other would-be entrepreneurs trying innovative ways to defraud the bank.

The thief got away with $90 000 plus his original $9000. Not a bad return on investment. None of this could have happened if the physical connection had been in place. The bank and other organisations need to find ways to *connect* with their key players in fuss-free ways. Beyond the physical connection is the importance of the *intangible* connection — knowing how others feel, why they feel that way, and what part you play in generating, exacerbating, or enhancing that feeling. Intangible connections are very complex. Their mastery relies on replacing assumptions with facts, and judgement with understanding.

| CHARACTERISTIC 7 • TANGIBLES & INTANGIBLES |

Well-read individuals realise that this world operates on several fronts. We generally understand that we move and operate within tangible and intangible parameters. Many would also agree that things that operate well in one domain are changing to the point where what was once tangible is becoming intangible, and vice versa. Respected observers have alerted us to the fact that things are switching camp — products are becoming services while things that were real are becoming virtual. Furthermore, those who once found riches from tangible assets are now beginning to appreciate the values of intangible assets.

The important aspect to this characteristic is that those who were in one camp are being pulled across to the opposite camp. Those who know how to survive and prosper in one camp do not necessarily understand what it takes to succeed in the opposite camp. For example, in the *tangible* world, when the weak and the strong unite they create synergy. In the *intangible* world, when the weak and the strong collide, the weak always win. This becomes important when trying to understand your current strengths and weaknesses, and what shape these might take after you've been forced to switch camps. (The power of tangibles and intangibles is explained in Chapter 12, "Come do the nanomation with me".)

| CHARACTERISTIC 8 • MARKET SPACE |

Once upon a time retailers, manufacturers, and service providers were required to become experts in their respective market*place*. They prospered when they learnt about their environment, their constituents, and their surrounding competitive pressures.

Over time, with the advent of globalisation, the Internet, and the freeing up of markets, organisations became bombarded with competitors that previously had not posed any threat because they either did not exist, or could not penetrate markets other than their own.

Discerning operators quickly realised that survival depended on a new level of understanding that encompassed the market *space* — namely, cyberspace, international space, and cross-border trading. Operating globally is no longer confined to export contracts and special distribution agreements. It now includes one-on-one trades with those who decide to transact on the basis of the *offer*, not on the basis of *geography*. That said, it became important to understand that the rules of the *market* differ from the rules of the *ether.* For example, when selling goods over the Internet, your customer might be shopping while you sleep. Your range of clothes has to cater for their climate, not only yours. Their preferred method of payment might be in a currency you know little about.

The exciting concept of trading within the market space has been widely discussed. What is little understood is the notion of market-*pace*. Organisations wishing to survive and compete in the accelerating networked world need to grasp the notion of market-pace because it is the *pace* of change, development, and attack that will sift the amateurs from the professionals.

There is no point in entering a race if you are ill-prepared or unaware of the energy that is required to keep pace. Today's markets demand the ability to: accelerate without warning; implement and cope with change; operate and think in real time; be connected in a complex and compliant environment; restrict complications; and have the flexibility to sway between tangible and intangible frameworks — all at a pace dictated by the market, within the rules of the market.

| **CHARACTERISTIC 9 • INFORMATION** |

Since the proliferation of computers in the workplace, managers have struggled to turn *data* into something useful. When they found ways to construct useful reports, they were quick to rejoice in the transformation, calling data "information".

Doubtless, the networked world feeds on information. However, there are two things that must be understood if we are to appreciate the nature of this two-edged sword. The first is that information-overload comes not from the fact that there is too much information, but from the fact that most of the information is not at all appropriate nor does it *inform*. Data cannot become information until it informs the recipient about matters relevant to the recipient. Therefore, information is nothing more than graffiti until it is customised to the user. This means that in*forma*tion must have *form* and structure.

The second important element is that survival depends on our ability to keep up with the market-pace. As such, information needs to become infor*motion*, meaning that it must have motion. It must be able to live and grow. Not only must information exist within the requirements of the user, and not only must it have form and structure, it must also be *connected* to its source so that it remains updated in real time, thereby providing the user with satisfactory and vital inputs for real-time thinking. This is a tall order, but it is incumbent upon the leader to make sure that systems are available to allow this to take place. Anything less than this would play into the hands of failure in the networked world.

| **CHARACTERISTIC 10 • CONVERGENCE** |

Convergence used to be subtle. It used to be the case that technologies, innovations, and improvements converged very slowly to construct new machines, new engines, new processes, and improved performance. Once this phenomenon was understood, the boardroom zealots started to force-fit elements and machines so that they could be converged into a new whiz-bang product. Within this, the "ER" craze was born wherein things were said to be better if they were faster, smaller, bigger, cheaper, lighter, and so it went.

Convergence became a way of finding permutations for the same set of components, so that they could be re-packaged and sold as a *new* product. These days organisations are deluded by the Internet and are there-fore losing sight of their core competencies. They are trying to make the Internet (Web) converge with their existing systems to arrive at all sorts of dubious electronic solutions that ultimately distract them.

The networked world has generated a myriad of social and business pressures. The shrewd will eventually realise that we must not become dazzled by *electronics in business*. Instead, it is more important to examine how business (or government) is conducted in the *electronic* net-worked world. Furthermore, the most important element to comprehend is that convergence ought not to focus on the *material* being brought together, but on what it is that the new combination produces. For example, ask your friends the following question: "What do you get when you combine copper, wire, paint, a resistor, and alu-minium, then have it powered by electricity?" After a series of clues, your colleagues might arrive at the correct answer — a toaster. This tricky question helps to illustrate the essence of convergence. The most important end product in this combination of material is not the toaster, but the *toast*. Ultimately, convergence ought to produce an outcome whose manifestation is greater than the sum of the parts. Using the toaster/toast analogy, you can see that convergent technologies that focus on the gadget (toaster) are less potent than those that are concerned with the outcome (toast).

It is important to understand what your organisation specialises in, and how it differentiates itself. What "toast" do you produce? Only when you can articulate your worth and your final outcome (whether this be a product or a service) can you truly benefit from a convergent technology. So, while others are blinded by the technology, you ought to focus on what you do best. Do not let the gadget squander your core competencies. Take what you do best and ignite it (not smother it) with technology. ∎

CHAPTER 22

BRANDED FOR *life*

IT'S THE LITTLE THINGS THAT COUNT

"HEY, NADER! WHAT DO YOU do for a job now, mate?", shouted an old classmate whom I had not seen for eleven years. We were at a reunion to celebrate the centenary of our college. I saw by his grin that he was making mischief. "I'm a futurist." With that, he expelled a belly laugh and looked around to find an audience for his retort. "You always were the weird one, Nader." The irony of his mockery was that he found my career a little daft in spite of the fact that he was an *historian*.

It is extremely respectable for someone to be an historian, yet it is peculiar to be a futurist. In a world that thrives on hope for the future, it seems strange that very few people learn how to befriend it. If the future is so important to so many people, why is it treated as a mysterious entity? Is the future not that which we help to mould? Do we not shape it by what we do today? If the answer is no, then what is the meaning of success? Is success not what we arrive at after we have planted the right seeds and invested well to secure it? Surely anyone who desires success is partnering with the present in the hope of arriving safely at the next place — a place not unlike this one, except that in the absence of its existence, we cannot give it a name, so we fearfully and respectfully call it "the future".

Perhaps in the past, when life was simpler, the notion of "tomorrow" focused heavily on nature's whims. Although nature still has a mind of it own, and still refuses to be tamed, we can deal with most of its tantrums. We can protect ourselves from most of its elements. We can heal ourselves of most of its diseases. We can lead ourselves, despite its distractions. Why, then, is it so strange that futurists should exist? Is it, perhaps, due to the reputation of fallen futurists who were erroneous in their predictions? Or is it due to the thankless nature of the profession whose more serious members found themselves in prison for most of their lives? Such tortured souls were locked up for daring to paint a picture that did not suit the aristocracy who stood to lose their fortunes or positions of power. Perhaps futurists were imprisoned as a public statement, or maybe even as a warning to mother nature, lest it contemplate the shattering of the comfortable status quo.

WHAT IS A FUTURIST?

There are vast differences between soothsayers, clairvoyants, psychics, diviners, mystics, prophets, analysts, forecasters, and futurists. For example, a prophet will envisage a better place and urge everyone to adopt new ways regardless of the sacrifices they would entail. A forecaster asks the leaders of the pack where they are heading, then formulates some assumptions based on emerging trends or rumoured investment. Often, what is forecast comes to fruition because the "mob" realigns its focus in fear of being left behind. For example, if a forecaster says "car makers will include an airbag in each new model", then enough airbags will be made in anticipation of demand. If there is no demand, a price war ensues, resulting in very cheap airbags that car makers would find attractive to purchase. *Voilà*! The forecast comes true.

Contrary to popular belief, a futurist is not someone who is devoid of practical applications. In fact, although merciless when it comes to the 101 excuses that managers give about why the status quo shall reign supreme, a futurist is someone who understands the current strengths and weaknesses of the here and now, and is able to see the strengths and weaknesses of the next destination. As such, a futurist is able to assess which of the two locations will dominate, and offer suggestions about what can be done to prepare for, and adapt to, the new environment, should it prove victorious. The hallmark of a futurist is understanding the differences between *fleeting* and *lasting* change.

The hallmark of a futurist is understanding the differences between fleeting and lasting change

A futurist understands that *force* and *power* are not to be reckoned with. In fact, the future is not something that needs to be constructed by us. It is not something that will seek our permission. It will do what it likes, to whom it likes, when it likes. The future will do unto us what it will. There is no stopping it. However, when speaking of "engineering the future", a futurist is showing how bridges can be built to facilitate pioneers and explorers to cross over so that they can undertake reconnaissance missions into the great unknown. By studying the new environment ahead of the pack, one is able to prepare for the future.

Preparation ahead of time will remove the sense of urgency that blinds many organisations when faced with the shock of it all. By understanding the new world, one is able to build solid foundations and flexible infrastructures so that one is able to react with purpose, not respond with surprise.

WHAT MAKES THE FUTURE?

Naturally, learning about the future starts by studying the past. It also requires an understanding of the present. However, what many observers do not realise is that it also requires a thorough understanding of the current peripheral environment. Whether one is forecasting, prophesying, anticipating, or predicting the future, there are important elements that can play a big part in how it shapes up. For example, regardless of the probability of what seems likely, the future is sometimes diverted by new laws, wild cards, and entrenched social taboos; and the impact of by-products, current demands, emergent necessities, and pent-up anxieties.

By understanding the new world, one is able to build solid foundations and flexible infrastructures so that one is able to react with purpose, not respond with surprise

Many inventions that have shaped our world came about as a result of someone's frustration with a set of circumstances. For example, Almon Strowger was an undertaker in Kansas City who was fed up with losing business to his competitors. He noticed that the local switchboard operator seemed to favour other undertakers, and would rarely connect callers to him. As a result, he decided to invent a switching system that would remove the need for discriminating operators. In 1891 he patented the automatic dialling system that we now use every day. Who would have thought that an undertaker would make such a contribution to the world of telecommunications?

Many lasting inventions were born as a result of coincidence, need, desperation, or simply by accident; as were microwave ovens, bubblegum, ice-cream cones, blue jeans, and rubber — a substance whose useful form was the result of accidental spillage, causing several chemicals to fuse on to a hot stove. Its inventor, Charles Goodyear, died a poor and humiliated man. The Goodyear Tyre and Rubber Company has no relation to this inventor. It was named in his honour as a mark of respect for his tenacity. Regardless of where you are now, it is highly likely that, within arm's reach, there is a product made from rubber, or a derivative, such as plastic.

We take these products for granted. However, there was a time when every expo and trade conference featured a hype merchant who pleaded with the masses to grasp the future potential of plastic. It took a long time before any such ideas were taken seriously. Furthermore, imagine the reaction to the idea of electricity. The concept of an invisible force squeezing itself inside thin wire left many in disbelief. How could electricity become useful in the kitchen and around the home? Most people were frightened of it. Some even suggested that it was evil, yet today we do not give it a second thought. The flawed reasoning that made people doubt the potential of rubber and electricity is still with us — except these days it is the Web and the Internet that they doubt.

SURPRISE ABSORPTION FACTOR

Understanding the future is one thing. Being able to survive it is another. An organisation's success relies on its ability to cope with surprises. Its buffer zone can be likened to a car's bumper bars. Some organisations, like some vehicles, can absorb sudden shocks, while others find the impacts unbearable. The terrains within the portals that lead to the future are turbulent, bumpy, and hazardous. As such, an organisation's Surprise Absorption Factor (SAF) will determine its likelihood of survival.

Understanding the future is one thing. Being able to survive it is another. An organisation's success relies on its ability to cope with surprises.

Innovative organisations and progressive societies think that they should focus on their ability to "change". They derive comfort from knowing that they are open-minded, agile, and willing to change. However, this thinking, although noble, is dangerous because in the networked world, it is not so much one's ability to change that determines survival. Rather, it is one's ability to adsorb the rude shocks. Those whose buffer zones are weak will topple. Agility will not only be measured by one's ability to move quickly, but also by one's ability to withstand a sudden and unexpected thud from behind. It is only *after* the storm has passed that one's ability or willingness to change becomes an important factor for survival.

The reason that one's Surprise Absorption Factor is more important than the "will to change" is that the future is not something that has ever sounded believable. Every generation has had to suffer this perplexing and hypnotic syndrome. With all the reasoning at its disposal, an organisation or society seems to think that the status quo is a modern one. With that comes an arrogance to assume that a modern environment is a perfect one where people are learned and infallible. The vicious cycle of confidence seems to suggest that if something is logical, it is believable. If it does not make sense, then it can't be real. Alas, the overriding characteristic about the future is that it *is* unbelievable. When a futurist describes something that people do embrace with enthusiasm and confidence, it is more likely that what the futurist is describing is the *current* state of affairs. The general litmus test about the future is that it is one that very few would be willing to believe. Hence, when you hear unbelievable statements, pause to consider what you might be overlooking.

RIGHT ANSWER, WRONG QUESTION

Although it can be exciting to find the answer, it is often more exhilarating to find the question. When hoping for a successful future in the networked world, asking the right questions will point the way. One of the most important questions that companies must ask themselves is: "What will be the single most important asset?"

The general rhetoric would have us believe that an organisation's employees are its most important asset. Although staff members can make or break an organisation, they are not assets because they do not belong to the enterprise.

Although it can be exciting to find the answer, it is often more exhilarating to find the question

Considering that an organisation's primary role is to create customers, while for customers, their primary concern when transacting is to find trustworthy organisations, it would seem reasonable to suggest that the most important asset will be the thing that can unite these two desires.

Observers of consumer behaviour say that modern shoppers are *smarter* and *better informed* than previously. This is a fallacy. Consumers today might have the capability to learn more about a product or service. They might even have the ability to access information faster. However, they are not better informed about your company and what you offer. They might know a little more about which

378

products are safe, and which might be unhealthy. The reason that consumers are not better informed is that they are busier, and have more choice, than ever before. They do not have time to research the options, let alone fathom the differences between new products and services that they do not fully comprehend. In the networked world, "attention" is the scarcest resource. To that end, anything that can assist consumers overcome their fears and anxieties when dealing with organisations will help to bridge the gap between the buyer and the seller.

The single most important asset, therefore, is the "brand". Herein lie opportunities amid misinformation.

I AM WELL, HOW ARE YOU?

When asking about one's heath, it seems that at first, one speaks of *general* health. It is in this single dimension that most business operators think of their brand.

What of physical, spiritual, or emotional health? And within each are subdivisions. For example, physical health delves into eyesight and hearing, among many other things.

Branding is just as complex. Each subdivision can cripple the whole organisation, and always requires surgical precision to design and maintain. From branding we arrive at brand awareness, brand recognition, brand positioning, brand values, brand recall, brand image, brand identity, and brand personality.

There is even another sub-layer below this level. For example, brand values branch into two areas. First, the term "values" refers to ethos — what the organisation stands for. Second, it also refers to a measure. This is demonstrated in the fashion industry where the designer-label garment commands a higher dollar value, over and above the true worth of the product.

Furthermore, brand values can have a measure other than dollars. The brand might be able to command a measure of "time". This is evidenced by the long period of time that car buyers are willing to wait for delivery. Although buyers of basic family sedans would not wait eight months for their new vehicle, buyers of luxury cars would, even though they might be unhappy about the delay.

Other measures of brand values might be "tolerance". For example, how tolerant would one be if a $2 plastic pen is faulty, compared with the tolerance level when a $900 pen ceases to function? Yet again, there is a twist to this because this ought not to suggest that the tolerance for product-failures always works against the premium brands. It is common for customers to have a higher measure of tolerance for the failure of the reputable-brand product because they might assume that they have experienced bad luck, not bad manufacturing.

PLACE YOUR BETS

The most important aspect in relation to the brand is what I call the "brand bet" — meaning what your customers are willing to bet about what you will or won't do in relation to what you have promised to do.

The most pertinent way in which I demonstrate this philosophy is to rise from a meeting, walk over to the light switch on the wall, and turn out the lights. Then, in semi-darkness I pose this question: "How many of you would bet $1000 that if I flick this switch on again, the lights would come back on?" Unanimously, people agree that the lights would illuminate the room once more. They are so confident, they are willing to bet a huge sum of money. The stability and reliability of light switches is very high. I turn the lights on, sit down, and pose my second question: "Supposing that my computer software displays several error messages, would you bet a thousand dollars that if I were to call the help desk for support, the phone would be answered within three rings?" No takers on that proposal. "Would you bet that I will *not* be put on hold?" Much laughter and merriment bubbles as people begin to understand the real meaning of brand bet.

"Well, what would you be willing to bet?" I ask. After jeers and nervous giggles, my audience generally settles for something like a thousand dollars on the assumption that: I would be forced to wait for approximately twenty-five minutes; the first person to take my call would not fully understand my question; the same person would try to suggest that the error could be a hardware fault; they would make a ludicrous suggestion such as ask me to remove all files and applications from my computer, leaving only their software installed, with a view to proving that the error was *not* caused by their software, and thereby hoping to exonerate themselves and find cause to hang up on me. My audience would be willing to bet another thousand dollars that if I were to insist on a resolution, I would be escalated to second-level help, only after I had agreed to pay a handsome fee, without any guarantees of a resolution.

With this example, you can see what I mean by brand bet. Organisations of all shapes and sizes can easily determine the value of their brand based on the confidence level of the consumer. This is a simple process. Contact customers at random, regardless of their disposable income. Perform the light-switch test, and ask them what they would seriously be willing to bet. Whatever that amount is becomes the base line. For example, if they bet $10 000, knowing full well that they would have to pay that amount if they were to lose, then $10 000 becomes their base line. Now, using the baseline figure, ask them what they would be willing to bet in relation to your product or service.

In my case, I am willing to bet $10 000 that if I go to the post office at 9:00 am, there would be a queue that stretches outside the front door. I would bet that if I landed in my hometown international airport at 6:00 am on a full flight, only five of the potential twenty-five immigration windows would be open for new arrivals. I would bet $5000 that despite booking a non-smoking room at my five-star hotel, the check-in clerk would deny any knowledge of such a request. I would bet $5000 that if I were to write a letter of complaint to the managing director (MD) of my Internet cable provider, the MD would not respond. Some underling would write to me on the MD's behalf, and three weeks later when I call to speak with the under-ling, that person would have moved on. I would bet $20 000 that from the moment I leave my house, I couldn't have a mobile-phone conversation for more than six minutes in my car without the line dropping out.

Regardless of how fancy your advertisements are, and no matter what values you espouse, it all boils down to what your customers are willing to bet on.

The confidence factor can be determined by asking customers what they would be willing to bet in relation to any of your promises. For example, you might say, "We produce the highest quality toasters." Now, take the base-line amount (say $10 000) and the bet amount (say $1000) to arrive at the confidence level, which in this case is only 10 per cent. If that is the average amount across a group of customers, then it can be said that your brand equity, as shown on your balance sheet, is only worth 10 per cent of its current value. For organisations whose brand sits as an intangible asset valued at $200 million, a reduction to 10 per cent of its value would remove $180 million from the asset register. Where would such organisations be today if they were re-valued using this formula? What would happen to their goodwill estimates?

Regardless of how fancy your advertisements are, and no matter what values you espouse, it all boils down to what your customers are willing to bet on

WHAT IS THE FUNCTION OF A BRAND?

There are many reasons for investing in the development of a brand. However, what is the single most important one? Some might be trying to impress future investors, not consumers. Others might be trying to appeal to certain people, hoping to show them that the organisation can identify with their tastes and beliefs.

For organisations that desire long-term prosperity, the single most important function of the brand is to reduce the advertising expense — which in turn means to reduce the sales cycle.

This philosophy might not sound plausible when one observes very large organisations that seem to spend more on advertising year after year. There are two reasons for the seemingly huge advertising investment. The first is a smart one that plants seeds for the future whereby the investment is focused on the long term — always nurturing and creating new believers. The second is a selfish and wasteful one born from an erroneous belief that one must have the largest market share, even if by one or two percentage points. Those who belong to this camp are the paranoid who lack confidence, and the greedy who lack patience. They spend far too much money trying to capture every possible stray; similar to the ways in which politicians try to capture every possible vote. The return on investment at that level is nonsensical, but easily justifiable in the corporate jungle where even half a point could mean the difference between life and death for the

CEO (or the nearest executive who can be blamed for the swing).

MARKET DOMINATION

There is a common maxim that says, "If you can't be the market leader, get out of the market."

This refers to the popular management strategy of market domination. These days, when a new CEO takes the reins, the executives are expected to report on the company's share of the market for each product category

Pulling out of markets due to lack of dominance is not prudent because you might never know what set of weaknesses contributed to your mediocrity

in each area. Where the company does not rank in the top three, the easiest thing is to pull the plug on that market.

For me, it is more important that I assess why my organisation is not doing so well, rather than just move out. Pulling out of markets due to lack of dominance is not prudent because you might never know what set of weaknesses contributed to your mediocrity.

Of course, there is the other nagging question about what it means to be the best in a market. There is corporate hysteria about market share. Everywhere you go you'll hear of executives chasing their tails to secure market share. Almost every business plan I have seen points to market dominance as one of its priorities.

As sure as people go around at Christmas chanting

"Merry Christmas" without a single thought to what this tribal lip-service is all about, they prance about at planning meetings saying, "Market share is important, and it must be achieved." Does anyone stop to ask why?

From what I have observed, many organisations want market share because they are haemorrhaging, and they have lost touch with their customers. They cannot count on any loyalty whatsoever because they know that they have not delivered on their promises. So, they want to replenish their customer base as fast as possible to make up for the many dissatisfied customers. When they lose customers, they blame the competitor. They do not stop for a minute to realise that their customers are fed up with them.

If you promise one thing and deliver another, your market will not give you a moment's rest. Focus on being true to your word, and your market will be kind to you.

Market ranking excites the analysts and logisticians. Market congruence excites customers.

Therefore, the new wisdom is, "Never mind market dominance. Set out to dominate the hearts and minds of your customers, one at a time."

How to Commit Brand Suicide

For a long time in the corporate world, the value of intangible assets was disregarded. Eventually, investors were convinced that what separated one company from the next were its reputation, its network, its infrastructure, and its brand. In due course, "expansion" became the order of the day, whereby conglomerates purchased huge factories to make more of the same product in order to satisfy the demands of consumers far and wide. After expansion came "diversification" whereby those who made scales to weigh vegetables eventually made typewriters and office equipment. The next wave was one of "branding"; as in to stamp one's logo on to merchandise of various shapes and sizes. It seemed easier to take the logo to the factory than to bring the factory to the logo.

It was easier for anonymous manufacturers to sell their wares to those who had the distribution channel and marketing expertise, than for them to try to re-invent the distribution network. They did not care that consumers would never know about their existence. They were phantom suppliers who made the products that others branded with their trademark.

Brand confusion is a messy business to rectify

After branding, the nineties brought the wisdom of "leverage". It seemed that everyone was trying to leverage their intangibles, whether they were relationships, brands, patents, or channels. To that end, the strangest of unions were formed. Manufacturers whose brand was synonymous with *products* soon derived most of their income from *services*. Those who became famous for their services switched camps to sell more products to customers they previously never thought to attract.

The word that will dominate the networked world is brand "portability" where not only will logos be used on a disparate range of products and services, they will also be used to migrate from one brand identity to the next. Here, the focus is not so much on changing a product range or capturing new markets, it's all about entering new territories that will force organisations to change their "identity". It's what undercover detectives do very well. They can dress up or dress down. They can look swish and mix with royalty or they can play rough and tumble in the ghettos. As with all such missions, they are dangerous.

Fiddling with brand identity is a very risky thing to do because it can easily fail. Brand confusion is a messy business to rectify. If organisations totally migrate to a new environment, they will be forced to let go of their roots (the very roots that comprised their lifeblood for years). Migration is harder for low-grade brands that are trying to break into the high-grade luxury market. The stigma of their past might haunt them for evermore.

It is not much easier for high-grade brands to move into the lower end of the market. Current customers would disown the brand because of the perceived "common" touch. Other migration issues relate to generation gaps, years of reputation and association, and levels of quality.

Brand portability is a great idea. However, beware that you do not commit brand suicide by daring (intentionally or accidentally) to undertake a wholesale sell-out of the brand values that have been firmly associated with your brand. Brand portability ought not to suggest anything other than taking the current set of rock-solid values and immovable identities, and applying them to new markets and/or new products. Portability is about extension and new applications, not defection.

Beware what you do in the name of brand portability. Sometimes, short-sightedness could prove to be very attractive, plausible, feasible, and profitable. As might be said of airlines that formed alliances in the nineties. It got to the point where passengers could insist on a Brand X flight, receive a Brand X ticket with all the hallmarks of Brand X, yet when they arrived at the terminal, they were forced to board a Brand Y aircraft. I was furious when this happened to me, mostly due to the fact that Brand Y allowed smoking in the cabin, when I had specifically and purposefully booked Brand X because it boasted about its non-smoking services. This was nothing more than brand suicide, no matter how the airlines might justify it, and no matter how they convince themselves that it makes sense. To those for whom it matters most, the move was naive and laughable. Yes, the managers of the day reaped their short-term rewards because they were able to show a reduction in costs. However, there will be a price to pay for their stupidity. Unfortunately, it will be the future managers who will inherit the disaster.

A QUESTION OF SURVIVAL

For those who are serious about building their brand, and delivering on their promises, Chapter 23, "The eight wonders of the networked world," addresses another of the important questions by outlining eight scenarios that will give clues about the best ways to engineer a successful future. ◘

THE EIGHT *wonders*
OF THE NETWORKED WORLD

PRE-EMPTING FUTURE CHALLENGES

R IVALRY IS A DESTRUCTIVE FORCE that shrouds itself in a playful mask. We observe it between teams, nations, cities, and families. What starts out as a bit of slap-and-tickle ends up a serious division between polarised groups. One-upmanship emerges as each party displays its supremacy while ridiculing the other.

Apart from the traditional interdepartmental rifts within organisations, there are serious divisions between those who "do and count" and those who "count and do". In other words, between those who make things happen (and then measure what happened) and those who wait for things to happen (and then comment on what took place).

Typically, this occurs between marketing and finance staff. While the marketing folk are pioneering, the finance fraternity is displeased that activity can take place before it has been *proved* to be feasible.

Rivalry is a destructive force that shrouds itself in a playful mask

The "prove it to me first" syndrome presupposes that we live in a "measurable" world. While some business operators find it impossible to make a decision unless its inputs and outputs can be calculated, others are quite happy to get on with the job and let the process of measurement keep track of the *past*, not restrict its movement into the *future*.

Ask CEOs if they would like to know (in advance) the major challenges that their organisation would face in the future, and you'll hear a resounding "yes" even though most of them would consider it a rhetorical question, similar to "would you like to know next week's winning lottery numbers?"

Some people are unable to seriously contemplate scenarios that cannot be punched into a computer spreadsheet. For them, possibilities can only be contemplated if they can be weighed up. This causes a communications breakdown between sales and marketing, between operations and finance, between design and manufacturing, between head office and field staff, and between the whole organisation and its customers. This is the result of rivalry between those who insist on proof, and futurists who are accused of having their head in the clouds.

While the marketing folk are pioneering, the finance fraternity is displeased that activity can take place before it has been proved to be feasible

In an effort to heal the wounds between the *logical* and the *creative* and between the *analysts* and the *visionaries*, here are eight questions that will point the way to a successful future.

Those who can embrace, and act upon, the essence and wisdom of these questions will place themselves in good stead to greet the future. Those who ignore them are likely to find the future less kind to their efforts.

These eight scenarios could give you clues about the future and what it might demand of you. By preparing for these eventualities, you will be in a better position to absorb surprises.

1) *What would happen if you had to pay for putting your customers on hold?*

If your organisation makes a habit of putting clients on hold, then consider that in the future, you might be liable to pay for the clients' time. Even if you estimate a modest dollar amount per hour, calculate what kind of exposure this would represent. Can you afford this kind of liability? If the figures alarm you, then you can engineer your future by doing something to fix the issues at their root. It is not a question of hiring more staff members to take more calls. It is a matter of working out why the call rates are high in the first place. Could it be that your products are not performing as they should be? Maybe your customers are so confused that they need help to decipher your product's installation instructions.

Whether or not laws will be passed in relation to this is not the point. Many organisations have boasted about how they have reduced their operating expenses. In many cases, all that they have managed to do is *shift* the expense from their camp to the customers'.

2) *What would happen if the money you receive from a customer freezes when your product fails?*

In the networked world, money will be linked to performance. This means that any product that you sell had better work. If it does not work, then the money you received from your customer will freeze in your bank account. Corporate wealth will be calculated on how well you deliver on your promise, not on how high your revenue is. Technologists might argue that it is neither feasible nor possible to produce fault-free products. That argument, although convenient, is unethical. When someone pays $100 for a product, that money is perfect money. It does not break down, it does not require service calls, it does not perish, and it does not stop working. Therefore, when manufacturers take the consumers' perfect money, what gives them the right to dish out rubbish? (For more on this subject, see Chapter 17, "Customer service — my foot!")

In the networked world, money will be linked to performance

3) *What would happen if those who did not like their job did not go to work tomorrow?*

Not long ago, employees who changed employers were considered to be a risk. These days, there is no stigma attached to wandering talent. Instead, the embarrassment befalls employers who are careless with staff. In certain industries, the choice exists for workers to move to a different company, to resign to start their own business or consulting practice, and to retire, if they are wealthy.

It had better be a matter of urgency for you to learn about your staff members' morale, their happiness, their contentment, and what it is that agitates them or makes them dislike their work environment. Once you have identified those who dislike their job, ask yourself what would happen to your business if they decided not to turn up to work. If your business would suffer as a result of this sudden rebellion, then you had better do something about the notions of fun, contentment, happiness, job satisfaction, and engagement. Are you engaging your people in your business and the industry? (For more on this subject, see Chapter 15, "Ready . . . aim . . . now what?")

4) *What would happen if you were forced to disclose your faults prior to making a sale?*

What if all the complaint statistics and product faults were available for your potential customers to inspect on the Web? This would mean that anyone could inspect the latest series of complaints and faults relating to a product before making a decision to purchase it.

Many of us know of horror stories about people who buy a product that breaks down within two days. Like the computer whose disk drive suddenly dies, taking with it all the files. Or the mobile phone whose tiny screen fades away — making it impossible to read a message or to see who is calling. What about the well-funded Internet network that shuts down without warning and no hint of compensation, leaving users without Internet access. Then there is the beloved laser printer whose tiny $2 motor that mixes the toner fails, rendering the whole machine useless, costing $110 to have a repair agent visit sometime between sunrise and sunset because "Sorry, we can't be more accurate than that." These are but some of the dozens of complaints that contribute to an organisation's death.

Once upon a time, product testing was done in labs. These days, the marketplace is used as the testing ground — at the consumers' expense and inconvenience.

Once upon a time, product testing was done in labs. These days, the marketplace is used as the testing ground — at the consumers' expense and inconvenience. I recall the days when my colleagues and I would not release a product until it had been dropped, poked, zapped, frozen, melted, tested, and tampered with at least 10 000 times. After that, the first batch was released to special clients who agreed to conduct further tests under strict conditions. Only after passing all these checks would a product be released to the masses. Back then, a five-year warranty was common for reputable brands. Modern executives are quick to remind me that, back then, profit margins were huge. What fascinates me is that they have not worked out why that was the case.

It is not uncommon for managers to be blinded by short-term revenue results. The sales manager is not measured on product quality, only on sales revenue. The repair centre does not care about how many faulty products it has to deal with, so long as its empire can grow to cope with the increase in demand. The help desk does not care about how many unnecessary calls it receives — the busier the phones, the more that it can justify its existence. This is the self-destructive nature of matrix management. (For more on matrix management, see Chapter 13, "Cut across the dotted line.")

Gather all your complaint statistics and product faults, and share these with a group of potential buyers. Then, ask them if they would still consider buying your product in view of what they now know. If your customers say that they would *hesitate*, you have a potential catastrophe brewing because very soon you will be forced to divulge such precious and damning information. What then? Can you do something about it now? Of course you can. This is how easy it is to engineer your future — if you care enough about your future.

5) *

Charlatans and crooks used to make outrageous offers to trick people into signing contracts. Eventually, authorities stepped in to protect consumers by insisting that all the conditions of a sale had to be divulged. These obligatory revelations were relegated to the back of contracts in fine print so small that very few people could read them, let alone understand them. Thereafter, the authorities stepped up their campaign to inject some truth in advertising by insisting that the asterisk be used to further highlight the potentially tricky areas.

* *What would happen if you were forbidden to use fine print?*

Regardless of what the law says, and irrespective of what you have to do to cover yourself, you need to look at

Brands have personalities and, as such, you need to ask if your brand has a personality that is attractive, warm, trustworthy, and meaningful; or is it full of hot air?

each offer you make, and contemplate what it would be like if you were unable to use fine print. Customers do not take kindly to "terms and conditions", especially when they are not in the spirit of the headline offer that caught their attention in the first place. For example, here is one of the hundreds of dubious offers that I see each week. It reads, "Any five garments can be dry-cleaned for $24.95*". The fine print reveals, "A surcharge applies for silks, pleats, dresses, dressing gowns, velvets, and lights. The offer excludes overcoats, skins, ski wear, and evening wear." This is all too hard.

The brands that people will bet on will be those that are safe to bet on. Brands have personalities and, as such, you need to ask if your brand has a personality that is attractive, warm, trustworthy, and meaningful; or is it full of hot air with complex and complicated twists and turns that very few people would want to be associated with? If your brand were a person, would it have many friends?

6) *What would happen if customers could record the conversation they are having with your staff members?*

"This call may be recorded for quality assurance purposes." How many times have you heard that as you waited on hold for someone to help? This message is a blatant lie. It was never the company's intention to improve the quality of its service. It was not even a warning to consumers. Instead, it was there to subtly remind the staff members that management might snoop on their calls to check their productivity. The guise of quality was a sneaky way to overcome union pressure and cries of infringement of workers' privacy.

What would happen to your reputation if, in fact, the controls were with the consumer —

If your brand were a person, would it have many friends?

meaning that a customer could choose to record the conversation with your organisation, and have that conversation up on the Web for all to access and listen to? How embarrassing would it be for your brand if the typical cold-shoulder approach to dealing with clients were digitally captured for the public to pass around as the joke-of-the-month e-mail?

There's a wise old saying that goes along the lines of "character is about not doing the wrong thing, even if you know that you'll never get caught". In this case, getting caught shouting at customers, humiliating them, or baffling them, will be only a matter of time. A simple unsavoury conversation, especially if it is one that people can easily identify with, will circle the globe within hours, causing more damage to your brand than you can possibly imagine. Therefore, beware how you train your staff members, and what you authorise them to do and say to customers over the phone.

7) What would happen if you no longer had a help desk in your organisation?

The day will come when help desks will disappear, simply because everyone will realise that they are useless. In fact, they were never established to help anyone in the first place. Help desks were born as a result of organisations dishing out substandard products and misinformation at a time when they were hungry to reach new markets, increase market share, and increase sales within a short period of time. The confused and frustrated customers who called to speak with senior managers were shunned. They were told to queue up and speak with a junior whose time was less precious than the executive's.

Help desks are a serious liability. They are impersonal, impractical, unhelpful, and downright infuriating — and that's only what the people who work at the help desk think. These poor staff members have to cope with customers who are at their wit's end. The staff members at the help desk do not have a thorough understanding of the overall organisation. Furthermore, they do not have the authority to make the necessary decisions that will fix the problems for the customers. And worse still, they do not have the authority to fix problems at their *roots*. They have to take call after call in relation to a problem that should never have been allowed to occur, let alone continue to occur.

Help desks will disappear because they remove the pain from those who *cause* the pain. Such abdication is dangerous and destructive.

*8) What would happen if customers had the opportunity to partici-
pate in an "exit poll" after each encounter with your organisation?*

It would be wrong to assume that in the networked
world customers will be more demanding. Although customers will have shorter tolerances for incompetence,
they will not care to demand any more from you because
they would not want to bother
with anyone who wastes their
time.

Do your customers really
want to do business with *you*?
In most cases, customers hang
around for convenience, not
loyalty. The moment that they
have an alternative, they will
take it if they are unhappy with
you. Their decision to switch

*Help desks will disappear
because they remove the
pain from those who
cause the pain.
Such abdication
is dangerous
and destructive.*

camps comes from a desire to vent their frustrations and
exercise their power over an unhappy relationship.

It's about time that organisations faced the question
of customer loyalty based not on how many customers
they have, but on how many they *would have* if their customers were given the opportunity to make a meaningful
protest. *This would have to be the most frightening question
that any organisation must contemplate.*

In the networked world, while your customers are
beating a path to your door, your competitors are beating a
door to your path. Hence, it would be myopic to keep your

eyes on traditional competitors. Competitors can come from anywhere. You will not know when and how they will strike. The weaker your relationship with your customers, the easier it will be for a competitor to lure them.

In the past, people did not necessarily want to order books on-line. They just did not want to waste their time talking with sales assistants whose response to every question was (and still is) the predictable phrase, "If it's not on the shelf, we don't have it." That kind of attitude kicked the customers away. The emergence of on-line shopping was not born of a desire to go shopping on-line. It was born out of frustration with long queues, ill-informed staff, crowds, noise, and chaotic, insecure car parks that offered no security and a sure bet that the car would be scratched by unruly shopping trolleys.

In the networked world, while your customers are beating a path to your door, your competitors are beating a door to your path

The decision-makers in an organisation have become so far removed from their customers and employees; they are now focused on charts and graphs plotted from surveys and questionnaires. They burden customers with inexplicable questions that statisticians plant for the purpose of control, balance, and contrast, all the while alienating the customer. It baffles me that hotels still ask questions like, "Was the radio working?"; "Was the water pressure in your shower adequate?"; "Was the air conditioner functioning satisfactorily?" Talk about shifting the burden. These days, hotels seem to expect the guests to go through a checklist, all under the guise of customer-satisfaction surveys. Why don't they check that everything is working before guests check in?

The most sensible survey will be the *exit poll* — a survey that asks customers what they think of an experience. The major difference between all other surveys and this one will be its immediacy. It will be conducted moments after an encounter or transaction, and the results will be plotted within seconds. The company will be able to assess its performance within minutes of every transaction. For example, after a telephone conversation or help desk enquiry, the customer will be given the opportunity to press a few buttons to cast a vote or express an opinion. Questions will be blunt and direct, such as: "Did we answer your query?"; "Would you like a senior official to contact you immediately to resolve your issues?"; "Do you think that we are a bunch of ratbags?"

Instantly, the results of the exit polls will be flashed on to the screen of several senior people within the organisation. Such immediacy will enable them to detect horrors as they happen. This level of attention will mean that organisations will be able to feel every pulse, and attend to tiny tremors, giving them an ability to address issues at their root.

This sharp method of operation is a far cry from waiting for survey results to be massaged, moulded, and carved into statistics whose meaning would have dissipated, rendering the whole ritual useless. (For more information about surveys and statistics, see Chapter 19, "You can only lie if you know the truth".) **N**

CHAPTER 24

A KICK UP THE
bottom line

WHAT'S MORE IMPORTANT THAN
THE MOST IMPORTANT?

THERE ARE PEOPLE WHO CANNOT accept that *future success* can be engineered. Upon reflection, they cannot remember having engineered their *current* state of affairs. Ironically, they *do* believe that *future failure* can be constructed.

For many people, success is like happiness — it is always somewhere else, but never here. Yet, for those who do know how to engineer their success, the process seems simple — despite the frustrations that come from obstructionists, non-believers, incompetent operators, unreliable hangers-on, and unethical colleagues.

For entrepreneurs, disappointment comes not from the frailty of others, nor from their own shortcomings, but from ignoring their own intuition. Their greatest remorse comes from knowing that their decrease in velocity was their own doing: they hesitated, skipped a beat, or allowed someone or something to distract them against their better judgement. For a genius at work, there is no greater regret than self-inflicted stupidity. My definition of stupidity is "knowing something, but not acting on that knowledge". On the other hand, I describe fools as "those who truly desire one thing, but do something that can never get them there",

For many people, success is like happiness — it is always somewhere else, but never here

because their real desire and their real action are in conflict.

This chapter will assist you to engineer your future by answering the question, "What is more important than the bottom line?" Those whose current bottom line seems satisfactory might ignore this question. Alas, this would be history repeating itself, whereby zealots hang on to a sinking ship — smug that they have a ship to hang on to.

THE TRIPLE SOMERSAULT

Over the years, experts have touted the need for organisations to pay attention to their "triple bottom line" — referring to traditional *economic* profitability, plus an organisation's *social* contribution, and its *environmental* impact and responsibility. The measure of these three (profit, society, environment) is called "the triple bottom line", and it is considered to be the future indicator of successful organisations. However, the triple bottom line is not the answer that a futurist would give.

In the networked world, we walk a wobbly tightrope. We are torn between *good* and *evil*. We are forced to embrace *complexity* in the face of uninvited *complication*. We are challenged to understand *speed* in the whirlwind of *acceleration*. We have to grasp the meaning of a *linked* society amid the push for a *connected* world. All these demands are taking place within *tangible* and *intangible* forces.

By understanding the characteristics of the networked world, you would realise that reverence for the bottom line is futile. Everyone knows that a "bottom line" is sometimes nothing more than a "bottom lie". Managers can manipulate corporate results to the extent that their ethics will stretch.

Smart operators understand that focusing on the end result is nowhere near as powerful as focusing on the *inputs*. Contrary to traditional methods and beliefs, it is what "comes in" that matters most. Hence, the only thing more important than the bottom line is the "top line".

> *Everyone knows that a "bottom line" is sometimes nothing more than a "bottom lie"*

The funnels that contribute to the top line are *staff*, *quality*, and *customers*. These three aspects construct the "triple top line".

IT STARTS AT THE TOP

"I don't care, just do it," bellowed a senior Vice President (VP) on the other side of the Atlantic. We were engaged in the ritual weekly conference call. Many of my colleagues admired the VP because he had a hands-off style that allowed each country manager to do what had to be done. He did not want to know about the nitty-gritty. He just wanted results.

Most of the managers liked their independence, and they understood what was expected of them. The phrase "I don't care, just do it" was code for "Do whatever you have to do, no matter how dirty it gets, regardless of how many bridges you have to burn, irrespective of how many careers you have to thwart. Just do it even if you are digging a grave for yourself because if we do not make 24 per cent growth this quarter, you're a dead duck."

That attitude reminded me of how I used to play chess at the age of eight. I played each move with no thought whatsoever to the subsequent move. I just took each turn as a totally isolated and independent challenge. Our VP did not care if we had to spill blood, pluck the heart from the organisation, or take a poison pill. His short-sightedness was only slightly less odious than that of the CEO whose myopia was frightening.

I did not fancy such a style of management. Sure, the hands-off approach was dandy, but what's the point of having a VP whose only role was to shout at us? I would have preferred a facilitator, a supporter, a mentor, a leader, a teacher, or a visionary. Instead, he was the highest paid paperboy in the company whose only task was to call each country, collect figures, shout, and hang up. No matter where I was in the world, I had to make myself available for that dreary conference call. At one time I was in Singapore after an exhausting trip that had taken me to India, Indonesia, Philippines, and several other time zones. The VP did not hesitate to wake me up at 4:00 am in Singapore to ask me, "Are you going to make the numbers?" In truth, he was not asking me anything. He was

You can hold your breath for a while, and even for a little longer. Eventually, the laws of nature kick in, and you kick the bucket.

reminding me that I had better have my finger on the pulse back home, and that I had better deliver. His only mode of negotiation was via threats and innuendoes. I said, "What will be, will be." As he hung up, I realised that I had hanged myself. However, the noose around my neck loosened when, two weeks later, the VP was discharged — not for his rudeness and stupidity, but for not being rude enough! In came the *next* VP, and the merry-go-round continued.

You can hold your breath for a while, and even for a little longer. Eventually, the laws of nature kick in, and you kick the bucket. The human body is good like that. It takes no nonsense. It forces us to pay the price for our excesses. Unfortunately, the "corporate body" is not so well engineered. When it suffers from stupidity and pollution, it cannot punish the perpetrator. It can only punish those left behind to suffer. The VPs and managers who cut off certain

Managers ought to be rewarded for the seeds they plant, not the crops they harvest

lifelines are often rewarded, not punished. They do not feel the effects of their ravenous corporate lifestyle; they do not care what kinds of stresses they place on the organisation. They get away with murder because they appear to be championing a good cause — results! In fact, they show everyone that they strive to "achieve" — and what could be nobler than achievement?

Burn the bridges

How you measure your performance will dictate how your people behave. If you plan to focus on the top line, you will have to destroy all mechanisms that measure the bottom line. Yes, destroy them! If you refuse to obliterate the current irrelevant measurement systems, they will rise and reclaim their position, and take a stronger grip than ever before — just as a fallen villain in a film struggles cunningly to reach for the nearby weapon. Never leave a weapon near a fallen victim, and never turn your back.

If you do not have the courage to destroy the bottom-line measurement system, you would be like a gambler who wants to give up gambling, but does not have the willpower to discard the deck of playing cards. Somehow the intention lacks conviction.

The golden goose

It would be naive to assume that achievement relates to bottom-line results. There is no gallantry in flogging the goose to deliver one last golden egg. *Managers ought to be rewarded for the seeds they plant, not the crops they harvest.*

In the networked world, the vital measure will be wealth-creation, not wealth-depletion. Successful managers will be those who can add value, not extract it. Their reputation will be measured by the overall health and well-being of the company, not by how many golden eggs they score per month. The real measure of someone's success could take years to determine. Therefore, in the networked world, bonuses and rewards will be calculated several years after an initiative, not immediately after a short-term gain.

When it comes to *staff*, ask if the people you employ are those whom you could trust (beyond a shadow of a doubt) to be dependable, ethical people. If your sycophantic subordinates have planted seeds of doubt in your mind about another employee, then I would wonder what they are trying to hide. If they can spread doubt in your mind, what kind of a manipulative game are they playing?

In the networked world, the vital measure will be wealth-creation, not wealth-depletion

The question of *quality* is a simple one. You are at liberty to produce any product to any specification you like. Your responsibility is to ensure that what you deliver is in line with what you promise. Anything less would be theft.

Finally, *customers* are vital to top-line results because most organisations could not exist without them. Do you treat your customers like they matter to the health of your organisation, or do you treat them like they matter to the bottom line? There's a big difference!

The triple top line will be the starting point for successful, healthy, and profitable organisations. Several volumes can be written about the triple top line. However, here is my challenge to any organisation that desires future success: undertake an audit to determine the number of hours that senior executives spend focusing on bottom-line issues, then be sure to inject just as much energy and time into top-line issues. If executives were to spend the same amount of time on *staff*, *quality*, and *customers*, the results would be so dynamic that market domination would be a foregone conclusion. **S**

ACKNOWLEDGMENTS

I
T IS CUSTOMARY TO ACKNOWLEDGE people who have helped an author. In my case it would be inappropriate to acknowledge those whom I have infuriated or lost as friends, for it is they who drove me to write this book. Most of them know who they are, and some are still living in their own bubble and might never know how they have contributed to this book.

How to Lose Friends and Infuriate People took eight years of hard work. The people whose initials are listed below have been instrumental in the production aspects of this book. They know that I treasure their faith and support.

Many thanks to you

AB • AD • AG • AH • AL • AM • AMD • AR • AT • BH • BM • BN • BS • CB • CD
CF • CL • CM • CN • CJMC • CT • CV • DB • DD • DH • DL • DMc • DMCF • DP
DR • DT • DW • EE • FC • FS • FW • GAS • GC • GB • GE • GG • GH • GJ • GJC
GM • GW • HDBW • HDW • HFL • HKK • HL • HT • IC • IK • IMc • INSL • IP
JB • JC • JCF • JD • JF • JG • JH • JK • JM • JMB • JMF • JN • JO • JPCF • JR
JS • JW • JY • KA • KBT • KH • KJ • KM • KMAc • KO • KS • LA • LB • LC • LF
LG • LM • LMc • LO • LPMB • MF • MG • MJ • MH • MM • MN • MP • MR • MS
MT • MW • ND • NN • NS • ON • PB • PC • PD • PF • PH • PL • PJ • PM • PMc
PR • PS • PW • RA • RAR • RC • RF • RK • RL • RM • RMc • RS • RSC • RW
RBW • SD • SL • SM • SR • SS • SV • TA • TCN • TF • TG • TH • TJ • TPC • TR
TWG • VC • VP • VS • WB • WH • WKJ • WS • WW • XX • YF • YH • YVD • ZN • ZS

(If two people have the same initials, only one listing is shown.
As a result, 69 initials have been omitted.)

INDEX